Computational Logic and Human Thinking

How to be Artificially Intelligent

The practical benefits of computational logic need not be limited to mathematics and computing. As this book shows, ordinary people in their everyday lives can profit from the recent advances that have been developed for artificial intelligence. The book draws upon related developments in various fields from philosophy to psychology and law. It pays special attention to the integration of logic with decision theory, and the use of logic to improve the clarity and coherence of communication in natural languages such as English.

This book is essential reading for teachers and researchers who want to catch up with the latest developments in computational logic. It will also be useful in any undergraduate course that teaches practical thinking, problem solving or communication skills. Its informal presentation makes the book accessible to readers from any background, but optional, more formal, chapters are also included for those who are more technically oriented.

ROBERT KOWALSKI is Emeritus Professor and Research Investigator in the Department of Computing at Imperial College London. In 2011 he received the IJCAI Award for Research Excellence for his contributions to logic for knowledge representation and problem solving, including his pioneering work on automated theorem proving and logic programming.

Computational Logic
and Human Thinking
How to be Artificially Intelligent

ROBERT KOWALSKI
Imperial College London

CAMBRIDGE
UNIVERSITY PRESS

CAMBRIDGE
UNIVERSITY PRESS

University Printing House, Cambridge CB2 8BS, United Kingdom

Cambridge University Press is part of the University of Cambridge.

It furthers the University's mission by disseminating knowledge in the pursuit of
education, learning and research at the highest international levels of excellence.

www.cambridge.org
Information on this title: www.cambridge.org/9780521194822

© R. Kowalski 2011

First published 2011

A catalogue record for this publication is available from the British Library

Library of Congress Cataloguing in Publication data
Kowalski, Robert.
Computational logic and human thinking : how to be artificially
intelligent / Robert Kowalski.
p. cm.
ISBN 978-0-521-19482-2 (hardback)
1. Computational intelligence.   2. Logic, Symbolic and mathematical – Famous
problems.   3. Rhetoric – Mathematics.   4. Communication – Philosophy.
5. Reasoning.   6. Critical thinking.   I. Title.
- Q342.K69   2011
511.3–dc22
2011002461

ISBN 978-0-521-19482-2 Hardback
ISBN 978-0-521-12336-5 Paperback

To Bob, John and Mary

Contents

Preface

The mere possibility of Artificial Intelligence (AI) – of machines that can think and act as intelligently as humans – can generate strong emotions. While some enthusiasts are excited by the thought that one day machines may become more intelligent than people, many of its critics view such a prospect with horror.

Partly because these controversies attract so much attention, one of the most important accomplishments of AI has gone largely unnoticed: the fact that many of its advances can also be used directly by people, to improve their own human intelligence. Chief among these advances is Computational Logic.

Computational Logic builds upon traditional logic, which was originally developed to help people think more effectively. It employs the techniques of symbolic logic, which has been used to build the foundations of mathematics and computing. However, compared with traditional logic, Computational Logic is much more powerful; and compared with symbolic logic, it is much simpler and more practical.

Although the applications of Computational Logic in AI require the use of mathematical notation, its human applications do not. As a consequence, I have written the main part of this book informally, to reach as wide an audience as possible. Because human thinking is also the subject of study in many other fields, I have drawn upon related studies in Cognitive Psychology, Linguistics, Philosophy, Law, Management Science and English Composition.

In fact, the variant of Computational Logic presented in this book builds not only upon developments of logic in AI, but also upon many other complementary and competing knowledge representation and problem-solving paradigms. In particular, it incorporates procedural representations of knowledge from AI and Computing, production systems from AI and Cognitive Science, and decision analysis from Management Science, Cognitive Psychology and Philosophy.

Because Computational Logic has so many applications and so many relations with other fields, the ideal, ultimate use of this book would be as a companion text for an undergraduate degree in practical thinking. Such a degree course would combine the traditional virtues of a liberal arts education with the argumentation skills of analytic philosophy, the rigours of scientific method and the modern benefits of information technology. It would provide the student with the transferable thinking and communication skills needed not only for more specialised studies, but also for problems that do not fall into neatly classified areas.

As far as I know, nothing approaching such a degree course exists today; and as far as I can see, no such degree course is likely to exist in the near future. Logic as an academic discipline, as it exists today, is fragmented between Mathematics, Philosophy and Computing. Moreover, the practical applications of Informal Logic are mostly buried inside other academic disciplines, like Law, Management Science and English Composition. None of these disciplines could host such a degree course on its own, and few of them would welcome such an expansion of logic in their own field.

Perhaps one day, an educational institution will make room for a degree course focusing on how to think. In the meanwhile, this book can be used as a supplement to more conventional courses. For those who have already completed their formal education, it can provide a glimpse into a possible future world.

In writing this book, I have taken pains to avoid misrepresenting the subject by over-simplification. For this reason, I have included a number of additional, more advanced chapters, which fill in some of the otherwise missing technical detail. These chapters can be safely skipped by the casual reader. Taken on their own, they provide a self-contained introduction and reference to the formal underpinnings of the Computational Logic used in this book.

I have also been sensitive to the fact that, because I address issues of English writing style, I am inviting attention to the inadequacies of my own writing style. In defence, let me argue that without the help of Computational Logic, my writing would be a lot worse.

When I started my undergraduate studies at the University of Chicago years ago, my writing was so bad that I failed the placement examination and had to take an extra, non-credit, remedial course. I finished the year with As in all my other subjects, but with a D in English writing skills. It took me years to diagnose the problems with my writing and to learn how to improve it. In the course of doing so, I learned more about practical logic than I did in any of my formal logic courses. I like to believe that my writing is a lot better today than it was during my first year in Chicago. But more importantly, I hope that the lessons I learned will also be helpful to some of the readers of this book.

I am very grateful to Tom Blackson, François Bry, Tony Burton, Keith Clark, Jacinto Davila, Phan Minh Dung, Maarten van Emden, Steffen Hoelldobler, Luis Pereira, Yongyuth Permpoontanalarp, Fariba Sadri, Keith Stenning, Dania Kowalska-Taylor, Sten-Ake Tarnlund, Jeff Thompson, Francesca Toni and Mike Tunstall for their valuable comments on earlier drafts of the book. Thanks also to Simon Taylor for the drawing of the fox and the crow.

Summary and plan of the book

Because this book ranges over a wide variety of topics, it is useful to summarise the relationships between the different chapters in one place. However, instead of placing this summary at the end of the book, where all of its terms will have already been explained in detail, I have decided to present it here, in keeping with the general spirit of the book that it is better to work backwards from your destination, than to stumble forward, wondering where you are going.

Therefore, this summary may be read either before or after the main body of the book. But it can also be read in parallel, to get a better orientation of how the individual chapters are related.

Introduction

In Artificial Intelligence, an *agent* is any entity, embedded in a real or artificial world, that can observe the changing world and perform actions on the world to maintain itself in a harmonious relationship with the world. Computational Logic, as used in Artificial Intelligence, is the agent's language of thought. Sentences expressed in this language represent the agent's beliefs about the world as it is and its goals for the way it would like it to be. The agent uses its goals and beliefs to control its behaviour.

The agent uses the inference rules of Computational Logic, applying them to its thoughts in logical form, to reason about the world and to derive actions to change the world for its own benefit. These inference rules include both forward reasoning to derive consequences of its observations, and backward reasoning to reduce its goals to subgoals and actions. The agent can also use forward reasoning to deduce consequences of candidate actions, to help it choose between alternative candidates.

Although the main purpose of Computational Logic is to represent an agent's private thoughts and to control its behaviour, the agent can also use Computational Logic to guide its public communications with other agents. By expressing its communications in a more logical form, a speaker or writer can make it easier for the listener or reader to translate those communications into thoughts of her own.

Chapter 1: Logic on the Underground

The London Underground Emergency Notice illustrates the way in which the meanings of English communications can be understood as thoughts in logical form. In Computational Logic, these thoughts have both a logical and computational character. Their logical character is apparent in their explicit use of logical connectives, like *any*, *if*, *and* and *not*; and their computational character is manifest in their use as procedures for reducing goals to subgoals. Because of this dual logical and computational character, sentences expressed in this form are also called *logic programs*.

The Emergency Notice also illustrates how the coherent use of English communications can be understood in terms of logical connections between the meanings of those communications and other thoughts in an agent's web of goals and beliefs. Once the agent has made the connections, the agent can activate them by forward or backward reasoning, when the need arises. Connections that are activated frequently can be collapsed into derived goals or beliefs, which can be used more directly and more efficiently in the future.

Chapter 2: The psychology of logic

The most influential and widely cited argument against logic comes from psychological experiments about reasoning with natural-language sentences in conditional form. The most popular interpretation of these experiments is that people do not have a natural general-purpose ability to reason logically, but have developed instead, through the mechanisms of Darwinian evolution, specialised algorithms for solving typical problems that arise in their environment.

In this chapter I discuss some of the issues involved in solving these reasoning tasks, and argue that one of the main problems with the experiments is that they fail to appreciate that the natural-language form of a conditional is only an approximation to the logical form of its intended meaning. Another problem is that the interpretation of these experiments is based upon an inadequate understanding of the relationship between knowledge and reasoning. In Computational Logic applied to human thinking, this relationship can be expressed rather loosely as an equation: *thinking = specialised knowledge + general-purpose reasoning*.

Chapter 3: The fox and the crow

Aesop's fable of the fox and the crow illustrates the backward reasoning of a clever fox, to generate a plan to achieve the goal of having the cheese of a not so clever crow. It contrasts the fox's *proactive*, backward reasoning with the crow's *reactive*, forward reasoning, to respond to the fox's praise by breaking out in song, thereby dropping the cheese to the ground, where the fox can pick it up. Both the fox and the crow reason in accordance with the inference rules of Computational Logic, but the fox has a better knowledge of the world, and has more powerful ways of using that knowledge for her own benefit.

If the crow knew as much as the fox and were able to reason *preactively*, thinking before he acts, then he could reason forward from the hypothetical performance of his candidate actions, predict their likely consequences and choose an alternative action, like flying away or swallowing the cheese, that achieves a better expected resulting state of affairs.

Chapter 4: Search

In Computational Logic, a *proof procedure* consists of a collection of inference rules and a search strategy. The inference rules determine both the structure of proofs and the *search space* of all possible proofs relevant to the solution of a goal. The *search strategy* determines the manner in which the search space is explored in the search for a solution.

Many different search strategies are possible, including both parallel strategies, which explore different parts of the search space at the same time, and best-first strategies, which aim to find the best solution possible in the shortest amount of time.

Chapter 5: Negation as failure

In the semantics of Computational Logic, the world is a positive place, characterised by the positive atomic sentences that are true at the time. Because the ultimate purpose of an agent's goals and beliefs is to manage its interactions with the world, the syntactic form of the agent's thoughts also has a corresponding positive bias. In many cases, syntatically negative thoughts arise from the *failure* to observe or derive positive information.

Negation as failure is a natural way to reason by *default* with incomplete information, deriving conclusions under the assumption that the agent knows it all, but then gracefully withdrawing those conclusions if new information shows that they do not hold. It also facilitates higher-level ways of organising goals and beliefs into hierarchies of rules and exceptions, in which the rules represent only the most important conditions, and the exceptions add extra conditions when they are needed.

Chapter 6: How to become a British Citizen

The British Nationality Act is a body of English sentences, which states precisely the conditions under which a person may acquire, renounce or be deprived of British Citizenship. The Act is designed to be both unambiguous, so there is little doubt about its intended meaning, and flexible, so that it can be applied to changing circumstances. Its English style resembles the conditional form of sentences in Computational Logic.

In addition to its use of conditional form, the British Nationality Act illustrates many other important features of Computational Logic, including the representation of rules and exceptions, and meta-level reasoning about what it takes for a person, like you or me, to satisfy the Secretary of State that the person fulfils the requirements for naturalisation as a British Citizen.

In contrast with the British Nationality Act, the University of Michigan Lease Termination Clause shows how an ambiguous, virtually unintelligible English text can be made understandable by reformulating it in Computational Logic style.

Chapter 7: The louse and the Mars explorer

Arguably, the most influential computational model of human thinking in Cognitive Psychology is the production system model, as illustrated in this chapter by the wood louse and the Mars explorer robot. Production systems combine a *working memory* of atomic facts with *condition–action rules* of the form *if conditions then actions*. The working memory is like a model of the current state of the world, and the rules are like an agent's goals and beliefs.

The condition–action rules are embedded in an _observation–thought–decision–action cycle_ and are executed by matching the conditions of rules with facts in the working memory and generating the actions of rules as candidate actions. This manner of execution is called _forward chaining_, which is similar to forward reasoning. If more than one candidate action is generated in this way, then a process, called _conflict resolution_, is used to decide between the candidates. The chosen action is then executed, changing the state of the working memory, simulating the way an agent's actions change the state of the world.

From a logical point of view, there are three kinds of condition–action rules: _reactive rules_, which are like instinctive stimulus–response associations; _goal-reduction rules_, which reduce goals to subgoals by forward chaining; and _forward reasoning rules_, which perform genuine logical forward reasoning.

Chapter 8: Maintenance goals as the driving force of life

The agent model presented in this book combines the functionalities of logic and production systems in a logical framework. The framework takes from production systems the _observation–thought–decision–action cycle_, but replaces condition–action rules by goals and beliefs in the logical form of conditionals. It replaces reactive rules by _maintenance goals_ used to reason forwards, goal-reduction rules by _beliefs_ used to reason backwards, and forward reasoning rules by _beliefs_ used to reason forwards.

In the logical agent model, the agent _cycle_ responds to observations of the environment by reasoning forwards with beliefs, until it derives a conclusion that matches one of the conditions of a maintenance goal. It reasons backwards, to check the other conditions of the maintenance goal. If all the conditions of the maintenance goal are shown to hold in this way, it reasons forwards one step, deriving the conclusion of the maintenance goal as an _achievement goal_. It then starts to reason backwards using its beliefs to reduce the achievement goal to a plan of candidate actions. It decides between different candidate actions, and starts to execute a plan. If necessary, it interrupts the execution of the plan, to process other observations, interleaving the plan with other plans.

Chapter 9: The meaning of life

The logical framework of the preceeding chapter views an agent's life as controlled by the changes that take place in the world, by its own goals and beliefs, and by the choices the agent makes between different ways of achieving its goals. The combination of its beliefs and its highest-level goals generates a hierarchy of goals and subgoals. However, for the sake of efficiency, this hierarchy may be collapsed into a collection of more direct stimulus–response associations, whose original goals are no longer apparent, but are implicit and emergent.

In AI and computing more generally, it is common for an intelligent designer to implement an artificial agent that does not contain an explicit representation of its higher-level goals. The designer is aware of the agent's goals, but the agent itself is not. As far as the agent is concerned, its life may seem to be entirely meaningless.

In this chapter, we contrast the seemingly meaningless life of an imaginary, artificial wood louse, with the more meaningful life of an intelligent agent, in which stimulus–response associations and awareness of higher-level goals are combined.

Chapter 10: Abduction

One of the main functions of an agent's beliefs is to represent causal relationships between its experiences. The agent uses these causal representations both *proactively* to generate plans to achieve its goals, and *preactively* to derive consequences of candidate actions to help it choose between alternative candidate actions. However, the agent can also use the same causal beliefs *abductively* to generate hypotheses to explain its observations, and to derive consequences of candidate hypotheses to help it choose between alternative hypotheses. This process of generating and choosing hypotheses to explain observations is called *abduction*.

Like default reasoning with negation as failure, abduction is *defeasible* in the sense that new information can cause a previously derived conclusion to be withdrawn.

Chapter 11: The Prisoner's Dilemma

The problem of deciding between alternative abductive explanations of an observation is similar to the problem of deciding between alternative actions, which is exemplified by the Prisoner's Dilemma. In this chapter, we see how an agent can use a combination of Computational Logic and decision theory to decide between alternatives. According to decision theory, the agent should choose an alternative that has the best expected outcome. The expected outcome of an action is determined by appropriately combining judgements of the utility (or desirability) of the action's consequences with judgements of the probability (or likelihood) that the consequence will actually happen.

Decision theory is a normative theory, which requires detailed knowledge of utilities and probabilities, but neglects the motivations of an agent's actions. In practice, agents more typically employ heuristic goals and beliefs (or rules of thumb), which approximate the decision-theoretic norms. But heuristics often go astray. When it is important to make smarter choices, it is better to use the more encompassing framework of the agent cycle, to analyse the motivations of actions and to ensure that a full range of alternatives is explored.

Chapter 12: Motivations matter

Decision theory leads to consequentialist theories of morality, which judge the moral status of actions simply in terms of their consequences. But in psychological studies and the law, people judge actions both in terms of their consequences and in terms of their motivations. We show how Computational Logic can model such moral judgements by using constraints to prevent actions that are deemed to be morally or legally unacceptable.

Chapter 13: The changing world

An agent's life is a continuous struggle to maintain a harmonious relationship with the ever-changing world. The agent assimilates its observations of the changing state of the world, and it performs actions to change the world in return.

The world has a life of its own, existing only in the present, destroying its past and hiding its future. To help it survive and prosper in such a changing environment, an intelligent agent uses beliefs about cause and effect, represented in its language of thought. In this chapter we investigate in greater detail the logical representation of such causal beliefs and the semantic relationship between this logical representation and the changing world.

Chapter 14: Logic and objects

Whereas in Cognitive Psychology production systems are the main competitor of logic, in Computing the main competitor is Object-Orientation. In the object-oriented way of looking at the world, the world consists of objects, which interact by sending and receiving messages. Objects respond to messages by using encapsulated methods, invisible to other objects, and inherited from general classes of objects.

Computational Logic is compatible with Object-Orientation, if objects are viewed as agents, methods are viewed as goals and beliefs, and messages are viewed as one agent supplying information or requesting help from another. Viewed in this way, the main contribution of Object-Orientation is twofold: it highlights the value both of structuring knowledge (goals and beliefs) in relatively self-contained modules, and of organising that knowledge in abstract hierarchies.

Chapter 15: Biconditionals

In this chapter we explore the view that conditional beliefs are biconditionals in disguise. For example, given *only* the two alternative conditions that can cause an object to look red:

> *an object looks red if the object is red.*
> *an object looks red if it illuminated by a red light.*

the two conditionals can be understood as standing for the biconditional:

> *an object looks red **if and only if***
> *the object is red **or** the object is illuminated by a red light.*

Both negation as failure and abduction can be understood as reasoning with such biconditionals as equivalences, replacing atomic formulas that match the conclusion by the disjunction of conditions (connected by *or*) that imply the conclusion.

Chapter 16: Computational Logic and the selection task

In this chapter we return to the problem of explaining some of the results of psychological experiments about reasoning with conditionals. We investigate the different ways that Computational Logic explains these results, depending on whether a conditional is interpreted as a goal or as a belief. If it is interpreted as a belief, then it is often natural to interpret the conditional as specifying the *only* conditions under which the conclusion holds. This explains one of the two main mistakes that people make when reasoning with conditionals, when judged by the standards of classical logic.

The other main mistake is that people often fail to reason correctly with negation. This mistake is explainable in part by the fact that an agent's observations are normally represented by positive atomic sentences, and that negative conclusions have to be derived from positive observations. In many cases this derivation is easier with conditional goals than with conditional beliefs.

Chapter 17: Meta-logic

In this chapter we explore how meta-logic can be used to simulate the reasoning of other agents, and to solve problems that cannot be solved in the object language alone. We illustrate this with a variant of the wise man puzzle, and with Gödel's theorem that there are true but unprovable sentences in arithmetic.

Conclusions of the book

This concluding chapter takes a step back from the details, and takes a broader look at the main aim of the book, which is to show how Computational Logic can reconcile conflicting paradigms for explaining and guiding human behaviour. It also suggests how Computational Logic may help to reconcile conflicts in other areas.

Chapter A1: The syntax of logical form

This additional, more formal chapter gives a more precise formulation of Computational Logic as a logic of sentences having the conditional form *if conditions then conclusion* or equivalently having the form *conclusion if conditions*. In its simplest form, the *conclusion* of a conditional is an *atomic expression*, consisting of a *predicate* and a number of *arguments*. The *conditions* are a conjunction (connected by *and*) of atomic expressions or the *negations* of atomic expressions.

In this chapter, I compare the conditional form of logic with standard classical logic. I argue that classical logic is to conditional logic, as natural language is to the language of thought. In both cases, there are two kinds of reasoning, performed in two stages. The first stage translates sentences that are unstructured and possibly difficult to understand into simpler sentences that are better structured. The second stage derives consequences of the resulting simpler sentences. The logic of conditional forms is the logic of such simpler and better structured sentences.

Chapter A2: Truth

Conditionals in Computational Logic represent an agent's goals and beliefs in its private language of thought. They also represent the meanings of its public communications with other agents, and for this reason they can be said to represent the *semantics* of natural-language sentences. However, sentences in logical form also have a *semantics* in terms of their relationship with states of the world.

This additional chapter makes a start on the discussion of this semantics, and of the relationship between truth in all models and truth in minimal models. It argues from the example of arithmetic that truth in minimal models is more fundamental than truth in all models.

Chapter A3: Forward and backward reasoning

This chapter defines the forward and backward rules of inference more precisely, and shows how they can be understood in semantic terms, as showing how the truth of one set of sentences implies the truth of another. This semantic point of view applies both to the use of these inference rules to determine truth in all models and to their use to generate and determine truth in minimal models.

Chapter A4: Minimal models and negation

This chapter shows how the semantics of negation as failure can be understood in terms of the minimal model semantics of Chapter A2.

Chapter A5: The resolution rule of inference

In this chapter we see that forward and backward reasoning are both special cases of the resolution rule of inference, and that resolution is the underlying mechanism for reasoning in connection graphs.

Resolution was originally presented as a machine-oriented rule of inference, whereas forward and backward reasoning are human-oriented ways of understanding human thinking. This combination of human and machine orientation is reflected in the fact that the human mind can be regarded as a computing machine whose software is a conditional form of logic and whose hardware is a connectionist form of resolution.

Chapter A6: The logic of abductive logic programming

This chapter provides most of the technical support for the combination of forward reasoning, backward reasoning and negation as failure, which are the basic inference rules of the Computational Logic used in this book.

The proof procedure presented in this chapter can be understood in semantic terms, as generating a minimal model in which an agent's goals and beliefs are all true. However, it can also be understood in argumentation terms, as generating an argument in favour of a claim, both by providing support for the claim and by defeating all attacking arguments with counter-arguments.

Introduction

Computational Logic has been developed in Artificial Intelligence over the past 50 years or so, in an attempt to program computers to display human levels of intelligence. It is based on Symbolic Logic, in which sentences are represented by symbols and reasoning is performed by manipulating symbols, like solving equations in algebra. However, attempts to use Symbolic Logic to solve practical problems by means of computers have led to many simplifications and enhancements. The resulting Computational Logic is not only more powerful for use by computers, but also more useful for the original purpose of logic, to improve human thinking.

Traditional Logic, Symbolic Logic and Computational Logic are all concerned with the abstract form of sentences and how their form affects the correctness of arguments. Although Traditional Logic goes back to Aristotle in the fourth century B.C., Symbolic Logic began primarily in the nineteenth century, with the mathematical forms of logic developed by George Boole and Gottlob Frege. It was enhanced considerably in the twentieth century by the work of Bertrand Russell, Alfred North Whitehead, Kurt Gödel and many others on its application to the Foundations of Mathematics. Computational Logic emerged in the latter half of the twentieth century, starting with attempts to mechanise the generation of proofs in mathematics, and was extended both to represent more general kinds of knowledge and to perform more general kinds of problem solving. The variety of Computational Logic presented in this book owes much to the contributions of John McCarthy and John Alan Robinson.

The achievements of Symbolic Logic in the past century have been considerable. But they have resulted in mainstream logic becoming a branch of mathematics and losing touch with its roots in human reasoning. Computational Logic also employs mathematical notation, which facilitates its computer implementation, but obscures its relevance to human thinking.

1

In this book, I will attempt to show that the practical benefits of Computational Logic are not limited to mathematics and Artificial Intelligence, but can also be enjoyed by ordinary people in everyday life, without the use of mathematical notation. Nonetheless, I include several additional, more technical chapters at the end of the book, which can safely be omitted by the casual reader.

The relationship between logic and thinking

Logic in all its varieties is concerned with formalising the laws of thought. Along with related fields such as Law and Management Science, it focuses on the formulation of *normative* theories, which prescribe how people ought to think. Cognitive Psychology is also concerned with thinking, but it focuses almost exclusively on *descriptive* theories, which study how people actually think in practice, whether correctly or not. For the most part, the two kinds of theories have been developed in isolation, and bear little relationship to one another.

However, in recent years, cognitive psychologists have developed *dual process* theories, which can be understood as combining descriptive and normative theories. Viewed from the perspective of dual process theories, traditional descriptive theories focus on *intuitive thinking*, which is associative, automatic, parallel and subconscious. Traditional normative theories, on the other hand, focus on *deliberative thinking*, which is rule-based, effortful, serial and conscious. In this book, I will argue that Computational Logic is a dual process theory, in which intuitive and deliberative thinking are combined.

But logic is concerned, not only with thinking in the abstract, but with thoughts represented in the form of sentences and with thinking treated as manipulating sentences to generate new thoughts. In Computational Logic, these logical manipulations of sentences also have a computational interpretation. Viewed in this way, Computational Logic can be regarded as a formalisation of the language of human thought.

Computational Logic and the language of thought

As used in Artificial Intelligence, Computational Logic functions first and foremost as an intelligent agent's *language of thought*. It includes a *syntax* (or grammar), which determines the *form* of the agent's thoughts, a *semantics*, which determines the *contents* (or meaning) of those thoughts, and an *inference engine* (or proof procedure), which generates (or derives or infers) new thoughts as consequences of existing thoughts. In this role, Computational Logic can be regarded as a *private language*, representing the agent's goals and beliefs, and helping the agent to regulate its behaviour. This private language is independent of, and more fundamental than, ordinary, natural languages like English.

However, in *multi-agent systems* in Artificial Intelligence, the private language of an individual agent also serves the secondary function of representing the meanings of its communications with other agents. These communications are expressed in a shared *public language*, which may differ from the private languages of individual agents. The task of a communicating agent is to translate thoughts from its private language into the public language, in such a way that the receiving agent can readily translate those public communications into appropriate thoughts in its own private language.

It would be easier if all agents shared the same private language, and if that private language were identical to the public language of the community of agents. This can be arranged by design in an artificial multi-agent system, but it can only be approximated in a society of human agents.

The distinction between private and public languages, which is so clear cut in Artificial Intelligence, has been proposed in the Philosophy of Language to explain the relationship between human thinking and communication. Many of these proposals, which for simplicity can be lumped together as "language of thought" (LOT) proposals, maintain that much human thinking can be understood as taking place in a language of thought. The most famous proposal along these lines is Fodor's hypothesis that the LOT is a private language, which is independent of the Babel of public languages (Fodor, 1975). Other proposals, notably Carruthers (2004), argue that a person's LOT is specific to the public language of the person's social community.

No matter where they stand on the relationship between private and public languages, most proposals seem to agree that the LOT has some kind of logical form. However, for the most part these proposals are remarkably shy about the details of that logical form. By comparison, the proposal that I present in this book – that Computational Logic can be regarded as a formalisation of the LOT – is shamelessly revealing. I draw the main support for my argument from the uses of Computational Logic in Artificial Intelligence. But I also draw support from the relationship between Computational Logic and normative theories of human communication.

Computational Logic and human communication

Much of the time, when we speak or write, we simply express ourselves in public, without making a conscious effort to communicate effectively. But when it really matters that we are understood – like when I am writing this book – we try to be as clear, coherent and convincing as possible. The difference is like the difference between descriptive and normative theories of thinking; and, as in the case of the two kinds of thinking, the two kinds of communication are studied mainly in different academic disciplines. Whereas linguistics is concerned with developing descriptive theories about how people use language in practice, rhetoric and allied disciplines such as English composition and critical thinking are concerned with *normative* theories about how people should use language to communicate more effectively.

In this book, I present a normative theory of intelligent thinking, communication and behaviour. But I pay attention to descriptive theories, because descriptive theories help us to understand where we are coming from, whereas normative theories show us where we are aiming to go.

The descriptive theory of communication that comes closest to a normative theory is probably relevance theory (Sperber and Wilson, 1986). It is based on a more general theory of cognition, which loosely speaking hypothesises that, given competing inputs from their environment, people direct their attention to those inputs that provide them with the most useful information for the least processing cost. Applied to communication, the theory hypothesises that, given a potentially ambiguous communication as input, readers or listeners translate the input into a logical form that maximises the amount of information it contains, while minimising the computational effort needed to generate that logical form.

Relevance theory is compatible with the hypothesis that Computational Logic, or something like it, is the logic of the language of thought. Like Computational Logic, relevance theory also has both logical and computational components. Moreover, it provides a link with such normative theories of communication as Joseph Williams' guides to English writing style (Williams, 1990, 1995).

One way to interpret Williams' guidance is to understand it in logical terms, as including the advice that writers should express themselves in a form that is as close as possible to the logical form of the thoughts they want to communicate. In other words, they should say what they mean, and they should say it in a way that makes it as easy as possible for readers to extract that meaning. Or to put it still differently, the public expression of our private thoughts should be as close as possible to the logical form of those thoughts.

If our private language and public language were the same, we could literally just say what we think. But even that wouldn't be good enough; because we would still need to organise our thoughts coherently, so that one thought is logically connected to another, and so that our readers or listeners can relate our thoughts to thoughts of their own.

Williams' guidance for achieving coherence includes the advice of placing old, familiar ideas at the beginning of a sentence and placing new ideas at its end. In a succession of sentences, a new idea at the end of a sentence becomes an old idea that can be put at the beginning of the next sentence.

Here is an example of his advice, which uses an informal version of the syntax of Computational Logic, and which incidentally shows how Computational Logic can be used to represent an agent's goals and beliefs to guide its behaviour:

> *You want to be more intelligent.*
> *You will be more intelligent if you are more logical.*
> *You will be more logical if you study this book.*
> *So (given no other alternatives) you should study this book.*

It may not be poetry, and you might not agree with it, but at least it's clear, coherent and to the point.

What is Computational Logic?

The version of Computational Logic presented in this book combines a simplified form of language for representing information with mechanical (or automatic) ways of using information to infer its consequences. Sentences in this language have the simple form of *conditionals*: *if conditions then conclusion* (or equivalently *conclusion if conditions*). The basic rules of inference are forward and backward reasoning.

Forward reasoning is the classical rule of inference (also called *modus ponens*) used to derive *conclusions* from *conditions*. For example, given the belief that in general *a person will be more logical if the person studies this book*, forward reasoning derives the *conclusion* that *Mary will be more logical* from the *condition* that *Mary studies this book*. Forward reasoning includes the special case in which an agent derives consequences of its observations, to determine how those consequences might affect its goals.

Backward reasoning works in the opposite direction, to derive *conditions* from *conclusions*. For example, given the belief that in general *a person will be more intelligent if the person is more logical* as the *only* way of concluding that a person will be more intelligent, backward reasoning derives the condition that *John should be more logical* from the conclusion *John will be more intelligent*. Backward reasoning can be regarded as a form of goal reduction, in which the *conclusion* is a goal, and the *conditions* are subgoals. Backward reasoning includes the special case in which an agent derives subgoals that are actions, which the agent can perform in the world.

Backward reasoning gives Computational Logic the power of a high-level computer programming language, in which all programs consist of goal-reduction procedures. Indeed, the programming language Prolog, which stands for Programming in Logic, exploits this form of computation mainly for applications in Artificial Intelligence.

Computational Logic, in the more general form that we investigate in this book, also includes the use of inference to help an agent choose between alternative courses of action. For example, having used backward reasoning to derive two alternative subgoals, say *John is more logical* or *John takes intelligence-enhancing drugs*, for achieving the goal *John is more intelligent*, John can use forward reasoning to infer the possible consequences of the alternatives before deciding what to do. In particular, if John infers the consequence that *John may suffer irreversible brain damage* if John chooses the second alternative, *John takes intelligence-enhancing drugs*, then it will encourage John to choose the first alternative, *John is more logical*, instead.

What is Artificial Intelligence?

Artificial Intelligence (AI) is the attempt to program computers to behave intelligently, as judged by human standards. Applications of AI include such problem areas as English speech recognition, expert systems for medical and engineering fault diagnosis, and the formalisation of legal reasoning.

The tools of AI include such techniques as search, Symbolic Logic, artificial neural networks and reasoning with uncertainty. Many of these tools have contributed to the development of the Computational Logic we investigate in this book. However, instead of concerning ourselves with Artificial Intelligence applications, we will focus on the use of Computational Logic to help ordinary people think and behave more intelligently.

Thinking of people in computational terms might suggest that people can be treated as though they were merely machines. On the contrary, I believe instead that thinking of other people as computing agents can help us to better appreciate our common nature and our individual differences. It highlights our common need to deal with the cycle of life in an ever-changing world; and it draws attention to the fact that other people may have other experiences, goals and beliefs, which are different from our own, but which are equally worthy of understanding, tolerance and respect.

Computational Logic and the cycle of life

The role of Computational Logic in the mind of an intelligent agent can be pictured approximately like this:

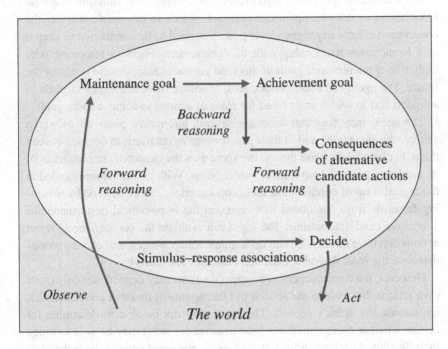

In this way of looking at the relationship between an agent and the world, the mind of the agent is a syntactic structure, which represents the agent's beliefs about the world as it is and its goals for the way it would like the world to be. These beliefs and goals are represented in the agent's private language of thought, whose sentences have the syntactic form of conditionals.

The world, on the other hand, is a semantic structure, which includes the agent's body, and gives meaning to the agent's thoughts. It is a dynamic structure, which is continuously changing, and exists only in the here and now. However, the agent can record its changing experiences in its language of thought, and formulate general beliefs about the causal relationships between its experiences. It can then use these beliefs, which explain its past experiences, to help it achieve its goals in the future.

The agent observes events that take place in the world and the properties that those events initiate and terminate. It uses forward reasoning to derive conclusions of its observations. In many cases, these conclusions are actions, triggered by instinctive or intuitive stimulus–response associations, which can also be expressed in the logical form of conditionals. The agent may execute these actions by reflex, automatically and immediately. Or it may monitor them by performing higher-level reasoning, as in dual process models of human thinking.

But whether an agent is tempted to react immediately with stimulus–response associations or not, the agent can reason forwards to determine whether the observation affects any higher-level goals that need to be maintained to keep it in a harmonious relationship with its environment. Forward reasoning with higher-level maintenance goals of this kind generates achievement goals for the future. The agent can reason backwards, to reduce these achievement goals to subgoals and to search in its mind for plans of actions to achieve these goals.

The agent may find that there are several, alternative plans all of which achieve the same goal; and, if there are, then the agent needs to decide between them. In classical decision theory, the agent uses the expected consequences of its candidate plans to help it make this decision. With its beliefs represented in the logical form of conditionals, these consequences can be derived by reasoning forwards from conditions that represent the hypothetical performance of alternative candidate actions. The agent can evaluate the consequences, reject actions that have unintended and undesirable consequences, and choose actions that have the most desirable expected outcomes (or utility).

However, the consequences of an agent's actions may depend, not only on its own actions, but also on the actions of other agents or on other conditions that are outside the agent's control. The agent may not be able to determine for certain whether these conditions hold in advance, but it may be able to judge their likelihood (or probability). In such cases, the agent can use the techniques of decision theory, to combine its judgements of probability and utility, and choose a course of actions having the highest expected utility. Alternatively, the agent may use more pragmatic, precompiled plans of action that approximate the decision-theoretic ideal.

Among the criteria that an agent can use to decide between alternative ways of accomplishing its goals, is their likely impact on the goals of other agents. Alternatives that help other agents achieve their goals, or that do not hinder the achievement of their goals, can be given preference over other alternatives. In this way, by helping the agent to understand and appreciate that other agents have their own experiences, goals and beliefs, Computational Logic can help the agent avoid conflict and cooperate with other agents.

This book aims to show that these benefits of Computational Logic, which have had some success in the field of Artificial Intelligence, also have great potential for improving human thinking and behaviour.

1
Logic on the Underground

If some form of Computational Logic is the language of human thought, then the best place to look for it would seem to be inside our heads. But if we simply look at the structure and activity of our brains, it would be like looking at the hardware of a computer when we want to learn about its software. Or it would be like trying to do sociology by studying the movement of atomic particles instead of studying human interactions. Better, it might seem, just to use common sense and rely on introspection.

But introspection is notoriously unreliable. Wishful thinking can trick us into seeing what we want to see, instead of seeing what is actually there. The behavioural psychologists of the first half of the twentieth century were so suspicious of introspection that they banned it altogether.

Artificial Intelligence offers us an alternative approach to discovering the language of thought, by constructing computer programs whose input–output behaviour simulates the externally visible manifestations of human mental processes. To the extent that we succeed in the simulation, we can regard the structure of those computer programs as analogous to the structure of the human mind, and we can regard the activity of those programs as analogous to the activity of human thinking.

But different programs with different structures and different modes of operation can display similar behaviour. As we will see later, many of these differences can be understood as differences between levels of abstraction. Some programs are closer to the lower and more concrete level of the hardware, and consequently are more efficient; others are closer to the higher and more abstract level of the application domain, and consequently are easier to understand. We will explore some of the relationships between the different levels later in the book, when we explore dual process theories of thinking in Chapter 9. In the meanwhile, we can get an inkling of what is to come by first looking closer to home.

If human thoughts have the structure of language, then we should be able to get an idea of that structure by looking at natural languages such as English. Better than that, we can look at English communication in situations where we do our best to express ourselves as clearly, coherently and effectively as possible. Moreover, we can be guided in this by the advice we find in books on English writing style.

For the purpose of revealing the language of thought, the most important advice is undoubtedly the recommendation that we express ourselves as clearly as possible – making it as easy as we can for the people we are addressing to translate our communications into thoughts of their own. Everything else being equal, the form of our communications should be as close as possible to the form of the thoughts that they aim to convey.

What better place to look than at communications designed to guide people on how to behave in emergencies, in situations where it can be a matter of life or death that the recipient understands the communication as intended and with as little effort as possible.

Imagine, for example, that you are travelling on the London Underground and you hear a suspicious ticking in the rucksack on the back of the person standing next to you. Fortunately, you see a notice explaining exactly what to do in such an emergency:

Emergencies

Press the alarm signal button
to alert the driver.

The driver will stop
if any part of the train is in a station.

If not, the train will continue to the next station,
where help can more easily be given.

There is a fifty pound penalty
for improper use.

The public notice is designed to be as clear as possible, so that you can translate its English sentences into your own thoughts with as little effort as possible. The closer the form of the English sentences to the form in which you structure your thoughts, the more readily you will be able to understand the sentences and to make use of the thoughts that they communicate.

The thoughts that the management of the Underground wants you to have are designed to make you behave effectively in an emergency, as well as to prevent you from behaving recklessly when there isn't an emergency. They are designed, therefore, not only to be clear, but to be to the point – to tell you what to do if there is an emergency and what not to do if there isn't one. But they are also intended to be coherent, so that you can easily relate the new thoughts that new sentences communicate to existing thoughts you already have in your head. These existing thoughts include both thoughts that were already there before you started reading and thoughts that might have been conveyed by earlier sentences in the text you are reading.

The Emergency Notice as a program

The purpose of the Emergency Notice is to regulate the behaviour of passengers on the London Underground. It does so in much the same way that a computer program controls the behaviour of a computer. In general, much of our human communication can be understood in such computational terms, as one human attempting to program another, to elicit a desired behaviour.

I do not mean to suggest that people should be treated as though they were merely machines. I mean to propose instead that thinking of people as computing agents can sometimes help us to communicate with them in more effective and more efficient terms. Our communications will be more *effective*, because they will better accomplish our intentions; and they will be more *efficient*, both because they will be easier for other people to understand, and because the information they convey will be easier for other people to use for their own purposes.

Understanding a communication is like the process that a computer performs when it *translates* (or *compiles*) a program written in an external *source language* into an internal *target language* that the computer already understands. When a computer compiles the source program, it needs both to translate individual sentences of the program into the target language and to place those sentences into a coherent internal structure expressed as a target program. Compiling a program is efficient when it can be done with as little processing as necessary. Analogously, understanding an English communication is *efficient* when compiling it from its English form into a mental representation can be done with as little effort as possible.

Using the information in a communication is like *executing* a target program, after it has been compiled. When a computer executes a program, it follows the instructions mechanically in a systematic manner. When a person uses the information in a communication, the person combines that information with other information that the person already has and uses the combined information to solve problems. People perform much of this process of using information systematically, automatically and unconsciously. Like a computer program, the information that people use to solve problems is *efficient* if it helps them to solve problems with as little effort as possible.

The computational nature of the Emergency Notice is most obvious in the first sentence:

> *Press the alarm signal button*
> *to alert the driver.*

This has the form of a *goal-reduction procedure*:

> *Reduce the goal of alerting the driver*
> *to the subgoal of pressing the alarm signal button.*

Goal-reduction procedures are a common form of human knowledge representation. They structure our knowledge in a way that facilitates achieving goals and solving problems. Here the thought communicated by the sentence is that the goal of alerting the driver can be reduced to the subgoal of pressing the alarm signal button.

To understand and make use of the goal-reduction procedure, you need to assimilate it into your existing goals and beliefs. For example, you might already know that there could be other ways of alerting the driver, such as shouting out loud. You probably know that alerting the driver is one way of getting help, and that there are other ways of getting help, such as enlisting the assistance of your fellow passengers. You probably recognise that if there is an emergency then you need to deal with it appropriately, and that getting help is one such way, but that other ways, such as running away or confronting the emergency head on yourself, might also be worth considering.

Goal-reduction procedures are also a common form of computer knowledge representation, especially in Artificial Intelligence. Liberally understood, they can serve as the sole construct for writing any computer program. However, almost all computer languages also use lower-level programming constructs. Most of these constructs bear little resemblance to human ways of thinking.

But there is one other construct that is even higher-level than goal reduction, and which may be even closer to the way humans structure their thoughts. This construct is exemplified by the logical form of the conditional sentences found in the second and third sentences of the Emergency Notice.

The logic of the second and third sentences

Many linguists and philosophers subscribe to some form of LOT hypothesis, the hypothesis that many of our thoughts have a structure that is similar to the structure of natural languages such as English. Most of those who subscribe to the hypothesis also seem to believe that the language of thought has a logical form. In this book, I will explore the more specific hypothesis that the language of thought has the logical form of conditional sentences. This hypothesis is supported by the English form of the second and third sentences of the Emergency Notice.

Indeed, the second and third sentences of the Emergency Notice both have the logical form of *conditionals* (also called *implications*). Conditionals are sentences of the form:

if conditions then conclusion

or equivalently: *conclusion if conditions*.

A more precise definition is given in the additional Chapter A1.

In the Emergency Notice, the second sentence is written with its conclusion first; and the third sentence is written the other way around, with its implicit conditions first.

In formal logic, it is normal to write conditionals in the forward direction *if conditions then conclusion*. This is why reasoning from conditions to conclusions is called *forward reasoning*, and why reasoning from conclusion to conditions is called *backward reasoning*. However, no matter whether conditionals are written conditions-first or conclusion-first, they have the same meaning. But we often write them one way rather than the other when we have one preferred direction of use in mind, or when we want to write them more coherently in the context of other sentences.

I have argued that the notice is designed to be as easy as possible to understand, and that as a consequence its external form should be a good indication of the internal form of its intended meaning. In particular, the external, conditional form of the second and third sentences suggests that their intended meaning also has the logical form of conditionals.

However, whatever the form of the LOT, one thing is certain: Its sentences are *unambiguous*, in that they mean what they say. In contrast, English sentences are often *ambiguous*, because they can have several different meanings. For example, the English sentence *the first passenger attacked the second passenger with a rucksack* has two possible meanings. Either *the first passenger carried out the attack with a rucksack* or *the second passenger had a rucksack, and the first passenger attacked the second passenger in some indeterminate manner.* The difference between the two meanings could make a big difference in a court of law.

Ambiguity is the enemy of clarity. It creates confusion, because the reader does not immediately know which of the several possible interpretations of the communication is intended; and it creates extra effort for the reader, because the reader has to explore different interpretations, to find an interpretation that makes the most sense in the context of the reader's background goals and beliefs.

You might be surprised, therefore, to discover that the second and third sentences of the notice are more ambiguous than they first appear. In particular, the second sentence does not explicitly state what the driver will actually stop doing. It is unlikely, for example, that:

> *The driver will stop causing the emergency*
> *if any part of the train is in a station.*

Instead, it is more likely that:

> *The driver will stop the train in a station*
> *if any part of the train is in the station.*

But even this interpretation does not fully capture the sentence's intended meaning. Understood in the context of the first sentence, the second sentence has an additional implicit condition, namely that the driver has been alerted to an emergency. Therefore, the intended meaning of the second sentence is actually:

> *The driver will stop the train in a station*
> *if the driver is alerted to an emergency*
> *and any part of the train is in the station.*

Without the additional condition, the sentence on its own literally means that the driver will stop the train whenever the train is in a station, whether or not there is an emergency. If that were the case, the train would never leave a station once it was there. To understand the sentence, the reader of the notice needs both general background knowledge about the way train drivers normally behave and specific knowledge about the context of the earlier sentences in the notice.

In the spirit of our interpretation of the second sentence, it should now be clear that the intended meaning of the third sentence is:

> *The driver will stop the train at the next station*
> *and help can be given there better than between stations*

if the driver is alerted to an emergency
and not any part of the train is in a station.

In natural language, it is common to leave out some conditions, such as *any part of the train is in the station*, that are present in the context. In more formal logic, however, the context needs to be spelled out explicitly. In other words, sentences in formal logic, to represent information unambiguously, need to stand on their own two feet, without relying for support on the context around them.

The web of belief

Because the meaning of individual sentences expressed in purely logical form does not rely on context, collections of sentences in logical form can be written in any order. In theory, therefore, if this book were written in purely logical form, I could write it – and you could read it – forwards, backwards, or in any other order, and it would still have the same meaning. In fact, you could take any text written as a sequence of sentences in logical form, write the individual sentences on little pieces of paper, throw them up in the air like a pack of cards, and pick them up in any order. The resulting sequence of sentences would have the same meaning as the text you started with.

In contrast, much of the work in writing a book like this is in trying to find an order for presenting the ideas, so they are as clear, coherent and convincing as possible. No matter whether I spell out all of the contexts of individual sentences in detail, I need to present those sentences in a coherent order, which relates consecutive sentences both to ideas you had before you started reading and to ideas you obtained from reading earlier sentences.

One way to achieve coherence is to follow Williams' advice of placing old, familiar ideas at the beginnings of sentences and new ideas at their ends. Sometimes, as a limiting case, if an "old" idea is particularly salient, because it has just been introduced at the end of the previous sentence, then the old part of the next sentence can be taken for granted and simply left out. This is what happens in the Emergency Notice, both in the transition from the first sentence to the second sentence, where the condition *the driver is alerted to an emergency* has been left out, and in the transition from the second sentence to the third sentence, where *any part of the train is in a station* has been left out.

If the language of thought is a logic of conditional forms, then the simplest way to achieve coherence is by linking the beginnings and ends of consecutive sentences by means of the conclusions and conditions of the thoughts they express, using such obvious patterns as:

> *If condition A then conclusion B.*
> *If condition B then conclusion C.*

and

> *conclusion C if condition B.*
> *conclusion B if condition A.*

The need for coherence in human communication suggests that the language of thought is not an unstructured collection of sentences, after all. Rather, it is a linked structure in which sentences are connected by means of their conclusions and conditions.

Connection graphs (Kowalski, 1975, 1979), which link conclusions and conditions of sentences in logical form, have been developed in Artificial Intelligence to improve the efficiency of automated reasoning. The links in connection graphs pre-compute much of the thinking that might be needed later. Here is a connection graph representing some of a person's goals and beliefs before reading the Emergency Notice:

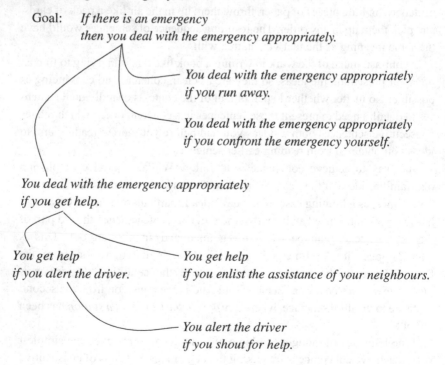

Goal: *If there is an emergency*
         then you deal with the emergency appropriately.

You deal with the emergency appropriately
if you run away.

You deal with the emergency appropriately
if you confront the emergency yourself.

You deal with the emergency appropriately
if you get help.

You get help
if you alert the driver.

You get help
if you enlist the assistance of your neighbours.

You alert the driver
if you shout for help.

Here is the same connection graph, augmented with additional beliefs, after the person reads the Emergency Notice, assuming the person believes everything written in the notice:

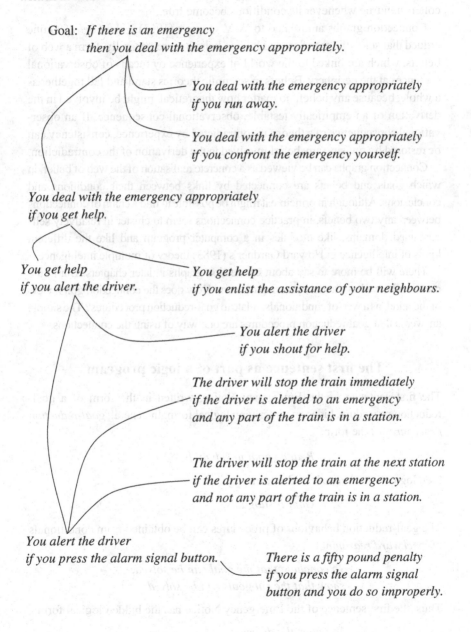

Goal: *If there is an emergency*
then you deal with the emergency appropriately.

You deal with the emergency appropriately
if you run away.

You deal with the emergency appropriately
if you confront the emergency yourself.

You deal with the emergency appropriately
if you get help.

You get help
if you alert the driver.

You get help
if you enlist the assistance of your neighbours.

You alert the driver
if you shout for help.

The driver will stop the train immediately
if the driver is alerted to an emergency
and any part of the train is in a station.

The driver will stop the train at the next station
if the driver is alerted to an emergency
and not any part of the train is in a station.

You alert the driver
if you press the alarm signal button.

There is a fifty pound penalty
if you press the alarm signal
button and you do so improperly.

We will see in later chapters that the kind of conditional represented by the sentence *if there is an emergency then you deal with the emergency appropriately* is a maintenance goal, which a person tries to make true by making its conclusion true whenever its conditions become true.

Connection graphs are related to W. V. Quine's (1963) *web of belief.* Quine argued that scientific theories, and human beliefs more generally, form a web of beliefs, which are linked to the world of experience by means of observational sentences at the periphery. Beliefs in scientific theories stand and fall together as a whole, because any belief, no matter how theoretical, might be involved in the derivation of an empirically testable, observational consequence. If an observational consequence of a theory is contradicted by experience, consistency can be restored by revising any belief involved in the derivation of the contradiction.

Connection graphs can be viewed as a concrete realisation of the web of belief, in which goals and beliefs are connected by links between their conditions and conclusions. Although in principle it might be possible to find a chain of connections between any two beliefs, in practice connections seem to cluster in relatively self-contained domains, like modules in a computer program and like the different kinds of intelligence in Howard Gardner's (1983) theory of multiple intelligences.

There will be more to say about connection graphs in later chapters. But in the meanwhile, we have a more pressing concern: How does the connection graph view of the mind, as a web of conditionals, relate to goal-reduction procedures? The simple answer is that goal-reduction procedures are one way of using the connections.

The first sentence as part of a logic program

The first sentence of the Emergency Notice, written in the form of a goal-reduction procedure, hides an underlying logical form. In general, *goal-reduction procedures* of the form:

> *Reduce goal to subgoals*

hide logical *conditionals* of the form:

> *Goal if subgoals.*

The goal-reduction behaviour of procedures can be obtained from conditionals by *backward reasoning*:

> *To conclude that the goal can be solved,*
> *show that the subgoals can be solved.*

Thus, the first sentence of the Emergency Notice has the hidden logical form:

> *You alert the driver,*
> *if you press the alarm signal button.*

Viewed in connection graph terms, backward reasoning is one way in which a thinking agent can use links between conditionals to direct its attention from one thought to another. Backward reasoning directs the agent's attention from a goal to a conclusion that matches the goal. For example:

Goal: *You deal with the emergency appropriately.*

You deal with the emergency appropriately if you get help.

The use of backward reasoning to turn conditionals into goal-reduction procedures is the basis of *logic programming*, which in turn is the basis of the programming language Prolog.

Backward reasoning contrasts with *forward reasoning*, which is probably more familiar to most people. Given a conditional of the form:

If conditions then conclusion.

and a collection of statements that match the conditions, forward reasoning derives the conclusion as a logical consequence of the conditions. For example, given the statements:

The driver is alerted to an emergency.
A part of the train is in a station.

forward reasoning uses the conditional:

The driver will stop the train immediately if the driver is alerted to an emergency and any part of the train is in a station.

to derive the conclusion that *the driver will stop the train immediately.*

Viewed in connection graph terms, forward reasoning directs attention from the conclusions of beliefs to a belief whose conditions are linked to those conclusions. For example:

The driver will stop the train immediately if the driver is alerted to an emergency and any part of the train is in a station.

The driver is alerted to an emergency.

A part of the train is in a station.

Backward reasoning is also called *top-down* reasoning, or *analysis*. Forward reasoning is also called *bottom-up* reasoning, or *synthesis*.

When and how to combine backward and forward reasoning are one of the main topics of this book. However, the connection graph view of the mind suggests that pure backward or forward reasoning are not the only ways of reasoning. Connections can also be activated in different parts of the mind simultaneously and in parallel (Cheng and Juang, 1987). Moreover, connections that are activated frequently can be short-circuited, and their effect can be compiled into a single goal or belief. For example, the link:

> *You deal with the emergency appropriately*
> *if you get help.*

> *You get help*
> *if you alert the driver.*

between two beliefs can be compiled into the single belief:

> *You deal with the emergency appropriately*
> *if you alert the driver.*

The fourth sentence as an inhibitor of action

In natural language, the logical form of conditionals is often hidden below the surface, sometimes appearing on the surface in procedural form, at other times appearing in declarative form. For example, the last sentence of the Emergency Notice is a declarative sentence, which hides its underlying conditional form:

> *There is a fifty pound penalty if*
> *you press the alarm signal button and*
> *you do so improperly.*

The sentence does not say that you will necessarily receive the penalty for improper use. So its conclusion, more precisely stated, is only that, under the condition that you use the alarm signal button improperly, *you will be liable to the penalty.* Backwards reasoning turns this conditional into a goal-reduction procedure:

> *To be liable to a fifty pound penalty,*
> *press the alarm signal button and*
> *do so improperly.*

It is very unlikely that a passenger would want to get a fifty pound penalty, and very unlikely, therefore, that the passenger would want to use the conditional as such a goal-reduction procedure. It is more likely that the passenger would use it to reason forward instead, to conclude that using the alarm signal button improperly could have an undesirable consequence.

In subsequent chapters, we will see two ways of dealing with the undesirability of the possible consequences of actions. The first is to use *decision theory*, associating probabilities and utilities with the consequences of actions, and choosing an action having the best expected outcome. The other is to use *deontic constraints* on actions, formulated in terms of obligations, permissions and prohibitions.

In standard logical representations, the deontic notions of *obligation, permission* and *prohibition* are accorded the same status as the logical connectives *and, or, if* and *not*, in so-called *deontic logics*. However, in the approach we take in this book, we treat obligations and prohibitions more simply as a species of goal. Obligations are represented by conditional goals whose conclusion the agent attempts to bring about if the conditions hold. Prohibitions (or constraints) are represented by conditional goals with conclusion *false*, whose conclusion the agent attempts to prevent, by ensuring that the conditions do not hold. In the case of the fourth sentence of the Emergency Notice, this prohibition could be stated in the form:

Do not be liable to a penalty.

Or, stated as a conditional goal: *If you are liable to a penalty then false.*

Although it may seem a little strange, we will see later that representing prohibitions and other constraints as conditional goals (with conclusion *false*) has the advantage that then they share the same semantics and the same rules of inference as other conditional goals. When used to reason forward and to derive the conclusion *false*, they eliminate any hypothesis or candidate action that leads to the derivation of *false*.

Thus, in conjunction either with the use of decision theory or with the use of deontic constraints, the fourth sentence acts as an inhibitor of action rather than as a motivator of actions. This explains why the sentence is written declaratively and not procedurally.

In fact, only the first sentence of the Emergency Notice is written in procedural form, and only this first sentence of the notice functions as a normal program, to evoke the behaviour that is desired of passengers on the Underground. The fourth sentence functions as a constraint, to prevent undesired behaviour.

The second and third sentences, on the other hand, describe part of a program to be executed by a different agent, namely by the driver of the train. These sentences are written declaratively and not procedurally precisely because they are to be executed by a different agent, and not by the agent observing the emergency. However, passengers can use these two sentences, like the fourth sentence, to derive the likely consequences of pressing the alarm signal button.

Programs with purpose

It is implicit that the purpose[1] (or goal) of the Emergency Notice is to explain how you can get help from the driver in an emergency. That is why the third sentence includes a phrase that explains why the driver does not stop the train immediately when it is not in a station, but waits to stop until the next station:

where help can more easily be given.

The notice makes sense because the first sentence, in particular, coheres with the goals and beliefs that you probably already had before you started reading the notice. For example, with such sentences as:

If there is an emergency then
deal with the emergency appropriately.

You deal with the emergency appropriately if
you get help.

You get help if you alert the driver.

Although I have deliberately written the second and third sentences here conclusion-first, because it is natural to use them conclusion-first, backwards, as procedures for dealing with emergencies, I have written the first sentence condition-first, because it is natural to use it condition-first, forwards, to respond to emergencies.

The first sentence also has the form of a conditional. But here its conclusion is written *imperatively* (*deal with the emergency appropriately*) rather than *declaratively* (*you deal with the emergency appropriately*). This follows English grammar, in which beliefs are expressed as declarative sentences, but goals, including commands and prohibitions, are expressed as imperative sentences.

The difference between goals and beliefs is that beliefs describe an agent's understanding of the world as it is, whereas goals describe the agent's view of the world as the agent would like it to be. This distinction between goals and beliefs has largely been neglected in symbolic, mathematical logic, because in Mathematics truth is eternal, and there are no actions that a mathematical theory can do to make a sentence become true. However, the distinction is important in Artificial Intelligence, because the ability to perform actions to achieve goals is an essential property of an agent's nature.

Ordinary natural languages distinguish between goals and beliefs by using imperative sentences for goals and declarative sentences for beliefs. However, in the Computational Logic used in this book, both kinds of sentences are expressed declaratively. For example, we represent the conditional-imperative sentence:

[1] The terms "goal" and "purpose" are interchangeable. Other terms that sometimes have the same meaning are "motivation", "reason", "interest", "desire", "objective", "mission", "target", "value", etc.

> *If there is an emergency then*
> *deal with the emergency appropriately.*

as the declarative sentence:

> *If there is an emergency then*
> *you deal with the emergency appropriately.*

We distinguish between goals and beliefs, not by means of syntax, but by assigning them to different categories of thought.

Where do we go from here?

This chapter has been intended to give an impression of the book as a whole. It shows how English sentences can be viewed in both computational and logical terms; and it shows how the two views are combined in Computational Logic.

Traditional logic, on which Computational Logic is based, has fallen out of fashion in recent years. Part of the problem is that its use of symbolic notation can give the impression that logic has little to do with everyday human experience. But another part of the problem is that it fails to address a number of issues that are important in human thinking and behaviour. These issues include the need:

- to distinguish between goals and beliefs
- to be open to changes in the world
- to combine thinking about actions with deciding what to do
- to combine thinking and deciding with actually performing actions
- to reason by default and with rules and exceptions.

We will see how Computational Logic addresses these issues in the following chapters. For the moment, we can picture the problem we face roughly like this:

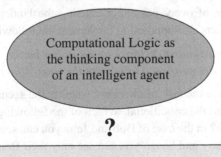

2

The psychology of logic

In this chapter, I will discuss two psychological experiments that challenge the view that people have an inbuilt ability to perform abstract logical reasoning. The first of these experiments, the "selection task", has been widely interpreted as showing that, instead of logic, people use specialised procedures for dealing with problems that occur commonly in their environment. The second, the "suppression task", has been interpreted as showing that people do not reason using rules of inference, like forward and backward reasoning, but instead construct a model of the problem and inspect the model for interesting properties. I will respond to some of the issues raised by these experiments in this chapter, but deal with them in greater detail in Chapter 16, after presenting the necessary background material.

To motivate the discussion of the selection task below, consider its potential application to the problem of improving security on the London Underground. Suppose that the management of the Underground decides to introduce a security check, as part of which security officers stick a label with a letter from the alphabet to the front of every passenger entering the Underground. Suppose that the security officers are supposed to implement the following conditional:

if a passenger is carrying a rucksack on his or her back,
then the passenger is wearing a label with the letter A on his or her front.

Imagine that you have the task of checking whether the security officers have properly implemented the conditional. Which of the following four passengers do you need to check? In the case of Bob and John you can see only their backs, and in the case of Mary and Susan you can see only their fronts:

Bob, who is carrying a rucksack on his back.
Mary, who has the label A stuck to her front.
John, who is carrying nothing on his back.
Susan, who has the label B stuck to her front.

Unfortunately, I have had only limited experience with trying this test myself. So I'm not entirely sure what to expect. But if you are like most ordinary people, and if the task I have asked you to perform is sufficiently similar to some of the psychological experiments that have been performed on ordinary people, then depending on how you interpret the task your performance may not be very logical.

If you were being logical, then you would certainly check Bob, to make sure that he has the label A stuck to his front; and most people, according to psychological studies, correctly perform this inference. So far so good.

But, if you were being logical according to the standards of classical logic, then you would also check Susan, because she might be carrying a rucksack on her back, in which case she would have the incorrect label B stuck to her front. Unfortunately, in many psychological experiments with similar reasoning tasks, most people fail to make this correct inference. If you were to make the same mistake in this version of the selection task, the failure could be disastrous, because Susan could be a terrorist carrying a bomb in a rucksack on her back. Not so good.

According to classical logic, those are the only cases that matter. It is not necessary to check Mary, because the conditional does not state that carrying a rucksack on the back is the *only* condition under which the letter A is stuck to a person's front. There could be other, alternative conditions, for example like carrying a hand grenade in a waist belt, that might also require the security officers to stick the letter A on a person's front. But you have not been asked to check whether Mary might be a terrorist. That is the security officers' job. You have been asked to check *only* whether the security officers have correctly implemented the one stated conditional. Checking to see whether Mary has a rucksack on her back is going beyond the call of duty. However, in many psychological experiments with similar tasks, most subjects do indeed perform this additional, logically unnecessary step.

It remains to consider the case of John, who has nothing on his back. Logically, it doesn't matter what letter he has stuck to his front. It could be the letter B, or even be the letter A. There is no need to check John at all. In psychological studies with similar tasks, most people also reason "correctly", concluding that the letter stuck to John's front is entirely irrelevant. Even most people who interpret the conditional as expressing the *only* condition under which the letter A is stuck to a person's front conclude that it is unnecessary to check John. (But if they really believed that the conditional expresses the *only* such condition, then they should check that the conclusion that John has the letter A stuck to his front doesn't hold under any other conditions, such as the condition that he has nothing on his back.)

You might think that the psychologists who devise these experiments would be disappointed with the evidence that most people appear not to be very logical. But many psychologists seem to be absolutely delighted.

The Wason selection task

The first and most famous of these experiments was performed by Peter Wason (1968). In Wason's experiment, there are four cards, with letters on one side and numbers on the other. The cards are lying on a table with only one side of each card showing:

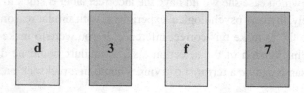

The task is to select those and only those cards that need to be turned over, to determine whether the following conditional holds:

If there is a d on one side,
then there is a 3 on the other side.

Variations of this experiment have been performed numerous times, mainly with college students. The surprising result is that only about 10% of the subjects give the logically correct solutions.

Almost everyone recognises, correctly, that the card showing *d* needs to be turned over, to make sure there is a 3 on the other side. This is a logically correct application of the inference rule *modus ponens*, which is also called *forward reasoning*. Most people also recognise, correctly, that the card showing *f* does not need to be turned over. Although, if you ask them why, they might say "because the conditional does not mention the letter *f*", which (as you will see in a moment) is not the right reason.

Many subjects also think, incorrectly, that it is necessary to turn over the card showing 3, to make sure there is a *d* on the other side. This is logically incorrect, because the conditional does not claim that having a *d* on one side is the *only* condition that implies the conclusion that there is a 3 on the other side. This further claim is expressed by the so-called *converse* of the conditional:

If there is a 3 on one side,
then there is a d on the other side.

The two conditionals are the *converse* of one another, in the same way that the two conditionals:

> *If it is raining, then there are clouds in the sky.*
> *If there are clouds in the sky, then it is raining.*

are also mutually converse. In fact (in case it's not obvious), the first conditional is true and the second conditional is false.

However, more disturbingly, only a small percentage of subjects realise that it is necessary to turn over the card showing 7, to make sure that *d* is not on the other side. It is necessary to turn over the 7, because the original conditional is logically equivalent to its *contrapositive*:

> *If the number on one side is not 3 (e.g. 7),*
> *then the letter on the other side is not d.*

Similarly, the second sentence in the pair of sentences:

> *If it is raining, then there are clouds in the sky.*
> *If there are no clouds in the sky, then it is not raining.*

is the contrapositive of the first sentence, and the two sentences are also logically equivalent. Notice that it is logically necessary to turn over the card showing 7 (because the number 3 is not the number 7), even though the original conditional does not mention the number 7 at all.

The obvious conclusion, which many psychologists draw, is that people are not logical, and that logic has relatively little to do with real human reasoning.

A variant of the selection task

Psychologists have shown that people perform far better when the selection task experiment is performed with a problem that is formally equivalent to the card version of the task but has meaningful content. The classic experiment of this kind considers the situation in which people are drinking in a bar, and the subject is asked to check whether the following conditional holds:

> *If a person is drinking alcohol in a bar,*
> *then the person is at least eighteen years old.*

Again there are four cases to consider, but this time instead of four cards there are four people. We can see what two of them are drinking, but not how old they are; and we can see how old two of them are, but not what they are drinking:

> *Bob, drinking beer.*
> *Mary, a senior citizen, obviously over eighteen years old.*

John, drinking cola.
Susan, a primary school child, obviously under eighteen years old.

In contrast with the card version of the selection task, most people solve the bar version correctly, realising that it is necessary to check Bob to make sure that he is at least eighteen years old, and to check Susan to make sure that she is not drinking alcohol, but that it is not necessary to check Mary and John.

Cognitive psychologists have proposed a bewildering number of theories to explain why people are so much better at solving such versions of the selection task compared with other, formally equivalent variations, like the original card version. The most generally cited of these theories, due to Leda Cosmides (1985, 1989), is that humans have evolved a specialised algorithm (or procedure) for detecting cheaters in social contracts. The algorithm has the general form:

If you accept a benefit,
then you must meet its requirement.

In the bar version of the selection task, the "benefit" is "drinking beer" and the "requirement" is "being at least eighteen years old".

Cosmides and her co-workers also argue that humans have evolved other specialised algorithms for dealing with other kinds of problems, for example an algorithm for avoiding hazards:

If you engage in a hazardous activity,
then you should take the appropriate precaution.

Stephen Pinker (1997) cites Cosmides' evolutionary explanation approvingly in his widely acclaimed book, *How the Mind Works*. He points out that the cheater algorithm explanation doesn't always justify the logically correct solution. For example, given the conditional *if he pays $20 he receives a watch*, subjects typically select the person who doesn't pay $20, to check he hasn't received a watch. But logically, this is unnecessary, because the conditional doesn't say that *he receives a watch only if he pays $20*. The conditional is entirely compatible, for example, with *a person receiving a watch if he takes early retirement*. Thus, according to Cosmides and Pinker, evolutionary algorithms explain human performance on selection tasks, whether or not that performance coincides with the dictates of classical logic.

At about the same time as Cosmides developed the evolutionary theory, Cheng and Holyoak (1985) put forward a related theory that people reason about realistic situations using specialised algorithms. But for Cheng and Holyoak, these algorithms are "pragmatic reasoning schemes". Chief among these pragmatic schemes are ones involving *deontic* notions concerned with permission, obligation and prohibition. In English these notions are typically signalled by the use of such words as "can", "should", "need" and "must". But these explicit linguistic signals can be omitted if the context makes it obvious that an obligation or prohibition is involved, as in the formulation of the bar version of the selection task above.

In fact, if Cheng and Holyoak are right, then the security check version of the selection task shouldn't be hard at all, because the most natural interpretation of the conditional:

If a passenger is carrying a rucksack on his or her back,
then the passenger is wearing a label with the letter A on his or her front.

is deontic:

If a passenger is carrying a rucksack on his or her back,
*then the passenger **should be** wearing a label with the letter A*
on his or her front.

But then the real problem isn't just how people reason with conditionals in logical form, but also how people interpret natural language conditionals and translate them into conditionals in logical form.

But both Cosmides and Cheng and Holyoak draw a different conclusion. They argue that people do not have an in-built, general-purpose ability for abstract logical reasoning, but instead employ specialised procedures for dealing with classes of practical problems that arise naturally in the world around them. I will discuss the selection task in greater detail in Chapter 16, but the relationship between general-purpose and special-purpose methods is too important not to address it here. It is part of the more fundamental relationship between knowledge representation and problem solving, which is one of the main themes of this book.

Thinking = knowledge representation + problem solving

In Artificial Intelligence, the ultimate goal of an agent is to maintain itself in a harmonious relationship with the world. For this purpose, intelligent agents employ a mental representation of the world and use that representation to respond to threats and opportunities that arise in their environment. They do so by observing the current state of the world, generating appropriate goals, reducing those goals to actions and performing actions, to change the world for their benefit. In Computational Logic, these mental representations are expressed in a logical language of thought; and both the generation of goals from observations and the reduction of goals to actions are performed by logical reasoning.

Thus, an intelligent agent needs both specialised knowledge (in the form of goals and beliefs) and general-purpose reasoning abilities (including forward and backward reasoning). The agent needs specialised knowledge, both to deal with everyday problems that occur as a matter of course, and to deal with problems that might never occur but could have life-threatening consequences if they do. But the agent also needs general-purpose reasoning, to be able to use its knowledge flexibly and efficiently.

The relationship between knowledge representation and reasoning is like the relationship between a computer program and program execution. Knowledge is like a computer program, consisting of specialised procedures for solving problems that are particular to a problem domain. Reasoning is like program execution, employing general-purpose methods to execute programs in any domain. In Computational Logic, programs are represented in logical form, and program execution is performed by applying rules of inference.

Compared with conventional computer programs, whose syntax consists of instructions for a machine, programs in logical form are much higher-level, in that their syntax more closely mirrors the semantic structure of the world that they represent. However, in Computational Logic the application of general-purpose inference rules to domain-specific knowledge behaves like specialised algorithms and procedures. This relationship can be expressed in the form of an equation:

$$algorithm = knowledge + reasoning.$$

I will argue later in this book that the kind of specialised algorithm involved in cheater detection can be viewed as combining a goal (or constraint) of the logical form:

> *if a person accepts a benefit*
> *and the person fails to meet its requirement*
> *then false.*

with general-purpose reasoning with goals that have the form of such conditionals. In general, given a goal of the logical form:

> *if conditions then conclusion.*

- reason forward to match an observation with a *condition* of the goal
- reason backward to verify the *other conditions* of the goal
- reason forward to derive the *conclusion* as an achievement goal.

In the special case where the achievement goal is *false* and therefore unachievable, then this pattern of reasoning detects violation of the goal. In the special case where the *other conditions* are properties that can be observed in the agent's environment, then the agent can attempt to verify these properties by actively attempting to observe whether or not they are true.

This analysis of the cheater detection algorithm applies without prejudice to the issue of whether or not people actually use such algorithms to solve selection tasks. Moreover, it is compatible with the argument of Sperber *et al.* (1995) that people are more likely to solve selection task problems in accordance with the norms of classical logic, the more natural it is for them to represent the conditional:

if conditions then conclusion
in the form: *it is not the case that*
conditions and not conclusion.
or equivalently: *if conditions and not conclusion then false.*

This analysis of the cheater detection algorithm is also compatible with the argument of Cheng and Holyoak (1985) and Stenning and van Lambalgen (2008) that people more readily solve selection task problems in accordance with classical logic if they interpret those problems in deontic terms. It is even compatible with Cosmides' argument that people use Darwinian algorithms, because the analysis is independent of the source of the agent's knowledge. The agent might have obtained its knowledge by learning it through its own experience, by learning it from parents, teachers or friends, or by inheriting it through the mechanisms of Darwinian evolution.

Although this analysis may explain some of the cases in which people reason correctly in terms of classical logic, it does not explain those cases, as in the card version of the selection task, where they reason with the converse of the conditional or where they fail to reason with the contrapositive. We will return to this problem in Chapter 16. But before we leave this chapter, we will look at another example that challenges the claim that people reason using logical rules of inference.

The suppression task

Consider the following pair of premises:

If she has an essay to write, then she will study late in the library.
She has an essay to write.

Most people correctly conclude:

She will study late in the library.

Suppose I now say in addition:

If the library is open, then she will study late in the library.

Given this additional information, many people (about 40%) suppress their earlier conclusion that *she will study late in the library.*

This problem was originally studied by Ruth Byrne (1989) and used as evidence to argue that people do not reason with logical rules of inference, such as *modus ponens* (forward reasoning), but reason instead by constructing and inspecting mental models, which are like architects' models or diagrams, whose structure is analogous to the structure of the situation they represent.

Mental models, as Johnson-Laird (1983) and Johnson-Laird and Byrne (1991) describe them, look a lot like the semantic structures that we investigate in later, mainly additional chapters. But they also look like sets of atomic sentences, and consequently are ambiguous by the rigorous standards of mathematical logic (Hodges, 1993, 2006). It would be easy to dismiss mental models as confusing syntax and semantics. But it might be a sign of a deeper relationship between syntax and semantics than is normally understood.

Indeed, somewhat in the spirit of mental models, I will argue later in this book that the appropriate semantics for Computational Logic is one in which semantic structures are represented syntactically as sets of atomic sentences. I will also argue that the kind of reasoning that is most useful in Computational Logic is the reasoning involved in generating such a synactically represented semantic structure, in order to make or show that a given set of sentences may be true. We will see that it is hard to distinguish between reasoning about truth in such syntactic/semantic structures and reasoning with purely syntactic rules of inference.

Like the Wason selection task, the suppression task has generated a wealth of alternative explanations. The explanation that comes closest to the approach of this book is the explanation of Stenning and van Lambalgen (2008) that solving problems stated in natural language is a two-stage process of first identifying the logical form of the problem and then reasoning with that logical form. The mistake that many psychologists make is to ignore the first stage of the process, assuming that if the syntax of a natural language statement already has an apparently logical form, then that apparent form is the intended form of the statement's meaning.

We saw a clear example of the difference between the apparent logical form of an English sentence and its intended logical form in Chapter 1, in the case of the second sentence of the London Underground Emergency Notice:

> *The driver will stop*
> *if any part of the train is in a station.*

where its intended meaning was:

> *The driver will stop the train in a station*
> *if the driver is alerted to an emergency*
> *and any part of the train is in the station.*

The intended meaning of the sentence contains both the missing object, *the train*, of the verb *stop* and an extra condition, coming from the context of the previous sentence *press the alarm signal button to alert the driver*. Because this missing condition is already present in the context, it is relatively easy for the reader to supply it without even noticing it isn't actually there.

Arguably, the situation in the suppression task is similar, in that the English-language sentence *if she has an essay to write, then she will study late in the library* is also missing an extra condition, namely *the library is open*, needed to represent the logical form of its intended meaning:

> *If she has an essay to write and the library is open,*
> *then she will study late in the library.*

But in the suppression task, the missing condition comes in a later sentence, rather than in an earlier one. In any case, it is hard to argue that the later sentence *if the library is open, then she will study late in the library* means what it actually says. Taken literally, the sentence says that she will study late in the library, whether or not she has an essay to write, as long as the library is open. It is also hard to argue that the sentence measures up to the standards of clarity advocated in books on good English writing style.

There are a number of ways that the task could be reformulated, to conform to better standards of English style. Perhaps the formulation that is closest to the original statement of the problem is a reformulation as a rule and an exception:

> *If she has an essay to write, she will study late in the library.*
> *But, if the library is not open, she will not study late in the library.*

Exceptions are a conventional way of adding extra conditions to a rule, after a simplified form of the rule has been presented. In general, rules and exceptions have the form:

Rule: *a conclusion holds if conditions hold.*
Exception: *but the conclusion does not hold if other conditions hold.*

Expressed in this form, the meaning of the rule depends upon the context of the exception that follows it. However, the rule can also be expressed context-independently, as strict logical form requires, by adding to the rule an extra condition:

Context-independent rule: *a conclusion holds if conditions hold*
                            and other conditions do not hold.

In the suppression task, the extra condition is equivalent to the positive condition *the library is open*.

We will see other examples of rules and exceptions in later chapters. We will see that the kind of reasoning involved in the suppression task, once its intended logical form has been identified, is a form of *default* (or *defeasible*) *reasoning*, in which the conclusion of a rule is deemed to hold by default, but is subsequently withdrawn (or suppressed) when additional information contradicting the application of the rule is given later.

Natural language understanding versus logical reasoning

Communicating effectively in natural language is a challenge not only for the writer (or speaker) but also for the reader (or listener). It is a challenge for the writer, who needs to express her thoughts as clearly, coherently and effectively as possible; and it is a challenge for the reader, who needs to construct a logical form of the communication, assimilate that logical form into his web of goals and beliefs, and act appropriately if necessary.

As we well know, the syntax of English sentences is only an imperfect conveyor of a writer's thoughts. In particular, English sentences frequently omit conditions (like *the driver is alerted to an emergency* and *the library is open*) and other qualifications (the driver will stop *the train*) needed to reconstruct their meaning. As a consequence, although a reader needs to use the syntax of English sentences to help him reconstruct their logical form, he cannot rely exclusively upon their syntax. In many cases, there can be several, alternative candidate logical forms for the same English sentence, and consequently the reader needs to draw on other resources to help him choose between the alternatives.

The only other resource a reader can draw upon are his own goals and beliefs, including the goals and beliefs he has extracted from previous sentences in the discourse, and including his beliefs about the writer's goals and beliefs. In choosing between the alternative meanings of a sentence, the reader needs to choose a logical form that is as coherent as possible with this context.

There are different ways to judge coherence. Obviously, a logical form that has no connections with the reader's understanding of the writer's goals and beliefs is less coherent than a logical form that does have such connections. A logical form that confirms this understanding is more coherent than a logic form that conflicts with this understanding. In a sequence of English sentences, a logical form that has connections with the logical forms of previous sentences is more coherent than a logical form that does not.

I have already argued, following Stenning and van Lambalgen, that the suppression task is a clear-cut case in which the first stage of solving the problem, namely constructing its logical form, is much harder than the second stage of reasoning with that logical form. In particular, it is hard because the writer has expressed one of the sentences in the converse form of its intended meaning. By comparison, the selection task is even more difficult, because both stages are hard.

The first stage of the selection task is hard, because the reader has to decide whether the conditional has any missing conditions, whether it is the only conditional having the given conclusion, and whether it is to be interpreted as a goal or as a belief. To help in making these decisions, the reader needs to assimilate the logical form of the conditional as coherently as possible into his existing goals and beliefs. Sperber *et al.* (1995) argue that, because there is so much variation possible in the first stage of the selection task, it is impossible to form any judgement about the correctness of the reasoning processes involved in the second stage. This view is also supported by the results of experiments by Almor and Sloman (2000) who showed that, when subjects are asked to recall the problem after they have given their solution, they report a problem statement that is consistent with their solution rather than with the original problem statement.

The second stage of the selection task is hard, mostly because negation is hard. For one thing, it can be argued that positive observations are more fundamental than negative observations. For example, we observe that a person is tall, fat and handsome, not that she is not short, not thin and not ugly. Such negative sentences have to be inferred from positive observations or assumptions, and the longer the chain of inferences needed to derive a conclusion, the harder it is to derive it.

We will look at reasoning with negation in greater detail in subsequent chapters. In the meanwhile, there is another issue, which goes to the heart of the relationship between logical and psychological reasoning, namely whether the given task is to be solved in the context of an agent's goals and beliefs, or whether it is to be solved in a context in which those goals and beliefs are temporarily suspended.

Reasoning in context

I argued above that, because natural language is ambiguous, readers often need to choose between alternative logical forms as a representation of the writer's intended meaning. The syntax of an English sentence is only one guide to that intended meaning. Coherence with the reader's existing goals and beliefs, including logical forms of earlier sentences in the same discourse, as well as the reader's beliefs about the writer's goals and beliefs, all play a part in helping to identify the intended logical form of a new sentence in the discourse.

Most of the time we understand communications intuitively, spontaneously and unconsciously, without being aware of these difficulties, relying perhaps more on our expectations of what the writer wants to say, than on what the writer actually says.

Sometimes, when communications have little connection with our own experience, they go in one ear and out the other, as though they were a kind of background noise. And sometimes we just understand sentences in our own, private way, only loosely connected to what the writer has written, and even more loosely connected to what the writer had in mind.

In contrast with sentences in natural language, sentences in logical form say exactly what they mean. But because different people have different goals and beliefs, the same sentence in logical form has different significance for different people. So, although a sentence may have the same meaning for different people when the sentence is regarded in isolation, it may have a different meaning (or significance) when the sentence is understood in the context of a person's goals and beliefs.

Assume, for example, that the sentence *Susan has a rucksack on her back* means exactly what it says, and is already in logical form. But if I believe that *Susan has a bomb in the rucksack* and you believe that *Susan has only her lunch in the rucksack*, then the same belief that *Susan has a rucksack on her back* has a different significance for the two of us.

Understanding sentences for their significance in the context of the reader's goals and beliefs is a higher kind of logic than understanding sentences in the isolated context of a psychological experiment. But most psychological studies of human reasoning make the opposite assumption: that logical reasoning means interpreting natural language problem statements context-independently, using only the sentences explicitly presented in the experiment.

Such ability to suspend one's own goals and beliefs and to reason context-independently, as studied in psychological experiments, is indeed an important and useful skill, but it is not quite the same as reasoning logically. In some cases, it is more like failing to see the wood for the trees.

Computational Logic is concerned with representing goals and beliefs in logical form and reasoning with those representations to solve problems that arise in the real world. Compared with representations in logical form, communications in natural language are generally only a poor approximation to the logical forms of those communications. As a consequence, reasoning tasks presented in natural language are often only an approximation to reasoning tasks performed on pure logical forms.

Before we conclude this chapter, we will look at yet another example that illustrates the confusion between natural language understanding and logical reasoning.

The use of conditionals to explain observations

The philosopher John Pollock (1995) uses the following example, not to argue that people are illogical, but to support the view that real logic involves a sophisticated form of argumentation, in which people evaluate arguments for and against a given conclusion. Here I use the same example to illustrate the difference between the apparent logic of the natural language statement of a problem and the underlying logic of the problem when it is viewed in the context of an agent's goals and beliefs.

Suppose I tell you that:

> *An object is red if it looks red.*

Try to suspend any other goals and beliefs you might have about being red and looking red, and treat the sentence as meaning exactly what it says. Now suppose I also tell you that:

> *This apple looks red.*

You will probably draw the obvious conclusion that *this apple is red*. Now suppose I say in addition:

> *An object looks red if it is illuminated by a red light.*

It is likely that you will now withdraw your previous conclusion.

The example is similar to the suppression task, because the third sentence can be interpreted as drawing your attention to a missing condition in the first sentence:

> *An object is red if it looks red and it is not illuminated by a red light.*

Pollock explains the example in terms of competing arguments for and against the conclusion that *this apple is red*. But there is an alternative explanation: namely, that you understand the first sentence in the context of your existing beliefs, which already include, perhaps naïvely, the belief that looking red is caused by being red, represented in the natural *effect if cause* form:

An object looks red if it is red.

Thus the first sentence of the discourse is the converse of your pre-existing causal belief. It tells you in effect that the writer believes that the *only* cause of an object looking red is that it actually is red. Given *only* this first sentence of the discourse, you conclude that the apple is red because that is the *only* way of explaining the observation that the apple looks red.

However, the third sentence of the discourse gives an additional possible cause for an object looking red. Either you already have this additional causal belief, and the writer is simply drawing your attention to it, or you add this new causal belief to your existing beliefs. In both cases the logical form of the third sentence is coherent with your existing beliefs. And in both cases you withdraw the assumption that being red is the only explanation for the apple looking red.

This way of thinking about the example views it as a problem of *abductive reasoning*, which is the problem of generating hypotheses to explain observations. Abductive reasoning is the topic of Chapter 10.

Conclusions

In this chapter, we considered the claim, supported by the selection task, that people reason by means of specialised algorithms rather than by means of general-purpose logic. I attacked this claim by arguing that it fails to appreciate that specialised algorithms combine specialised knowledge with general-purpose reasoning.

Following Sperber *et al.* (1995) and Stenning and van Lambalgen (2008), I argued that the discussion of psychological experiments of reasoning often fails to pay adequate attention to the first stage of solving such problems, which is to translate them from natural language into logical form. Moreover, it fails in particular to take into account the need for those logical forms to be coherent with the reader's other goals and beliefs.

However, even taking these arguments into account, there remain problems associated with the second stage of reasoning with the resulting logical forms. Some of these problems, as illustrated by both the suppression task and the red light examples, have to do with the relationship between conditionals and their converse. Other, more difficult problems have to do with reasoning with negation. Both kinds of problems, reasoning with converses and reasoning with negation, will be taken up in later chapters.

We also considered the argument, supported by the suppression task, that people reason by means of mental models rather than by means of rules of inference. In the more advanced Chapters A2, A3, A4 and A6, I will argue that forward and backward reasoning can both be viewed as determining truth in minimal models. This observation lends support to a variant of the mental model theory of deduction, reconciling it with the seemingly contrary view that people reason by means of rules of inference.

3

The fox and the crow

In this chapter we revisit the ancient Greek fable of the fox and the crow, to show how the proactive thinking of the fox outwits the reactive thinking of the crow. In later chapters, we will see how reactive and proactive thinking can be combined.

The fox and the crow are a metaphor for different kinds of people. Some people are *proactive*, like the fox in the story. They like to plan ahead, foresee obstacles, and lead an orderly life. Other people are *reactive*, like the crow. They like to be open to what is happening around them, take advantage of new opportunities, and be spontaneous. Most people are both proactive and reactive, at different times and to varying degrees.

The fox and the crow

Most people know the story, attributed to Aesop, about the fox and the crow. It starts, harmlessly enough, with the crow perched in a tree with some cheese in its beak, when along comes the fox, who wants to have the cheese.

Goal: *The fox has cheese.*
Beliefs: *The crow has cheese.*
An animal has an object
if the animal is near the object
and the animal picks up the object.
The fox is near cheese if the crow sings.
The crow sings if the fox praises the crow.

In this version of the story, we consider the fox's point of view. To model her proactive way of thinking, we represent her goals and beliefs in logical form:

Goal: *I have the cheese.*

Beliefs: *the crow has the cheese.*

> *An animal has an object*
> *if the animal is near the object*
> *and the animal picks up the object.*
>
> *I am near the cheese*
> *if the crow has the cheese*
> *and the crow sings.*
>
> *the crow sings if I praise the crow.*

As you can see, the fox is not only a logician of sorts, but also an amateur physicist. In particular, her belief about being near the cheese if the crow sings combines in a single statement her knowledge about her location relative to the crow with her knowledge of the laws of gravity. Reasoning informally, the single statement can be derived from other more fundamental statements in the following way:

> The fox knows that if the crow sings,
> then the crow will open its beak
> and the cheese will fall to the ground under the tree.
>
> The fox also knows that, because the fox is under the tree,
> the fox will then be near the cheese.

> Therefore, the fox knows she will be near the cheese if the crow sings.

The fox is also an amateur behavioural psychologist. Being a behaviourist, she is interested only in the crow's external, input–output behaviour, and not in any internal methods that the crow might use to generate that behaviour. In particular, although the fox represents her own beliefs about the crow in logical terms, she does not assume that the crow also uses logic to represent any beliefs about anything. As far as the fox is concerned, the crow's behaviour might be generated by means of condition–action rules without any logical form. Or his behaviour might even be "hardwired" directly into his body, without even entering into his mind.

Like the fox's belief about being near the cheese if the crow sings, the fox's belief that the crow will sing if the fox praises the crow might also be derived from other, more fundamental beliefs. They might be derived perhaps from more general beliefs about the way some naïve, reactive agents respond to being praised, without thinking about the possible consequences of their actions.

The fox also has ordinary common sense. She knows that an animal will have an object if she is near the object and picks it up. As with her other beliefs, she can derive this belief from more basic beliefs. For example, she can derive this belief from the simpler belief that an animal will have an object if the animal picks up the object, by combining it with the constraint that to pick up an object the animal has to be near the object (ignoring other constraints like the weight and size of the object).

The fox holds this belief about the conditions under which she will have an object as a general law, which applies universally to any animal and to any object (although she doesn't seem to know that the law also applies to robots, unless she views robots as another species of animal). She also knows enough logic to be able to *instantiate* the general law, in other words, to apply it to special instances of animals and objects, such as the fox and the cheese respectively.

The fox's beliefs as a logic program

The fox's beliefs have not only logical form, but they also have the more specialised form of conditionals:

> *conclusion if conditions.*

Both the conclusion and the conditions are written in declarative form. The conditionals are written backwards, conclusion first, to indicate that they can be used to reason backwards, from conclusions to conditions. Using backward reasoning, each such conditional behaves as a goal-reduction procedure:

> *to show or make the conclusion hold,*
> *show or make the conditions hold.*

Even "facts", which record observations, like the belief that the crow has the cheese, can be viewed as conditionals that have a conclusion, but no conditions:

> *conclusion if nothing.*

Or in more logical terms:

> *conclusion if true.*

Such facts also behave as procedures:

> *to show or make the conclusion hold, show or make*
> *true hold.*

or:　　　　　　*to show or make the conclusion hold, do nothing.*

Therefore, the fox's beliefs can be used as a collection of procedures:

to have an object, be near the object and pick up the object.
to be near the cheese, check the crow has the cheese
and make the crow sing.
to make the crow sing, praise the crow.
to check that the crow has the cheese, do nothing.

Notice that the subgoals in these procedures are expressed in the imperative mood. This manner of expression is risky. What do you do if you have two alternative procedures for achieving the same goal? For example:

to have an object, make the object.

There is no problem with a declarative formulation:

An animal has an object if the animal makes the object.

But the two procedures, with two imperatives, create a conflict. We will see later in Chapter 7 that the need for conflict resolution, to choose between conflicting imperatives, also arises with condition–action rules. However, in the meanwhile, we can avoid such explicit conflicts by treating the subgoals of procedures, not as imperatives, but as recommendations:

to have an object, you can be near the object
and you can pick up the object.
to have an object, you can make the object.

You wouldn't get very far with such irresolute language in the army, but at least you would avoid the need for conflict resolution. However, let's not worry about these niceties for now, and return to our story of the fox and the crow.

The fox can use these procedures (whether expressed imperatively or as recommendations), one after the other, to reduce the top-level goal *I have the cheese* to the two action subgoals *I praise the crow and I pick up the cheese*. Together, these two actions constitute a plan for achieving the top-level goal.

Backward reasoning in connection graphs

The fox's reduction of her original goal to the two action subgoals can be visualised as searching for a solution in the connection graph that links her top-level goal to the web of her beliefs. Of course, the totality of all her beliefs is bound to be huge, and the search would be like looking for a needle in a haystack. However, the strategy of backward reasoning guides the search, so that she needs to consider only relevant beliefs whose conclusion matches the goal.

Starting from the original, top-level goal and following links in the graph, the fox can readily find a subgraph that connects the goal either to known facts, such as *the crow has the cheese*, or to action subgoals, such as *I praise the crow* and *I pick up the object*, that can be turned into facts by executing them successfully in the real world. This subgraph is a *proof* that, if the actions in the plan succeed, and if the fox's beliefs are actually *true*, then the fox will achieve her top-level goal. The fox's strategy for searching the graph, putting the connections together and constructing the proof is called a *proof procedure*.

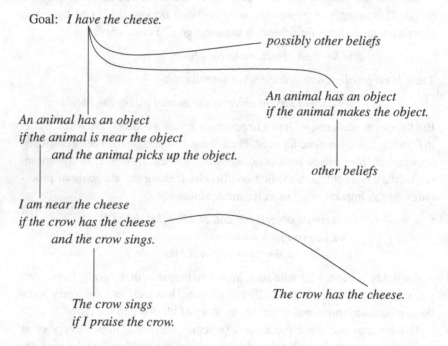

Goal: *I have the cheese.*

possibly other beliefs

*An animal has an object
if the animal makes the object.*

*An animal has an object
if the animal is near the object
        and the animal picks up the object.*

other beliefs

*I am near the cheese
if the crow has the cheese
        and the crow sings.*

The crow has the cheese.

*The crow sings
if I praise the crow.*

Backward reasoning is performed by matching (or better *unifying*) a goal with the conclusion of a conditional and deriving the conditions of the conditional as subgoals. For example, the top-level goal:

>   *I have the cheese.*

matches the conclusion of the conditional:

>   *An animal has an object
>   if the animal is near the object and the animal picks up the object.*

Backward reasoning derives the two subgoals:

>   *I am near the cheese and I pick up the cheese.*

by *instantiating* the general terms *the animal* and *the object* with the specific terms *I* and *the cheese* respectively.

The second of these two subgoals is an action, which matches the conclusion of no conditional in the connection graph. It can be solved only by performing it successfully. However, the first subgoal can be reduced to other subgoals by three further steps of backward reasoning. The final result of this chain of backward reasoning is a logical proof that the fox has the cheese if she praises the crow and picks up the cheese.

In traditional logic, it is more common to present proofs in the forward direction. In this case, a traditional proof would look more like this:

	I praise the crow.
Therefore:	*the crow sings.*
	The crow has the cheese.
Therefore:	*I am near the cheese.*
	I pick up the cheese.
Therefore:	*I have the cheese.*

Although forward reasoning is a natural way to present proofs after they have been found, backward reasoning is normally a more efficient way to find them. Both forward and backward reasoning involve search; but given a goal to be solved, backward reasoning is goal-directed and focuses attention on beliefs that are relevant to the goal.

The connection graph pictured above illustrates only a fraction of the beliefs that are potentially relevant to the goal. Some of the links, like the one linking the top-level goal to the belief that *an animal has an object if the animal makes the object* do not feature in the plan that the fox eventually finds to solve her goal. The belief is relevant to the goal, because its conclusion matches the goal. But for simplicity, I have ignored, for now, the possibility that the fox might explore this alternative way of solving her top-level goal.

In a more realistic representation of the graph, there would be many more such potentially relevant links. Some of them might lead to other solutions, for example to the solution in which the fox climbs the tree and snatches the cheese from the crow. Others might lead to useless or even counter-productive attempted solutions, for example the fox leaping at the crow, but frightening him away in the process.

The fox needs both a strategy to guide her search for solutions and a strategy to compare solutions and decide between them. We will discuss the problem of searching for solutions in Chapter 4, and the problem of deciding between solutions in later chapters.

But, first, notice that, in addition to other links, which lead to other ways of trying to solve the top-level goal *I have the cheese*, there is another way of trying to solve the goal, which doesn't even make it, as a link, into the graph, namely by trying to use the fact *the crow has the cheese*. Remember this fact is actually a kind of degenerate conditional *the crow has the cheese if true*, which behaves as the simple procedure *to check that the crow has the cheese, do nothing*. This procedure could be used to try to solve the top-level goal *I have the cheese*, by trying to identify (match or unify) the two specific terms *I* and *the crow*. If this identification were possible, backward reasoning with the fact would solve the top-level goal in one step.

We have been using the related terms *identification, instantiation, matching* and *unification* informally. These terms have precise definitions, which are presented in Chapter A3. For the purposes of this example, it suffices to note that these definitions preclude the possibility of identifying different specific terms with one another. So, unless the fox is having an identity crisis, she cannot match the conclusion of the degenerate conditional *the crow has the cheese if true* with her goal *I have the cheese*. The connection graph does not include a link between the fact and the goal, because it pre-computes unifying instantiations, and recognises that the identification of the specific terms *I* with *the crow* is impossible. This pre-computation is independent of the different purposes to which such a link might contribute.

Thus backward reasoning, connection graphs and a host of other techniques developed in the field of Automated Reasoning in Artificial Intelligence significantly reduce the amount of search that an agent needs to perform to solve its goals. But even with all of these refinements, the problem of search is inescapable, and we will return to it in Chapter 4, where it gets a whole chapter of its own.

The end of the story of the fox and the crow?

For a logic extremist, this would be the end of the story. For the extremist, there is no difference between the fox's world and the fox's beliefs about the world, and no difference between the fox's plan for getting the cheese and the fox's actually having it.

However, common sense tells us that there is more to life than just thinking. In addition to thinking, an agent needs to observe changes in the world and to perform actions to change the world in return. Logic serves these purposes by providing the agent with a means of constructing symbolic representations of the world and of processing those representations to reason about the world. We can picture this relationship between the world and logic in the mind of an agent like this:

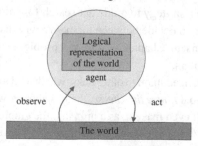

Representation and meaning

This relationship can be looked at in different ways. On the one hand, sentences in logical form *represent* certain aspects of the agent's experience of the world. On the other hand, the world is an *interpretation*, which gives *meaning* (or *semantics*) to sentences expressing the agent's goals and beliefs.

This notion of *meaning*, by the way, is quite different from the meaning that we were concerned with before, when we understood *meaning* as the thoughts that people attempt to communicate by means of sentences in natural language. There, the meaning of a public sentence was a private sentence in the communicator's language of thought. Here, it is the meaning of that private sentence in relationship to the world. These relationships between different kinds of meaning can be pictured like this:

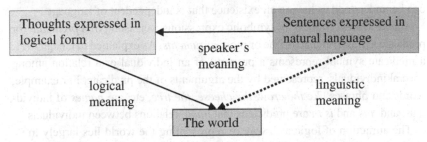

Whereas before we were concerned with so-called *speaker's meaning*, here we are concerned with *logical meaning*. Linguists and philosophers are also concerned with *linguistic meaning*, understood in terms of the relationship between natural language sentences and the world. But in my opinion, ordinary natural language communications are too imprecise and too clumsy to have a meaning that is independent of the logical meaning of their speaker's meaning.

We can better understand the notion of logical meaning if we consider it in general terms, as a relationship between sentences in logical form and *interpretations* (sometimes also called *models* or *possible worlds*), including artificial and imaginary worlds, like the world in the story of the fox and the crow. An *interpretation* is just a collection of *individuals* and *relationships* among individuals. For simplicity, properties of individuals are also regarded as relationships.

An interpretation in traditional logic normally corresponds to a single, static state of the world. For example:

> In the story of the fox and the crow, the fox, crow, cheese, tree, ground under the tree, and airspace between the crow and the ground can be regarded as individuals; and someone having something can be regarded as a relationship between two individuals. The sentence "The crow has the cheese." is true in the interpretation at the beginning of the story and false in the interpretation at the end of the story.

The simplest way to represent an interpretation in symbolic form is to represent it by the set of all the atomic sentences that are true in the interpretation. In this example we might represent the interpretation at the beginning of the story by the atomic sentences:

> *the crow has the cheese.*
> *the crow is in the tree.*
> *the tree is above the air.*
> *the air is above the ground.*
> *the tree is above the ground.*
> *the fox is on the ground.*

The difference between such atomic sentences and the interpretation they represent is that in an interpretation the individuals and the relationships between them can be understood as having an existence that is independent of language.

Atomic sentences are only symbolic expressions, consisting of a *predicate* (or predicate symbol) and zero, one or more *arguments*. As explained in Chapter A1, a predicate symbol represents a property of an individual or a relation among several individuals, represented by the arguments of the predicate. For example, words and phrases like *the crow, the cheese, the tree*, etc. are *names* of individuals, and *has* and *is in* are predicates that *name* relations between individuals.

The attraction of logic as a way of representing the world lies largely in its ability to represent regularities (or rules) by means of conditional sentences. For instance, in the atomic sentences above, the fact that *the tree is above the ground* can be derived from the more basic facts that *the tree is above the air* and *the air is above the ground*, given the conditional:

> *one object is above a second object*
> *if the first object is above a third object*
> *and the third object is above the second object.*

Or, looking at it differently, the conditional is *true* in the interpretation represented by the atomic sentences.

The ultimate purpose of interpretations is to determine whether sentences are *true* or *false*. In the case of an agent embedded in the real world, beliefs that are *true* are normally more useful than beliefs that are *false*. Goals that are easy to make *true* are normally more useful than goals that are difficult to make *true*.

In general, the problem of determining the truth value of a non-atomic sentence in an interpretation reduces to the problem of determining the truth values of simpler sentences. For example:

> A sentence of the form *conclusion if conditions* is *true*
> if *conditions* is *false* or *conclusion* is *true*.

A sentence of the form *everything has property P* is *true*
if for every individual *T* in the interpretation, *T has property P* is *true*.

Backward reasoning with such meta-sentences (sentence about sentences) eventually reduces the problem of determining the truth value of an arbitrary sentence to the problem of determining the truth values of atomic sentences alone.

Thus, for the purpose of determining whether arbitrary sentences are *true* or *false*, it is unnecessary to know what are the real individuals and relationships in an interpretation. It is sufficient merely to know which atomic sentences are *true* and which atomic sentences are *false*.

We will investigate semantics in greater detail in the more advanced Chapter A2, and the representation of changing states of the world in Chapter 13. But before we leave this chapter:

What is the moral of the story of the fox and the crow?

Presumably Aesop's fable had a purpose – a lesson that it is not safe to take another agent's words and actions at face value, without trying to understand the agent's underlying goals and intentions. Or, even more simply, that before you do something you should think about its possible consequences.

The crow in Aesop's fable reacts to the fox's praise spontaneously – without thinking, you could say. A more intelligent crow would monitor his intended actions, before performing them, to determine whether they might have any unintended and undesirable consequences.

If only the crow knew what the fox knows, then the crow might have been able to reason *preactively* as follows:

> *I want to sing.*
> *But if I sing, then the fox will be near the cheese.*
> *If the fox is near the cheese and picks up the cheese,*
> *then the fox will have the cheese.*
> *Perhaps the fox wants to have the cheese and therefore will pick it up.*
> *But then I will not have the cheese.*
> *Since I want to have the cheese, I will not sing.*

This line of reasoning uses some of the same beliefs as those used by the fox, but it uses them forwards rather than backwards. We will investigate this dual use of beliefs for both backward and forward reasoning in future chapters. In the meanwhile, we note that, whether or not the use of logic might seem to be the most natural way to think, it can often help us to think and behave more effectively.

4

Search

It is a common view in some fields that logic has little to do with search. For example, Paul Thagard (2005) in *Mind: Introduction to Cognitive Science* states on page 45: "In logic-based systems, the fundamental operation of thinking is logical deduction, but from the perspective of rule-based systems, the fundamental operation of thinking is search."

Similarly, Jonathan Baron (2008) in his textbook *Thinking and Deciding* writes on page 6: "Thinking about actions, beliefs and personal goals can all be described in terms of a common framework, which asserts that thinking consists of *search* and *inference*. We search for certain objects and then make inferences from and about the objects we have found." On page 97, Baron states that formal logic is not a complete theory of thinking because it "covers only inference".

In this book, we see the inference rules of logic as determining a *search space* of possible solutions of goals, and *search strategies* as determining *proof procedures* for finding solutions of goals. But like Baron, we also see the need to use the inference rules of logic to infer consequences of candidate solutions. Moreover, we also distinguish *thinking*, which generates solutions and infers their consequences, from *deciding*, which evaluates solutions and chooses between them. In Chapter 8, we will see that rule-based systems, championed by Thagard, can also be understood in logical terms.

The relationship between search and backward reasoning is easy to see when the search space generated by backward reasoning is pictured as an *and–or tree*. Nodes in the tree represent atomic goals, with the top-level goal at the top of the tree. There are two kinds of arcs: *or-arcs* linking an atomic goal with all the alternative ways of solving the goal, and *and-arcs* connecting all of the subgoals in the same alternative.

There is a clear relationship between such and–or trees and connection graphs. Or-arcs correspond to links in a connection graph, and and-arcs correspond to the conjunction of all the conditions in a conditional. Here is the and–or tree for the fox's goal of having the crow's cheese:

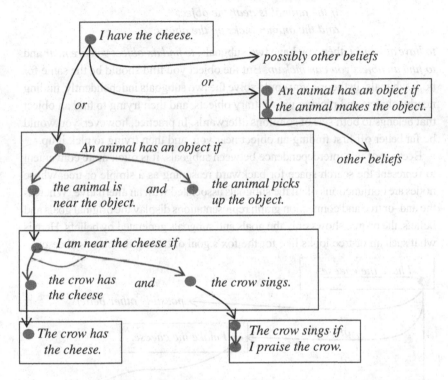

And–or trees have been used extensively for problem solving in Artificial Intelligence, especially for two-person games, such as chess. In game playing, or-arcs represent the first player's alternative moves, and and-arcs represent all of the second player's possible reponses. To win the game, the first player must have a move that defeats every move of the second player.

In very large games, such as chess, it is impossible for a player to search the tree completely before deciding on the next move. However, even in such games, it is often possible to compute an approximate measure of the value of a node, and to use that measure to guide the search for the best solution within the time and other resources available. The minimax search strategy, for example, uses such a measure to choose a move that minimises the value of the best moves for the other player. Similar search strategies can be used for more general and–or trees corresponding to backward reasoning in connection graphs.

In conventional and–or trees, the subgoals associated with the same alternative are independent of one another. But in connection graphs, subgoals are often interdependent. For example, if you are an animal and you try to use the belief:

> *an animal has an object*
> *if the animal is near the object*
> *and the animal picks up the object.*

to have an object, then you have two subgoals, *to find an object you are near* and *to find an object you can pick up.* But the object you find should be the same for both subgoals. In theory, you could solve the two subgoals independently, finding nearby objects and picking up arbitrary objects, and then trying to find an object that belongs to both sets of solutions afterwards. In practice, however, you would be far better off first finding an object near you, and then trying to pick it up.

Because of this interdependence between subgoals, it is often more convenient to represent the search space for backward reasoning as a simple or-tree, whose nodes are conjunctions of all the subgoals associated with an alternative. Whereas the and–or tree and connection graph representations display the original goals and beliefs, the or-tree shows only the goals and subgoals generated by beliefs. Here is what such an or-tree looks like for the fox's goal of having the crow's cheese:

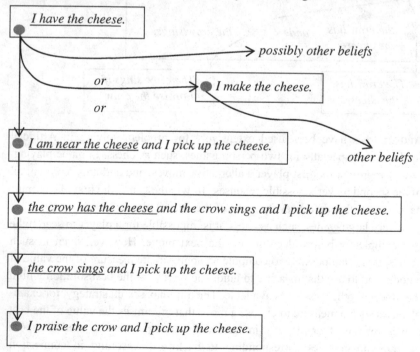

The underlined subgoal in each node is the subgoal selected for goal reduction, which gives rise to the next level of nodes lower in the search space.

Because of their simplicity, it is easy to see how to define a variety of search strategies for searching or-tree search spaces. The most naïve strategy is to search *breadth-first*, level by level, first generating all nodes one step away from the top-level goal, then all nodes two steps away, etc. If there is any solution to the top-level goal, then breadth-first search is guaranteed to find the shortest solution. But breadth-first search is combinatorially explosive. If every node has two alternative successor nodes, one level lower in the tree, then if the shortest solution involves two goal reductions, the search strategy needs to generate only $2^2 = 4$ branches. If it involves 10 goal reductions, it needs to generate $2^{10} = 1024$ branches. But if it involves 50 goal reductions, then it needs to generate $2^{50} = 1,125,899,906,842,624$ branches. No wonder many critics believe that AI is impossible.

There are two ways around the problem. One is to use a better search strategy. The other is to use a better search space. We will come back to the second way later. But first consider the same situation as before, in which every node has two successors, but now suppose that half of the branches contain a solution, say at the same level 50 steps away from the top-level goal. Then, on average, depth-first search needs to generate only 100 nodes to find the first solution.

Depth-first search is the opposite of breadth-first search, it explores only one branch at a time, backtracking to try other branches only when necessary. It is very efficient when the search space contains lots of solutions. But it can go disasterously wrong if it contains infinite branches and they are explored before alternative finite branches containing solutions. Here is a connection graph for a simple example:

Goal: *Who will go to the party?*

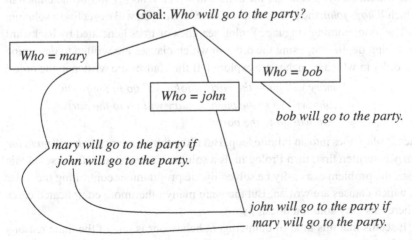

Now consider the or-tree search space for the same problem:

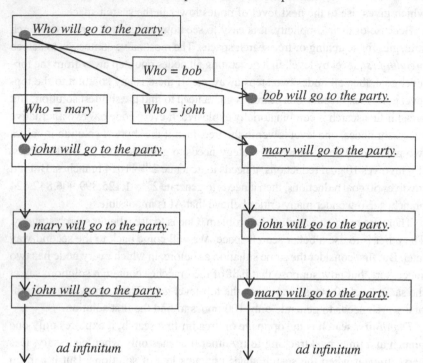

If you are interested in finding only one solution, and you do a breadth-first search, then you find your answer *Who = bob* in one step. But it you do a depth-first search, and you consider the branch in which *Who = mary* or the branch in which *Who = john*, then you can go on forever, but you will never find a solution.

The programming language Prolog searches or-trees generated by backward reasoning depth-first, using the order in which clauses are written to determine the order in which branches are explored. If the clauses are written in the order:

> *mary will go to the party if john will go to the party.*
> *john will go to the party if mary will go to the party.*
> *bob will go to the party.*

then Prolog goes into an infinite loop. But if the third sentence *bob will go to the party* is written first, then Prolog finds a solution in one step. Of course, in this case, the problem can easily be solved by the programmer controlling the order in which clauses are written. But there are many other more complicated cases where this easy solution doesn't work.

It seems that this kind of unintelligent behaviour is one of the main reasons that logic programming languages, like Prolog, went out of fashion in the

1980s. Many alternative solutions to the looping problem and related inefficiencies have been explored since the 1970s, but the one that seems to have been the most effective is the use of *tabling* (Sagonas *et al.*, 1994), which is now incorporated in several Prolog systems.

Tabling maintains subgoals and their solutions in a table. When a previously generated subgoal is re-encountered, the search strategy reuses solutions from the table, instead of redoing inferences that have already been performed. In the example just given, if it generates the subgoal *mary will go to the party* and later generates it again, it will recognise the loop, fail and backtrack to an alternative branch of the search space.

The problem of search is a well-developed area of Artificial Intelligence, featuring prominently in such introductory textbooks as those by Russell and Norvig (2010), Poole and Mackworth (2010) and Luger (2009). The search strategies described in these books apply equally well to the problem of searching for solutions in Computational Logic. For the most part, these search strategies are general-purpose methods, such as depth-first, breadth-first and best-first search.

Best-first search

Best-first search strategies are useful when different solutions of a problem have different values. For example, assuming that the fox in our story judges that having the crow's cheese is more valuable than making her own food, she could use best-first search to guide her search for the best solution.

To use best-first search, you need to be able to evaluate and compare different solutions. For example, if you want to go from A to B, then you might prefer a travel plan that takes the least time, costs the least money or causes the least harm to the environment. No single plan is likely to be best for all of these attributes, so you may have to weigh and trade one attribute off against the other. Given such weights, you can use the weighted sum of the values of the attributes as a single measure of the overall value of a solution.

It is often possible to extend the measure of the value of a complete solution to a measure of the value of a partial solution. For example, suppose you want to travel from Bridgeport in Connecticut to Petworth in England, and you are exploring a partial travel plan that involves flying from New York to London, but haven't figured out the rest of the plan. You know that the best cost of any complete travel plan that extends the partial plan will need to include the cost of the flight. So you can add together the cost of the flight with an estimate for the best costs of any additional travel, to estimate the cost of the best travel plan that includes this partial plan.

Best-first search uses this measure of the value of partial solutions to direct its search for complete solutions. The breadth-first variant of best-first search does this by picking a branch that has currently best value, and generating its successor nodes. Under some easily satisfied conditions, the first solution found in this way is guaranteed to be the best (optimal) solution.

Although such best-first search is better than simple breadth-first search, it suffers from similar disadvantages. It too is computationally explosive, especially when there are many solutions that differ from one another only slightly in value. These disadvantages can be avoided to some extent by a depth-first version of best-first search, which like simple depth-first search, explores only one branch of the search space at a time.

The depth-first version of best-first search keeps a record of the best solution found so far. If the current branch is not a solution, and the branch can be extended, then it extends the branch by generating a successor node that has the highest estimated value. However, if the estimated value of the extended branch exceeds the value of the best solution found so far (if there is one), then the extended branch terminates in failure and the search strategy backtracks to an earlier alternative.

If the current branch is a new solution, then the search strategy compares its value with the value of the best solution found so far (if there is one), and it updates its record of the currently best solution. In this way, the search strategy can be terminated at any time, having generated the best solution that can be found within the computational resources available.

Both variants of best-first search complement the use of decision theory for choosing the best solution, once it has been found. The depth-first variant has the further advantage that it interprets "best solution" more realistically as "the best solution given the computational resources available". Morever, its measure of the value of solutions and of partial solutions can be extended to include not only their utility, but also the probability of their actually achieving their expected outcomes. The resulting measure of value as expected utility, combining utility and probability, integrates best-first search into a classical decision-theoretic framework.

The connection graph of an agent's goals and beliefs can also help with best-first search, by associating with links statistical information about the degree to which the links have proved useful in the past. This information can be used to increase or decrease the strength of connections in the graph. Whenever the agent solves a new goal, it can increase the strength of links that have contributed to the solution, and decrease the strength of links that have led it down the garden path. The strength of links can be used for best-first search, by activating stronger links before weaker links.

The strength of links can be combined with activation levels associated with the agent's current goals and observations. Activation levels can be spread through the graph in proportion to the strength of links, reasoning bidirectionally both backwards from the goals and forwards from the observations. Any candidate action subgoal whose level of activation exceeds a certain threshold can be executed automatically.

The resulting action execution combines a form of best-first search with a form of decision-theoretic choice of best action, in an algorithm that resembles a connectionist model of the brain. An agent model employing this approach has been developed by Pattie Maes (1990). The model does not use logic or connection graphs explicitly, but it can be understood in such purely logical terms.

Connection graphs can also be used to combine search with compiling general-purpose goals and beliefs into more efficient special-purpose form. This is because very strong links between goals and beliefs behave as though the links were goals or beliefs in their own right. Generating these goals or beliefs explicitly and adding them to the graph short-circuits the need to activate the links explicitly in the future. For example, the fox's specialised belief that *the crow sings if I praise the crow* can be generated from such more general-purpose beliefs as:

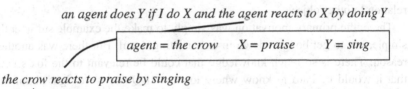

an agent does Y if I do X and the agent reacts to X by doing Y

agent = the crow   X = praise   Y = sing

the crow reacts to praise by singing

I will argue later in Chapter 9 that this kind of compiling links into new goals and beliefs can be viewed in some cases as a kind of compiling of conscious thought into subconscious thought.

Knowledge representation matters

But efficient search strategies and other general-purpose problem-solving methods are only half the story of what it takes to solve problems efficiently. The other half of the story concerns knowledge representation. In our story of the fox and the crow, in particular, we have employed a simplified representation, which vastly over-simplifies the knowledge representation issues involved.

To start with, the representation completely ignores temporal considerations. It is obvious that the action of an agent picking up an object initiates the property of the agent possessing the object afterwards. This property continues to hold until it is terminated by some other action or event, such as the agent giving the object away, losing it or consuming it. Thus, to be more precise, we should have expressed the relationship between picking up an object and possessing it more like this:

an animal has an object at a time
if the animal is near the object at an earlier time
and the animal picks up the object at the earlier time
and nothing terminates the animal having the object between the two times.

In fact, as we will see in Chapter 13, this representation combines in a single belief a more basic law of cause and effect (that a state of possession is initiated by picking up an object) with a constraint (that a precondition of picking up an object is being near the object).

The representation of cause and effect is sufficiently complex that we give it detailed consideration in Chapter 13. But, even ignoring such considerations, there are still major knowledge representation issues at stake. In fact, we skirted around these issues earlier when we argued informally that the fox might derive the belief *I am near the cheese if the crow has the cheese and the crow sings* from more basic beliefs concerning the laws of gravity and her location in relation to other objects.

There, the primary motivation was simply to make the example sufficiently simple, not to get bogged down in excruciating detail. But there was another reason: There is so much knowledge that could be relevant to the fox's goal that it would be hard to know where to stop. If Quine were right about the web of belief, that every belief is connected to every other belief, an agent would potentially need to consider all of its beliefs, in order to solve any goal that might arise in its environment. It is this knowledge representation problem, more than any problem to do with general-purpose reasoning, that is the major bottleneck in developing Artificial Intelligence. Arguably, it is also the biggest problem for understanding and improving human intelligence. To put it more directly, knowledge is more important than raw problem-solving power.

Probably the most ambitious attempt to address this knowledge representation problem is the Cyc Project (Lenat and Guha, 1989; Panton *et al.*, 2006), which has assembled a collection of several million assertions encoding the common-sense knowledge of human experience. Assertions in Cyc are formulated in a variety of Computational Logic, similar to the one investigated in this book, and its inference engine is based primarily on backward reasoning.

Cyc organises its knowledge in collections of micro-theories, concerning such separate domains as science, society and culture, climate and weather, money and financial systems, health care, history and politics. These micro-theories, in turn, are organised in hierarchies, in which micro-theories lower in the hierarchy inherit assertions from more abstract micro-theories higher in the hierarchy. Micro-theories in Cyc are like classes in object-oriented computer programming languages and like modules in some computational theories of the mind. We will have more to say about such classes and modules later in Chapter 14.

5

Negation as failure

It's easy to take negation for granted, and not give it a second thought. Either it will rain or it won't rain. But definitely it won't rain and not rain at the same time and in the same place. Looking at it like that, you can take your pick. Raining and not raining are on a par, like heads and tails. You can have one or the other, but not both.

So it may seem at first glance. But on closer inspection, the reality is different. The world is a positive, not a negative place, and human ways of organising our thoughts about the world are mainly positive too. We directly observe only positive facts, like this coin is showing heads, or it is raining. We have to derive the negation of a positive fact from the absence of the positive fact. The fact that this coin is showing heads implies that it is not showing tails, and the fact that it is sunny implies, everything else being equal, that it is not raining at the same place and the same time.

From an agent's point of view, an observation can be passive or active. A *passive observation* is an observation over which you have no control. The world forces it upon you, and you have to take it on board, like it or not. Because our conceptualisation of the world consists of positive facts, these passive observations are positive, atomic sentences.

An *active observation*, on the other hand, is one that you actively perform to determine the value of some atomic predicate. If the predicate contains no variables,[1] then the result of the observation is either *true* or *false*. If it contains

---

[1] Variables in symbolic logic are similar to variables in mathematics, but more precise. In mathematics, it is common to make no distinction between the different roles that the variable X plays in the two equations: $2X=2$, $X+Y=Y+X$. In the first equation X is an *unknown*, and implicitly, the equation represents the *existentially quantified* goal of showing that there exists an X such that $2X=2$, namely the value $X=1$. However, in the second equation X and Y stand for arbitrary numbers, and implicitly the equation represents the *universally quantified* sentence expressing that for any pair of numbers X and Y it doesn't matter in which order you add them, the result is the same.

variables whose values are unknown, then either the observation succeeds and returns values for the unknowns, or the observation fails and returns a negative observation. In either case, you can use the result and just forget about it, or you can record it for possible future use. For example:

> You look out the window and fail to see any raindrops falling from the sky. You conclude that it is not raining.

> It is just before bedtime and time for a midnight snack, but you are on a diet. You pause to monitor the sensations in your body. Failing to feel pangs of hunger, you decide you are not hungry, and stick to your diet. You are lucky this time. Not only has the active observation of the state of your body returned a negative response, but you have not been attacked by unprovoked, "passive" feelings of hunger.

> You are a robot looking for life on Mars, moving one step at a time on uncertain terrain. Every time you move forward one step, you observe and record how far you have gone. If your attempt to move has failed, then you have observed that you haven't moved at all.

We will see later that negative observations can be represented by means of constraints, which are conditional goals with conclusion *false*. But in the meanwhile here are a couple of examples:

	if raining then false.
i.e.	*it is not the case that it is raining.*
	if I am hungry then false.
i.e.	*it is not the case that I am hungry.*

We will also see that negative observations can be derived from positive observations, using constraints. For example:

Observation:	*the grass is wet.*
Constraint:	*if an object is wet and the object is dry then false.*
i.e.	*it is not the case that*
	an object is wet and the object is dry.
Forward reasoning:	*it is not the case that the grass is dry.*

Mental representations have a positive bias

In the semantics of Computational Logic, it is convenient to identify the world, at any given point in time, with the set of all the atomic sentences that are true in the world at that time. This is the source of our positive observations. It gives our goals and beliefs a positive bias too, because the main function of our mental representations is to help us deal with the world around us. Even emotionally negative thoughts, like being lonely, sad or disgruntled, which reflect the way we feel about our situation in the world and which affect the decisions we make, have logically positive mental representations.

Further evidence that our mental representations have a positive bias is in the way we record information in history books and computer databases. For example:

> We record that Columbus discovered America in 1492 – not in 1493, not in 2010, not in any other year, but *in and only in* 1492.

> The last train to leave London Victoria for Pulborough, West Sussex from Monday to Friday, between 17 May 2010 and 12 December 2010 is at 22:52 – not 22:51 and not 22:53. If you arrive at Victoria at 22:53 and you miss the train, then it's your fault, and not the fault of the timetable.

But mental representations involve more than just records of positive facts. They also involve the use of conditionals to represent facts more compactly by means of general rules. Since the facts are positive, the conclusions of the conditionals used to derive the facts are positive too. For example, the time of the last train to Pulborough could be represented by means of a conditional whose conclusion gives the time and whose conditions restrict the days of the week and the calendar period:

> *the last train from victoria to pulborough leaves at 22:52 on a day*
> *if the day is a weekday and the day is in the period*
> *between 17 may 2010 and 12 december 2010.*

Of course, to complete the representation, the conditional would need to be augmented with additional, lower-level conditionals with positive conclusions to represent the days of the week and the days in the period between two days.

This use of conditionals to represent data more compactly is associated with deductive databases and the database family of languages called Datalog. But most conventional computer databases either store the data explicitly or compactify it by using conventional, low-level computer programming techniques.

Conditionals in logic programming and in the programming language Prolog can also be used to represent programs and to execute them by systematically reducing goals to subgoals. But programs, no matter what language they are written in, also have a positive bias. For example, they compute positive arithmetic relationships like addition and multiplication, and not negative relationships like non-addition and non-multiplication. For one thing, it would be hard to know where to draw the line. Sure:

$$2 + 2 \neq 1 \text{ and } 2 + 2 \neq 5.$$

But what about : $\quad 2 + 2 \neq a\ pot\ of\ gold?$

Where do goals and beliefs come from?

To do justice to the role that negation plays in our goals and beliefs, we would need to tackle larger issues concerning the nature and sources of all our goals and beliefs. The argument about the primacy of positive information, presented so far, relates only to beliefs that are obtained first-hand from experience, that generalise experience, or that are computed by programs. It ignores two other important sources of goals and beliefs, namely those that we may have been born with, and those that we may have obtained second-hand as the result of the testimony, persuasion or coercion of other agents.

These other sources of goals and beliefs often do have an essentially negative character in the form of constraints. For example:

Nothing is both big and small.
No number is both odd and even.
No letter is both a vowel and a consonant.
Do not drink alcohol in a bar if you are under eighteen years old.
Do not harm a person who is not threatening any harm.
Do not steal.
Do not talk with your mouth full.

We will see later that such constraints play an important role in monitoring and eliminating both candidate actions and candidate explanations of observations. In the meanwhile, however, we will focus on the simpler source of negative information, which is from the failure to derive positive information.

Negation as failure and the closed-world assumption

The derivation of negative conclusions from the lack of positive information about a predicate is justified by a belief or assumption that we have all the positive information that there is to be had about the predicate. This applies both to the conclusions we derive by actively observing the world, and to the conclusions we derive by consulting our beliefs. For example:

You look for your keys in their usual place, and you cannot find them. On the assumption that you have done a thorough investigation, you conclude that they are not in their usual place.

If you believe that Christopher Columbus discovered America in 1492, and you believe that a person can discover something *only* once, then it follows that Christopher Columbus did not discover America in 2010 or in any year other than 1492.

If you believe that the last train is at 22:52, and you believe that the *only* trains on a given day are between the first and last train, then there is no train scheduled to leave at 22:53 or at any other time after 22:52 on the same day.

If you believe that you know how to add two numbers, that every pair of numbers has *only* one sum, and that when you add *2 + 2* you get *4*, then you can conclude that *2 + 2 ≠ a pot of gold.*

Deriving a negative conclusion from the failure to solve a positive goal is called *negation as failure* in logic programming:

> *to show that the negation of a positive sentence holds,*
> *show that the positive sentence does not hold.*

Negation as failure extends the much simpler *if–then–else* statement of more conventional programming languages. Analogues of the *if–then–else* statement are also familiar in natural languages like English. For example, the second and third sentences of the London Underground Emergency Notice are expressed in a variant of the *if–then–else* form:

> *if any part of the train is in a station,*
> *then the driver will stop the train,*
> *else the driver will stop the train at the next station.*

The use of negation as failure to derive a negative conclusion is justified by the *closed-world assumption* that you have complete knowledge about all the conditions under which the positive conclusion holds. It might better be called the *closed-mind assumption*, since an agent's beliefs are not held externally in the world, but internally in its mind. The assumption can be represented as a meta-belief:

> *the negation of a sentence holds*
> *if the sentence does not hold.*

This meta-belief is a meta-sentence, because it talks about sentences. It can also be understood as an *epistemic* or *autoepistemic* sentence,[2] because it can be phrased in terms of what an agent knows or believes:

> *the negation of a sentence holds*
> *if I do not know (or believe) that the sentence itself holds.*

The term *epistemic* comes from the same root as *epistemology*, the study of knowledge.

As we will see in Chapter 17, the language of Computational Logic can be extended to include goals and beliefs that are meta-logical or epistemic. Because

---

[2] Epistemic logic and meta-logic are very similar when understood informally, but they are very different when they are formalised. The relationship between them is touched upon in later chapters, but to some extent is still an open research issue.

the closed-world assumption has conditional form, it can be used to reason backwards or forwards, like any other conditional. Backward reasoning with the closed world assumption is equivalent to negation as failure. Therefore, negation as failure is a natural complement to the use of backward reasoning in general. Given a conditional with negative conditions of the form:

positive conclusion if positive conditions and negative conditions

backward reasoning uses the conditional as a goal-reduction procedure:

> *to show or make the positive conclusion hold,*
> *show or make the positive conditions hold and*
> *show or make the negative conditions fail to hold.*

To illustrate the negation as failure rule (abbreviated *naf*), suppose that we are trying to decide on whether or not to go to a party and suppose:

> *mary will go if john will go.*
> *john will go if bob will not go.*

Suppose we are interested in whether *mary will go*. Then we can reason backwards as follows:

Initial goal:	*mary will go.*
Subgoal:	*john will go.*
Subgoal:	*bob will not go.*
	Naf: *bob will go.*
	Failure: *no!*
Success:	*yes!*

In accordance with the closed-world assumption, because we have no way of showing that *bob will go*, it follows that *bob will not go*, and therefore that *mary will go*.

The same conclusion that *mary will go* can also be derived by reasoning forward, once we get off the ground by starting with the assumption that *bob will not go*:

Assume:	*bob will not go.*
Forward reasoning:	*john will go.*
Forward reasoning:	*mary will go.*

Now suppose Bob decides to be difficult. Believing that *mary will go*, he decides to go as well. Let's see what Mary thinks about that:

Initial goal:	*mary will go.*
Subgoal:	*john will go.*
Subgoal:	*bob will not go.*
	Naf: *bob will go.*

Success: *yes!*
Failure: *no!*

So it seems that Bob will be going to the party on his own. The addition of the new information that *bob will go* defeats the previous argument that *mary will go*. It similarly defeats any attempt to show that *john will go*.

This property of negation as failure and the closed-world assumption is called *defeasibility* or *non-monotonicity*.[3] It is a form of *default reasoning*, in which an agent jumps to a conclusion, but then withdraws the conclusion given new information that leads to the contrary of the conclusion.

Looked at in this way, the closed-world assumption is not so close-minded after all, because any conclusion obtained with its aid is always subject to revision. It is as though the conclusion had an extra, hidden auto-epistemic qualification, *as far as I know*. For example:

Conclusion: *Mary and John will not go the party, as far as I know.*

The development of logics for default reasoning has been one of the most important achievements of Artificial Intelligence. Most of the research has been concerned with exploring alternative "semantics" of default reasoning and with developing efficient proof procedures. The closed-world assumption is an informal semantics, but it needs to be refined to deal with more difficult cases, as the following example shows.

Suppose that Bob is now out of the picture, but Mary and John are still having trouble deciding what to do:

> *mary will go if john will go.*
> *john will go if mary will go.*

Initial goal: *mary will go.*
Subgoal: *john will go.*
Subgoal: *mary will go.*
ad infinitum   . . .

Since it cannot be shown that *mary will go*, it follows from the closed-world assumption that *mary will not go*. Similarly *john will not go*. *As far as we know.*

The example shows that default reasoning can involve the need to reason with an infinite amount of resources. For this reason, the semantics is said to be *non-constructive*. However, in this as in many other cases, the infinite chain of

---

[3] *Monotonicity* in mathematics means that the more you put into a system, the more you get out. Classical logic is monotonic in this sense. Default reasoning is *non-monotonic*, because putting in more information can result in previously derived conclusions being withdrawn.

reasoning needed to show that a negative conclusion holds can be detected finitely by noticing that the same subgoal reoccurs as a subgoal of itself. But in the general case, infinite failure cannot be detected by finite means.

This is an example of the same phenomenon underlying Kurt Gödel's (1931, 1951) proof of the incompleteness theorem, which states that there exist true, but unprovable sentences of arithmetic. We will return to this issue in Chapters 15, 17 and A2. Moreover in Chapter 15, we will investigate a finite, constructive version of negation as failure and discuss its relationship with proof in arithmetic.

An intelligent agent needs to have an open mind

Granted that we tend to view the world in positive terms, and to derive negative conclusions from the failure to show positive conclusions, it doesn't follow that we need to have a closed mind about everything. We can distinguish between *closed predicates*, about which we have complete knowledge, and *open predicates*, about which our knowledge is incomplete. Closed predicates are appropriate for concepts that we use to organise and structure our thoughts, and which do not directly represent our interactions with the world. They include predicates that classify observations and actions into more abstract categories, like emergencies and getting help, as well as more complex predicates, like being eligible for Housing Benefit and being a British Citizen.

But there are other predicates about which it makes no sense to believe that we have complete knowledge. These are open predicates that describe states of affairs in the external world about which we have little or no experience. Did it rain last night in Port Moresby in Papua New Guinea? In the event of my applying for naturalisation as a British Citizen, will the Secretary of State deem fit to grant me a certificate of naturalisation? Was a child found abandoned in the UK born to parents at least one of whom was a British Citizen? You would have to be self-confident to the point of recklessness to believe you could use the closed-world assumption to answer all such questions.

Relaxing the closed-world assumption

Many of the benefits of reasoning with the closed-world assumption can be achieved more modestly without assuming that we know it all, but by the selective use of conditions of the form *cannot be shown* in otherwise normal conditionals. For example, the closed-world assumption can be applied selectively to a single *particular sentence*, formalising an agent's meta-belief that *if the particular sentence were true, then the agent would know (and believe) that the particular sentence is true; otherwise the sentence is false.* This can be stated in the same form as the more general closed-world assumption, but restricted to the single *particular sentence* rather than applied to all atomic sentences. Robert Moore (1985) gives the following example of such a selective closed-world assumption:

> "Consider my reason for believing that I do not have an older brother. It is surely not that one of my parents once casually remarked, 'You know, you don't have any older brothers'. Nor have I pieced it together by carefully sifting other evidence. I simply believe that if I did have an older brother I would surely know about it, and since I don't know of any older brothers, I must not have any."

Moore's belief that he does not have an older brother follows from the selective closed-world assumption:

> *I do not have an older brother*
> *if I cannot show that I have an older brother.*

Default reasoning

From the selective closed-world assumption, it is only a small step to full-blown default reasoning without the closed-world assumption. Instead of limiting expressions of the form *cannot be shown* to closed-world and selective closed-world assumptions, they can be used in the conditions of any conditional. The *negation as failure inference rule* can be generalised accordingly:

> *to show that a sentence cannot be shown*
> *show that all ways of trying to show the sentence result in failure.*

Consider the belief that a person is innocent unless proven guilty, and suppose that Bob is accused of robbing the bank.

> *a person is innocent of a crime*
> *if the person is accused of the crime*
> *and it cannot be shown that*
> *the person committed the crime.*

> *a person committed an act*
> *if another person witnessed the person commit the act.*

> *bob is accused of robbing the bank.*

Clearly, there are other conditions, besides there being a witness, that may lead an agent to believe that a person committed a crime, for example DNA evidence of the person's involvement in the crime. But it is hard to identify and consider all of these other possibilities from the outset. In the next section, we will see how default reasoning makes it easier to deal with such additional possibilities incrementally by successive approximation.

However, given the simplified representation above, negation as failure can be used to determine whether Bob is innocent. Here we assume the taxonomic knowledge that *robbing a bank* is *a crime* and *a crime* is *an act*:

Initial goal: *bob is innocent of robbing the bank.*

Subgoals: *bob is accused of robbing the bank and*
it cannot be shown that bob committed robbing the bank.

Subgoal: *it cannot be shown that bob committed robbing the bank.*

Naf: *bob committed robbing the bank.*

Subgoals: *another person witnessed bob commit robbing the bank.*

Failure: *no!*

Success: *yes!*

The negation as failure inference rule shows that Bob cannot be shown to have robbed the bank. But without the closed-world assumption, it does not follow that Bob actually did not rob the bank! He did not rob the bank, only so far as we know.

But suppose that we are given the additional information:

john witnessed bob commit robbing the bank.

The application of the negation as failure rule now succeeds, and the previous conclusion that he is innocent no longer holds.

Missing conditions

In everyday language, it is common to state only the most important conditions of a general statement (or rule) explicitly, and to leave it implicit that other unstated conditions may also apply. For example, we commonly say:

all birds fly.

i.e.   *an animal can fly if the animal is a bird.*

rather than: *an animal can fly if the animal is a bird*
and the animal is not a penguin
and the animal is not unfledged
and the animal is not injured.

But instead of revising our statement when it becomes apparent that it was an over-simplification, we more commonly correct ourselves in seemingly contradictory, separate statements. We say for example:

an animal cannot fly if the animal is a penguin.
an animal cannot fly if the animal is unfledged.
an animal cannot fly if the animal is injured.

We saw an even more confusing example of this in the suppression task, where the first statement is an over-generalisation, and the second statement attempts to draw attention to a missing condition of the first sentence:

> *she will study late in the library if she has an essay to write.*
> *she will study late in the library if the library is open.*

The example is confusing because it doesn't play the correction game in the standard way. The standard way is to seemingly contradict yourself, by stating missing conditions in separate sentences whose conclusion is contrary to the conclusion of the first sentence:

Over-simplification: *a conclusion holds if conditions hold.*
Correction: *the conclusion does not hold if other conditions hold.*
Intended meaning: *a conclusion holds if conditions hold*
                    and other conditions do not hold.

There are logics that give semantics and provide proof procedures for reasoning directly with sentences in this seemingly contradictory form. These semantics and proof procedures are typically defined in terms of arguments, what it means for arguments to attack and defend one another, and what it means for a set of arguments collectively to defeat an attack. In these semantics and associated proof procedures, there are ways to ensure that a correction defeats an original over-simplification.

However, in the version of Computational Logic in this book, it is simpler to re-express the original over-simplification more precisely from the start, with an explicit condition stating that the contrary of the conclusion does not hold:

Restated rule: *a conclusion holds if conditions hold*
                    and it is not the case that the conclusion does not hold.

It might seem that the two negations *it is not the case that* and *does not hold* would cancel one another out, but in fact they don't. The first negation *it is not the case that* is negation as failure, and the second negation *does not hold* can be reformulated as a positive predicate. This second kind of negation is sometimes called *strong negation.*[4]

Strong negation is commonly used to represent the opposite of one of the positive predicates in a pair of *antonyms* or *contraries*, like *wet* and *dry*, *tall* and *short*, *big* and *small*, *good* and *bad*. Using strong negation, *not wet* is equivalent to *dry* and *not good* is equivalent to *bad*. We will see other examples of strong negation later in the book.

---

[4] Strong negation was introduced into logic programming in Gelfond and Lifschitz (1988).

The advantage of restating rules with missing conditions in the more precise formulation is that additional conditions can be added to the rule in separate sentences without the appearance of seeming contradiction. For example, here is a restatement of the suppression task example in the more precise formulation, with separate corrections, to take into account different conditions that might prevent a student from studying late in the library:

> *she will study late in the library*
> *if she has an essay to write*
> *and it is not the case that*
> *she is prevented from studying late in the library.*

> *she is prevented from studying late in the library*
> *if the library is not open.*
> *she is prevented from studying late in the library*
> *if she is unwell.*
> *she is prevented from studying late in the library*
> *if she has a more important meeting.*
> *she is prevented from studying late in the library*
> *if she has been distracted.*

Here, *being prevented from studying late in the library* is a positive predicate, which is the contrary of *studying late in the library*. Its meaning and associated rules of inference would be unchanged if it were replaced by the strongly negated predicate *she will not study late in the library.*

However, no matter how the corrections are expressed, they can be compiled into a representation in which all of the qualifying conditions are stated explicitly:

Intended meaning: *she will study late in the library*
> *if she has an essay to write*
> *and the library is open*
> *and she is not unwell*
> *and she doesn't have a more important meeting*
> *and she hasn't been distracted.*

The only problem with this compiled representation, as simple as it is, is that it has to be changed every time a new missing condition is identified. The formulation is lower-level than the higher-level rule and exceptions formulation. It requires less sophisticated problem-solving resources, and is therefore more efficient. But the formulation as a higher-level rule and exception is easier to develop and maintain.

The relationship between the two formulations is another example of the relationship between a higher-level and a lower-level representation, which is a recurrent theme in this book. In this case, the higher-level rule acts as a simple first approximation to the more complicated lower-level rule.

In many cases, when a concept is under development, the complicated rule doesn't even exist, and the higher-level representation as a rule and exceptions makes it easier to develop the more complex representation by successive approximation. In other cases, when a complicated rule already exists, for example in the case of existing legislation, the rule and exception form makes it easier to communicate the rule to other agents. By isolating the most important conditions of the rule, and highlighting them in the general rule, the less important conditions can be mentioned in separate corrections/exceptions when and if the need later arises. Public communications of regulations are a good example. The following example is from the UK Citizen's Advice Bureau website:

> Housing Benefit is a benefit for people on a low income to help them pay their rent. You may be able to get Housing Benefit if you are on other benefits, work part-time or work full-time on a low income.

The word "may" in the second sentence indicates that there are other conditions that also need to be satisfied to get Housing Benefit, but they are not significant enough to be mentioned in an introduction.[5] The sentence is a simplified rule that is subject to unstated exceptions. Here is a partial representation of the logic of the two sentences:

> *a person gets help to pay rent if the person receives housing benefit.*
>
> *a person receives housing benefit*
> *if the person is on other benefits*
>   *or the person works part-time*
>   *or the person works full-time on a low income*
> *and it is not the case that*
>   *the person is ineligible to receive housing benefit.*

The representation is partial because it does not represent the "constraint" that Housing Benefit is for people on a low income. This constraint can be treated as an exception:

> *a person is ineligible to receive housing benefit*
> *if the person is not on a low income.*

We will see a number of other examples of rules and exceptions when we look at the British Nationality Act. But first we will look briefly at an example that illustrates the way rules and exceptions can be organised into hierarchies.

---

[5] In more traditional logic, the word "may" is more commonly regarded as a modal operator in modal logic.

Hierarchies of rules and exceptions

Consider the following informal statement of the example:

Rule 1: All thieves should be punished.
Rule 2: Thieves who are minors should not be punished.
Rule 3: Any thief who is violent should be punished.

Here the intention is that rule 2 is an exception to rule 1, and rule 3 is an exception to rule 2. In argumentation terms, rule 2 attacks arguments constructed using rule 1, and rule 3 defends arguments constructed using rule 1, by attacking arguments constructed using rule 2. These intentions and argument attack relations can be compiled into the lower-level rules:

> *a person should be punished*
> *if the person is a thief and the person is not a minor.*

> *a person should be punished*
> *if the person is a thief and the person is a minor*
> *and the person is violent.*

In this compiled representation it is not necessary to write explicitly that:

> *a person should not be punished if the person is a thief*
> *and the person is a minor and the person is not violent*

if we treat the predicate *a person should be punished* as a closed predicate.

The compiled rules can be decompiled into higher-level rules and exceptions in several ways. Here is one such representation:

> *a person should be punished*
> *if the person is a thief*
> *and it is not the case that*
> *the person is an exception to the punishment rule.*

> *a person is an exception to the punishment rule*
> *if the person is a minor*
> *and it is not the case that*
> *the person is an exception to the exception to the punishment rule.*

> *a person is an exception to the exception to the punishment rule*
> *if the person is violent.*

Notice that the positive predicates *a person is an exception to the punishment rule* and *a person is an exception to the exception to the punishment rule* cannot be written as the more obvious predicates *a person should not be punished* and *a person should be punished* respectively. If they were, then the top-level rule would also be an exception to the exception, which is not what is intended.

Suppose, for example, that Bob is a thief:

Initial goal: *bob should be punished.*
Subgoals: <u>*bob is a thief*</u> *and*
               it is not the case that
               bob is an exception to the punishment rule.
Subgoals: *it is not the case that*
               bob is an exception to the punishment rule.

    Naf: *bob is an exception to the punishment rule.*
    Subgoals: <u>*bob is a minor*</u> *and it is not the case that*
               bob is an exception to the exception
               to the punishment rule.
    Failure: *no!*

Success: *yes!*

It cannot be shown that Bob is an exception to the punishment rule, because it cannot be shown that he is a minor. Suppose, instead, that Mary is a thief, who is also a minor:

Initial goal: *mary should be punished.*
Subgoals: <u>*mary is a thief*</u> *and*
               it is not the case that
               mary is an exception to the punishment rule.
Subgoals: *it is not the case that*
               mary is an exception to the punishment rule.

    Naf: *mary is an exception to the punishment rule.*
    Subgoals: <u>*mary is a minor*</u> *and it is not the case that*
               mary is an exception to the exception
               to the punishment rule.
    Subgoal: *it is not the case that*
               mary is an exception to the exception
               to the punishment rule.

        Naf: *mary is an exception to the exception*
                   to the punishment rule.
        Subgoals: <u>*mary is violent.*</u>
        Failure: *no!*

    Success: *yes!*

Failure: *no!*

I'm sure you can figure out for yourself what happens to John, who is a thief, a minor, violent and prone to fits of jealousy.

Conclusions

In this chapter, I have argued the case for the primacy of positive predicates, starting with the claim that the state of the world at any given time is characterised by the atomic sentences that are true in the world at that time. Consequently, passive observations, over which an agent has no control, are invariably represented by positive atomic sentences. However, active observations, which an agent can perform to determine the value of some predicate, can result in negative observations, as the result of the failure to obtain a positive result.

Active observations, whether they return a positive or negative result, can be used to solve the problem at hand and can be forgotten, or they can be recorded for future use. We will see in later chapters that negative observations can be recorded by means of constraints, or can be derived from positive observations by means of constraints.

The primacy of positive predicates extends to an agent's beliefs, which typically have the form of conditionals with positive atomic conclusions. However, negations of atomic predicates can occur as conditions of conditionals and can be solved by means of negation as failure, justified by the closed-world assumption – that the agent knows all there is to know about the predicate of the condition. The closed-world assumption can be relaxed, by replacing negative conditions by weaker conditions that positive predicates *cannot be shown*. But whether or not the assumption is relaxed in this way, the resulting beliefs are defeasible, in the sense that new information can defeat previously derived conclusions and can cause them to be withdrawn.

A common application of defeasible reasoning, also called default reasoning, is to reason with rules and exceptions. In these applications, it is often natural to represent the conclusion of an exception as the negation of the conclusion of the general rule; and it is often common to neglect to qualify the general rule with an explicit condition expressing that the rule is subject to possible exceptions. Semantics and proof procedures, often of an argumentation-theoretic form, can be provided for beliefs in this form. However, it is simpler to define semantics and proof procedures for precise rules with explicit conditions stating that contrary conditions do not hold.

We have seen that rules and exceptions can be compiled into lower-level rules in which all of the qualifying conditions of the exceptions are incorporated into the rules. But just as importantly, lower-level rules can often be decompiled into higher-level rules and exceptions. These higher-level rules are easier to develop, maintain and communicate to other agents.

Unfortunately, there is more to negation than we have been able to cover in this chapter. We need to deal with negation by means of constraints, and we have to investigate the kind of reasoning with contrapositives that is involved in problems like the selection task. We also need to see how negation can be understood in terms of biconditionals. These are topics for later chapters. The semantics of negation as failure is investigated in greater detail in the more advanced Chapter A4.

6

How to become a British Citizen

In this chapter we return to the topic of Chapters 1 and 2: the relationship between logic, natural language and the language of thought. We will look at the law regulating British Citizenship, which is the British Nationality Act 1981 (BNA), and see that its English style resembles the conditional style of Computational Logic (CL) (Sergot *et al.*, 1986).

The BNA is similar to the London Underground Emergency Notice in its purpose of regulating human behaviour. But whereas the Emergency Notice relies on the common sense of its readers to achieve its desired effect, the BNA has the power of authority to enforce its provisions. The BNA differs from the Emergency Notice also in its greater complexity and the more specialised nature of its content.

Nonetheless, like the Emergency Notice, the BNA has been written in an English style that has been chosen to be as easy as possible for its intended audience to understand. Arguably therefore, like the Emergency Notice, its linguistic form is likely to reflect the form of the private, mental language in which its readers represent their own thoughts.

We will see that the most obvious similarity between the BNA and CL is their shared use of conditional sentences (or rules) as the main vehicle for representing information. But we will also see that the BNA, like ordinary English, uses a variety of grammatical forms to express the conditions of conditionals, often inserting them into the conclusions. More importantly, we will see that the BNA highlights the need for logical features in CL that we have seen only in toy examples until now. The most important of these features are negation and meta-level reasoning. We will also use the BNA as an excuse to delve into the more formal side of CL.

In addition to studying the BNA for clues to the logic of the language of human thought, we will also see examples where expressing the BNA in CL form can make its natural language expression easier to understand. In contrast with the BNA, we will look at the University of Michigan lease termination clause, which was studied by University of Michigan law professor Layman Allen and his colleague Charles Saxon (1984) as an example of ambiguous English, and will see how its language can be improved by expressing it in CL form.

The British Nationality Act 1981

The following examples from the BNA illustrate the representation of time, default reasoning and meta-level reasoning about belief.

Acquisition by birth

The first subsection of the BNA deals with acquisition of citizenship by virtue of birth in the United Kingdom after commencement (1 January 1983, the date on which the Act took effect):

1.-(1) A person born in the United Kingdom after commencement shall be a British citizen if at the time of the birth his father or mother is -
  (a) a British citizen; or
  (b) settled in the United Kingdom.

The English of this clause can be considered an informal variant of CL form, even to the extent of expressing its conclusion before (most of) its conditions, which is the conventional syntax for logic programs used to reason backwards. The biggest difference from CL syntax is that it inserts the logical conditions born in the United Kingdom after commencement into the middle of its logical conclusion a person shall be a British citizen. Syntactically, these conditions are a variant of the restrictive relative clause who is born in the United Kingdom after commencement.

Restrictive relative clauses are similar in syntax to non-restrictive relative clauses, but their semantics is entirely different. *Restrictive relative clauses* add extra conditions to conditionals. *Non-restrictive relative clauses* add extra conclusions. Grammatically, non-restrictive clauses are supposed to be set apart from the rest of the sentence by commas, but restrictive clauses are supposed to be tied to the phrase they qualify without any commas. But most of the time, it seems that writers and readers ignore the rules of grammar, and rely instead upon their background knowledge to determine the intended meaning.

For example, the following two sentences are punctuated correctly. The relative clause is restrictive in the first sentence, and non-restrictive in the second sentence:

> *A British citizen who obtains citizenship by providing false information may be deprived of British citizenship.*

> *A British citizen, who is an EU citizen,*
> *is entitled to vote in EU elections.*

In CL, the logical form of the two clauses is dramatically different:

a person may be deprived of British citizenship
if the person obtains citizenship by providing false information.

a person is entitled to vote in EU elections
if the person is a British citizen.

a person is an EU citizen if the person is a British citizen.

Some grammarians also insist that the correct relative pronoun for restrictive relative clauses is *that* rather than *which* or *who*. According to them, the first sentence in the pair of sentences above should be written:

A British citizen that obtains citizenship by providing false information
may be deprived of British citizenship.

But in British English, this rule is largely ignored these days. In any case, if it is important that your readers understand what you write, then it is better not to rely on such subtle grammatical devices as the presence or absence of commas, and the supposed differences of meaning between *that* and *which*, which few readers know or care about. It is better to express yourself in an English form that more closely resembles the logical form of the thought you wish to convey. For example, do not write:

A British citizen, who has the right of abode in the UK,
owes loyalty to the Crown.

or

A British citizen that has the right of abode in the UK
owes loyalty to the Crown.

But, depending on what you mean, write:

All British citizens have the right of abode in the UK
and owe loyalty to the Crown.

or

A British citizen owes loyalty to the Crown
if the citizen has the right of abode in the UK.

The use of relative clauses is one way in which the syntax of English differs from the syntax of conditionals in logical form. Another difference is the way in which it represents *variables*. Symbolic forms of CL use symbols, like X and Y for variables, which range over classes of individuals. Variables are distinct from constants, which represent unique individuals.

English uses the combination of an *article*, like *a* and *the*, and a *common noun*, like *person, animal, object* and *thing*, as a sorted or typed variable. It uses the articles *a* and *an*, as in *an animal* and *a person*, for the first use of a variable; and it uses the article *the*, as in *the animal* and *the person*, for subsequent uses of the same variable. It uses *proper nouns*, like *Mary, Felix* and *Venus*, which are usually capitalised, as constants, to represent individuals. Individuals can also be represented by definite descriptions, as in the phrase *the strongest man on earth*.

Putting all these considerations about relative clauses and variables together, and taking the liberty to introduce one or two other refinements, we obtain the following more precise, but still relatively informal CL representation of subsection 1.1:[1]

> *X acquires british citizenship by subsection 1.1 at time T*
> *if   X is a person*
> *and   X is born in the uk at time T*
> *and   T is after commencement*
> *and   Y is a parent of X*
> *and   Y is a british citizen at time T or*
> *   Y is settled in the uk at time T*

Notice that the condition *X is a person* prevents cats and dogs from claiming British Citizenship. However, it is unnecessary to add the condition *Y is a person*, because if *X* is a person then any parent of *X* is also a person. Notice also that the condition *Y is a parent of X* is short for *Y is a mother of X or Y is a father of X*.

This representation uses the Prolog convention in which capitalised words or letters, such as *X, Y* and *T*, stand for variables, which is why *british* and *uk* have been written in lower case. This is the opposite of the English convention in which upper case is used for proper nouns and names, and lower case is used for common nouns. Just for the record, this is one of the ways a die-hard mathematical logician might write 1.1:

$$\forall X(\forall T(\exists Y(b(X, uk, T) \land c(T) \land d(Y, X) \land (e(Y, T) \lor f(Y,T))) \rightarrow a(X, 1.1, T))).$$

Representation of time and causality

The English formulation of subsection 1.1 is precise about the temporal relationships among the conditions of 1.1, but does not state the temporal relationship between the conditions and the conclusion. In other words, it does not say when a person satisfying the conditions of 1.1 actually is a British Citizen. I have used the term *acquires british citizenship* as a kind of place-holder, which can accommodate different relationships between these times. Anticipating Chapter 13, about the representation of time and change, this is as good a place as any to propose a likely intended relationship:

---

[1] Notice that this has the propositional form *A if (B and C and D and (E or F))*, which is equivalent to two separate conditionals: *A if B and C and D and E* and *A if B and C and D and F*.

> *a person is a british citizen at a time*
> *if* *the person acquires british citizenship at an earlier time*
> *and* *it is not the case that*
> *the person ceases to be a british citizen between the two times.*

This should remind you of the relationship between picking up an object and having the object at a later time, which was mentioned briefly at the end of Chapter 4. In both cases, these relationships are instances of a more general, abstract relationship. Here is a statement of that relationship in the *event calculus* (Kowalski and Sergot, 1986):

> *a fact holds at a time*
> *if* *an event happened at an earlier time*
> *and* *the event initiated the fact*
> *and* *it is not the case that*
> *an other event happened between the two times and*
> *the other event terminated the fact.*

The different special cases can be obtained by adding information about specific types of events initiating and terminating specific types of facts. For example:

> *the event of a person acquiring british citizenship initiates*
> *the fact that the person is a british citizen.*

> *the event of a person being deprived of british citizenship terminates*
> *the fact that the person is a british citizen.*

> *the event of an animal picking up an object initiates*
> *the fact that the animal has the object.*

> *the event of an animal dropping an object terminates*
> *the fact that the animal has the object.*

Notice that in the case of an animal picking up an object, our earlier representation in Chapter 4 of the relationship:

> *an animal has an object at a time*
> *if the animal is near the object at an earlier time*
> *and the animal picks up the object at the earlier time*
> *and nothing terminates the animal having the object between the two times.*

contains an additional condition that *the animal is near the object at an earlier time*. In the event calculus, this additional condition can be expressed as a separate constraint:

> *if an animal picks up an object*
> *and it is not the case that the animal is near the object at a time*
> *then false.*

In general, the event calculus constraint expresses that an event is possible if all its preconditions hold. We will discuss the representation of preconditions of events later in Chapter 13.

The use of the term *fact* in the event calculus axiom can be stretched to cover, not only ordinary facts, which are atomic sentences, but also more general sentences, which are initiated by events like the commencement of an act of parliament. For example:

> *the commencement of an act of parliament initiates a provision*
> *if the provision is contained in the act.*

> *the repeal of an act of parliament terminates a provision*
> *if the provision is contained in the act.*

The treatment of events and sentences as individuals is an example of *reification*. The corresponding phenomenon in English is *nominalisation*, in which a verb, such as *commence* is turned into a noun, such as *commencement*. Reification is a powerful tool, which has proved to be indispensible for knowledge representation in Artificial Intelligence. But it worries some philosophers, who view it as populating the world with individuals of questionable existence.

Acquisition by abandonment

The second subsection of the BNA also employs reification, in this case to reify the purposes of subsection 1.1:

1.-(2) A new-born infant who, after commencement, is found abandoned in the United Kingdom shall, unless the contrary is shown, be deemed for the purposes of subsection (1)-
   (a) to have been born in the United Kingdom after commencement; and
   (b) to have been born to a parent who at the time of the birth was a British citizen or settled in the United Kingdom.

It might seem a little strange to devote the very second sentence of the BNA to such a hopefully uncommon case, when there are so many simpler and more common cases to consider. But what better, more coherent place is there for a provision referring to the purpose of subsection 1.1 than immediately after 1.1 itself? Somewhat more awkward, from our point of view, is that subsection 1.2 combines so many other complex logical features in a single rule that it's hard to know where to begin in picking its logic apart.

Perhaps the easiest place to start is with the notion of *purpose*. It is clear that *purpose* is just another name for *goal*. But in logic programming, the conclusion of a conditional, used to reason backwards, is treated as a goal and its conditions are treated as subgoals. Accordingly, the conclusion of a conditional identifies its purpose. Thus we can interpret the phrase the purposes of subsection (1) as a reference to the logical conclusion of 1.1, namely to acquire British Citizenship. The phrase could equally well have been expressed less dramatically as the conclusion of subsection (1).

Moreover, the phrases 1.2.a and 1.2.b are exactly the logical conditions of 1.1. Therefore, translating *unless* as *if not*, we can paraphrase subsection 1.2 in the form:

The conclusion of 1.1 holds for a person
if the person is found newborn abandoned in the uk after commencement
and the contrary of the conditions of 1.1 are not shown to hold for the person.

The paraphrased sentence combines in a single sentence the use of meta-language to talk about the conclusions and conditions of sentences with the object-language to talk about states of affairs in the world. The use of meta-language treats sentences as individuals, and is another example of reification. We shall return to the issue of meta-language both later in this chapter and in Chapter 17.

The other notable feature of 1.2 is its use of the phrase unless the contrary is shown. We have seen the use of the similar phrase *cannot be shown* for default reasoning before. The phrase *cannot be shown* has nice theoretical properties; but, as we have seen, it includes the need to expend a potentially infinite amount of resources trying to show that something is the case. The phrase *is not shown* is more practical, because it assumes that only a finite amount of effort has been spent, but it suffers from the imprecision of not specifying how much effort is needed. Moreover, it does not cater for the possibility that new information or additional effort might make it possible to show conditions that could not be shown before.

Ignoring these concerns and exploiting the fact that the contrary of born in the UK is born outside the UK, and the contrary of born after commencement is born on or before commencement, we can rewrite 1.2 as:

A person found newborn abandoned in the uk after commencement
shall be a british citizen by section 1.2
if it is not shown
that the person was born outside the uk
and it is not shown that
the person was born on or before commencement
and it is not shown that
both parents were not british citizens at the time of birth
and it is not shown that
both parents were not settled in the uk at the time of birth

This gives us two logical paraphrases of subsection 1.2. However, I suspect that, of the two, the combined object-language/meta-language representation is probably the easier to understand.

Rules and exceptions

The phrases *is not shown* and *cannot be shown* are forms of negation that can be implemented by variants of negation as failure. The BNA also includes the use of negation to represent exceptions to rules. For example:

> 40.-(2) The Secretary of State may by order deprive a person of a citizenship status if the Secretary of State is satisfied that deprivation is conducive to the public good.
> 40.-(4) The Secretary of State may not make an order under subsection (2) if he is satisfied that the order would make a person stateless.

As we saw in Chapter 5, the exception can be compiled into the conditions of the rule:

> 40.-(2) The Secretary of State may by order deprive a person of a citizenship status if the Secretary of State is satisfied that deprivation is conducive to the public good,
> and he is not satisfied that the order would make the person stateless.[2]

English typically distinguishes between rules and exceptions by presenting the rule before its exceptions, and introducing the exceptions by such words or phrases as "but", "however" or "on the other hand". In the following provision 12.1 of the BNA, the signal that the rule is subject to exceptions is given by the vague qualification, subject to subsections (3) and (4):

> 12.-(1) If any British citizen of full age and capacity makes in the prescribed manner a declaration of renunciation of British citizenship, then, subject to subsections (3) and (4), the Secretary of State shall cause the declaration to be registered ...
> 12.-(3) A declaration made by a person in pursuance of this section shall not be registered unless the Secretary of State is satisfied that the person who made it will after the registration have or acquire some citizenship or nationality other than British citizenship; ...

---

[2] The condition *he is not satisfied that the order would make the person stateless* is not equivalent to the arguably more natural condition *he is satisfied that the order would not make the person stateless*. The "more natural condition" is equivalent to a stronger version of 40.-(4): The Secretary of State may not make an order under subsection (2) **unless** he is satisfied that the order would **not** make a person stateless.

12.-(4) The Secretary of State may withhold registration of any declaration made in pursuance of this section if it is made during any war in which Her Majesty may be engaged in right of Her Majesty's government in the United Kingdom.

12.3 is a straightforward exception to 12.1, expressing in effect a condition under which the Secretary of State may not cause a declaration of renunciation to be registered. 12.4 is also an exception, but its effect depends on whether the Secretary of State actually decides to exercise permission to withhold registration. Taking the difference between these two exceptions into account, the intended combined meaning of 12.1, 12.3 and 12.4 can be compiled into a single rule:

The Secretary of State shall cause a declaration of renunciation
of British citizenship to be registered
if the declaration is made by a British citizen of full age and capacity
and the declaration is made in the prescribed manner
and the Secretary of State is satisfied that after the registration the person will
have or acquire some citizenship or nationality other than British citizenship;
and it is not the case that
the declaration is made during a war in which Her Majesty is engaged
in right of Her Majesty's government in the United Kingdom
and the Secretary of State decides to withhold the registration.

Notice that the rule can be further simplified by replacing the condition the Secretary of State is satisfied that after the registration the person will have or acquire some citizenship or nationality other than British citizenship by the equivalent condition the Secretary of State is satisfied that after the registration the person will not be stateless.

Section 12 contains another rule and exception, which on the face of it is even more complicated:

12.-(2) On the registration of a declaration made in pursuance of this section the person who made it shall cease to be a British citizen.

12.-(3) ... ; and if that person does not have any such citizenship or nationality on the date of registration and does not acquire some such citizenship or nationality within six months from that date, he shall be, and be deemed to have remained, a British citizen notwithstanding the registration.

However, much of the complication disappears if the rule and exception are compiled into a single rule defining termination of citizenship:

the event of registering a declaration of renunciation by a person terminates
the fact that the person is a british citizen
if the registration was made on date T1

and the person has some citizenship or nationality
other than british citizenship on date T2
and T1 ≤ T2 ≤ T1 + six months.

Understood in the context of the event calculus, the termination rule takes effect at the time of registration only if the person renouncing citizenship is a citizen or national of some other country within six months following the registration. The complexity is due, not to the logical form of the rule, but to its content, whereby a state of affairs in the past (termination of citizenship) is caused in part by a state of affairs in the future (possession of some other citizenship or nationality).

How to satisfy the Secretary of State

The provisions in the BNA for depriving a person of British Citizenship and for registering a renunciation of British Citizenship involve seemingly inscrutable references to satisfying the Secretary of State. However, under the assumption that the Secretary of State is a rational person, not all of these references are as impenetrable as they may seem. Consider, for example, the main provision for acquiring British Citizenship by naturalisation:

6.-(1) If, on an application for naturalisation as a British citizen made by a person of full age and capacity, the Secretary of State is satisfied that the applicant fulfils the requirements of Schedule 1 for naturalisation as such a citizen under this sub-section, he may, if he thinks fit, grant to him a certificate of naturalisation as such a citizen.

At the top-most level, this has the logical form:

> *the secretary of state may grant a certificate of naturalisation*
> *to a person by section 6.1*
>   *if   the person applies for naturalisation*
>   *and the person is of full age and capacity*
>   *and the secretary of state is satisfied that*
>   *the person fulfils the requirements of schedule 1*
>   *for naturalisation by 6.1*
>   *and the secretary of state thinks fit*
>   *to grant the person a certificate of naturalisation.*

The first two conditions are simple object-level conditions concerning the state of the world. But the last two conditions are epistemic or meta-level conditions concerning the Secretary of State's state of mind. In theory, the last condition is totally inscrutable and can only be given as part of the input for a given case. However, in practice, an expert lawyer might be able to predict with a high degree of certainty how the Secretary of State will decide new cases based on the lawyer's knowledge of previous decisions in similar, old cases.

The third condition is more interesting, because the BNA includes a specification of the requirements for naturalisation that an applicant must fulfil to the satisfaction of the Secretary of State. If the Secretary of State's state of mind were entirely impenetrable, there would be no point in specifying these requirements. The schedule is quite long, and it is convenient therefore to summarise and paraphrase its contents:

a person fulfils the requirements of schedule 1 for naturalisation by 6.1
   if   either the person fulfils the residency requirements
        of subparagraph 1.1.2
        or the person fulfils the crown service requirements
        of subparagraph 1.1.3
   and   the person is of good character
   and   the person has sufficient knowledge
        of english, welsh, or scottish gaelic
   and   the person has sufficient knowledge about life in the uk
   and either the person intends to make his principal home in the uk
        in the event of being granted naturalisation
      or the person intends to enter or continue in crown service or
        other service in the interests of the crown in the event of being
        granted naturalisation.

On the assumption that the Secretary of State is a rational person and that all rational people understand the meaning of the words if, or and and as they occur in schedule 1 in the same way, it can be shown that:

the secretary of state is satisfied that
a person fulfils the requirements of schedule 1 for naturalisation by 6.1
  if either *the secretary of state is satisfied that*
      the person fulfils the residency requirements of subparagraph 1.1.2
     or *the secretary of state is satisfied that*
      the person fulfils the crown service requirements of subparagraph 1.1.3
  and *the secretary of state is satisfied that*
      the person is of good character
  and *the secretary of state is satisfied that*
      the person has sufficient knowledge
      of english, welsh, or scottish gaelic
  and *the secretary of state is satisfied that*
      the person has sufficient knowledge about life in the uk
  and either *the secretary of state is satisfied that*

> the person intends to make his principal home in the uk
> in the event of being granted naturalisation
> or *the secretary of state is satisfied that*
> the person intends to enter or continue in crown service or
> other service in the interests of the crown in the event of being
> granted naturalisation.

The result is an explicit, though tedious statement of what it takes to satisfy the Secretary of State concerning the requirements for naturalisation. We will see how to derive this explicit form in Chapter 17.

As we have seen, compared with ordinary English, the language of the BNA is extraordinarily, and at times even painfully precise. Its precision is due in large part to its use of conditional form, which helps to eliminate ambiguity.

A syntactic expression is *ambiguous* when it has several distinct identifiable meanings. For example, the word *he* is ambiguous in the following pair of sentences:

> *The Secretary of State deprived Bob Smith of his British citizenship.*
> *He was very upset about it.*

Ambiguity can be eliminated simply by replacing the ambiguous expression by a precise expression that represents its intended meaning; for example, by replacing the word *he* in the second sentence above either by *the Secretary of State* or by *Bob Smith*.

The conditional form of CL helps to reduce the ambiguity associated with such relative clauses as *who was born in the UK*. As we have seen, restrictive relative clauses add extra conditions to conditionals, whereas non-restrictive relative clauses add extra conclusions.

Ambiguity is distinct from, but often confused with *vagueness*. Ambiguity arises when a syntactic expression has several distinct interpretations, all of which can be expressed explicitly. Vagueness, on the other hand, arises when a concept, like *newborn infant* has no crisp, hard and fast definition. Logic tolerates vagueness, but does not tolerate ambiguity. It accommodates vague concepts as conditions of conditionals, simply by not attempting to define them in the conclusions of other conditionals.

Although, like ambiguity, vagueness causes problems of interpretation, it is often useful in practice, because it allows the law to evolve and adapt to changing circumstances. Arguably, however, except for its use in poetry, humour and deception, ambiguity serves no other useful purpose.

Whereas the syntax of the BNA is expressed in explicit conditional form, the syntax of the University of Michigan lease termination clause below is both unstructured and highly ambiguous. The termination clause was originally investigated by Allen and Saxon to illustrate the use of propositional logic to formulate a precise interpretation of an ambiguous legal text. Significantly, the intended interpretation identified by Allen and Saxon has the conditional form associated with Computational Logic.

The University of Michigan lease termination clause

The clause consists of a single sentence, which I advise you not to try to understand until I first explain why the sentence in this form is virtually impossible to understand:

> "**The University may terminate this lease** when the Lessee, having made application and executed this lease in advance of enrollment, is not eligible to enroll or fails to enroll in the University or leaves the University at any time prior to the expiration of this lease, or for violation of any provisions of this lease, or for violation of any University regulation relative to Resident Halls, or for health reasons, **by providing the student with written notice of this termination 30 days prior to the effective time of termination**; unless life, limb, or property would be jeopardized, the Lessee engages in the sales or purchase of controlled substances in violation of federal, state or local law, or the Lessee is no longer enrolled as a student, or the Lessee engages in the use or possession of firearms, explosives, inflammable liquids, fireworks, or other dangerous weapons within the building, or turns in a false alarm, **in which cases a maximum of 24 hours notice would be sufficient**".

In fact, I could not resist trying to make your task a little easier by highlighting the two conclusions, the first of which is split into two halves, separated by its various conditions.

The sentence is hard to understand, because it has the ambiguous form:

> *A if B and B', C or D or E or F or G or H*
> *unless I or J or K or L or M in which case A'.*

The sentence is ambiguous for the same reason that the arithmetic expression $1 + 1 \times 2$ is ambiguous. In mathematics and mathematical logic, such ambiguities are resolved by the appropriate use of parentheses, either $1+(1 \times 2)$ or $(1 + 1) \times 2$ in the case of the arithmetic expression.

In the case of the termination clause, the subclauses $A, A', B, B', C, D, E, F, G, H, I, J, K, L$ and M can be grouped together by means of parentheses in many different ways. Some of these groupings are logically equivalent. After accounting for these equivalences, Allen and Saxon identified approximately 80 questions that would need to be asked to disambiguate between the different interpretations. As a result of their analysis they identified the intended interpretation as having the unambiguous logical form:

(A if (not (I or J or K or L or M) and ((B and B' and (C or D))
or E or F or G or H)) and A' if (I or J or K or L or M)).

This formal representation can be simplified if we rewrite it in the syntax of
conditionals, and if we assume that the second conditional states the *only*
conditions under which the conclusion A' holds. Using this assumption, we
can replace the condition *not (I or J or K or L or M)* by *not A'*, obtaining the
conditionals:

A	if	*not A' and B and B' and C.*		A'	if	I
A	if	*not A' and B and B' and D.*		A'	if	J
A	if	*not A' and E.*		A'	if	K
A	if	*not A' and F.*		A'	if	L
A	if	*not A' and G.*		A'	if	$M.$

The repetition of the conclusions A and A' is a little tedious, but at least it makes
the meaning crystal clear. In English, we can obtain a similar effect without the
tedious repetition by signalling the disjunction of the different conditions with
the phrase "one of the following conditions holds":

The University may terminate this lease by providing the student with
written notice of this termination 30 days prior to the effective time of termination
if the University may not terminate this lease
     with a maximum of 24 hours notice
and one of the following conditions holds:

1) The Lessee, having made application and executed this lease in
    advance of enrollment, is not eligible to enroll
    or fails to enroll in the University.
2) The Lessee leaves the University at any time
    prior to the expiration of this lease.
3) The Lessee violates any provisions of this lease.
4) The Lessee violates any University regulation
    relative to Resident Halls.
5) There are health reasons for the termination.

The University may terminate this lease
with a maximum of 24 hours notice
if one of the following conditions holds:

1) Life, limb, or property would be jeopardized.
2) The Lessee engages in the sales or purchase of controlled substances in
    violation of federal, state or local law.
3) The Lessee is no longer enrolled as a student.
4) The Lessee engages in the use or possession of firearms, explosives,
    inflammable liquids, fireworks, or other dangerous weapons within the
    building.
5) The Lessee turns in a false alarm.

There are two reasons why you may not be entirely satisfied with this rewriting of the sentence. First, why would the University want to restrict itself, in cases where it is allowed to give 24 hours notice, so that it does not have the discretion of giving 30 days notice instead? This is probably a mistake, due to the complex wording of the original sentence, which even its writers may not have fully understood.

Second, what does it mean to say that the University may terminate this lease with a maximum of 24 hours notice? The word maximum here suggests that in such cases the University may terminate the lease with less than 24 hours notice. Surely, in all fairness, the student deserves a minimum of 24 hours to get her things together and to vacate her room.

So how could the lawyers who drafted the lease make such a big mistake? Perhaps they meant that, upon receiving such notice, the student would have a maximum of 24 hours to vacate the halls of residence. If so, the intention could have been achieved more correctly and more simply by expressing the conclusion in a parallel form to the alternative conclusion that the University may terminate a lease with 30 days notice. The parallel form would mention neither the term maximum nor minimum:

> The University may terminate this lease by providing the student with notice of this termination 24 hours prior to the effective time of termination.

Part of the moral of the story is to do as every good book on English writing style advises: Express similar ideas in similar ways.

Summary

Both the BNA and the University of Michigan lease termination clause illustrate, in their very different ways, the usefulness of expressing information in conditional form. Arguably this is because, not only are conditionals close to the language of human thought, but also close to the laws that govern both our natural and social worlds.

The BNA shows that we still have some way to go to understand the subtleties and complexities of meta-level reasoning and of different kinds of negation. However, the University of Michigan lease termination clause shows that, even without those complexities, the syntactic form of conditionals can help not only to clarify the intended meanings of English sentences, but also to uncover unintended meanings.

In the next chapter, we explore production systems, which are widely regarded in Cognitive Psychology as the most convincing computational model of the mind. In the following chapter, we will see how Computational Logic reconciles logic and production systems.

7

The louse and the Mars explorer

Logical Extremism, which views life as all thought and no action, has given logic a bad name. It has overshadowed its near relation, Logical Moderation, which recognises that logic is only one way of thinking, and that thinking isn't everything.

The antithesis of Logical Extremism is Extreme Behaviourism, which denies any "life of the mind" and views Life instead entirely in behavioural terms. Behaviourism, in turn, is easily confused with the condition–action rule model of thinking.

Behaviourism

If you were analysing the behaviour of a thermostat, which regulates the temperature of a room by turning on the heat when it is too cold and turning off the heat when it is too hot, you might *describe* the thermostat's input–output behaviour in condition–action rule terms:

> *If the current temperature is C degrees*
> *and the target temperature is T degrees*
> *and C < T − 2°*
> *then the thermostat turns on the heat.*

> *If the current temperature is C degrees*
> *and the target temperature is T degrees*
> *and C > T + 2°*
> *then the thermostat turns off the heat.*

But you wouldn't attribute the thermostat's behaviour to a mind that consciously manipulates such descriptions to *generate* its behaviour.

In the same way that you could view the thermostat's external behaviour without committing yourself to a view of its internal operation, the behaviourist views agents in general. Thus, in the story of the fox and the crow, a behaviourist, unable to examine the fox's internal, mental state, would view the behaviour of the fox in the same way that we view the behaviour of the thermostat:

> *If the fox sees that the crow has cheese, then the fox praises the crow.*
> *If the fox is near the cheese, then the fox picks up the cheese.*

The behaviourist's description of the fox in the story begins and ends with the fox's externally observable behaviour. The behaviourist justifies her refusal to attribute any internal, mental activity to the fox, by the fact that it is impossible to verify such attributions by the scientific method of observation and experimentation.

According to the behaviourist, the fox could be a purely reactive agent, simply responding to changes in the world around her. If, in the course of reacting to these changes, the fox gets the cheese, then this result might be merely an indirect, emergent effect, rather than one that the fox has deliberately aimed to bring about by proactive thinking.

The behaviourist also sees no reason to distinguish between the behaviour of a thermostat and the behaviour of a human. The behaviourist might use a conditional:

> *If a passenger observes an emergency on the underground,*
> *then the passenger presses the alarm signal button*

to *describe* the behaviour of a passenger on the underground. But the use of such a description says nothing about how the passenger actually *generates* that behaviour. As far as the behavourist is concerned, pressing the alarm signal button whenever there is an emergency might be only an instinctive reaction, of whose purpose the passenger is entirely unaware.

Behaviourism is indirectly supported by Darwinism, which holds that organisms evolve by adapting to their environment, rather than by a goal-oriented process of self-improvement.

Behaviourism also shares with condition–action rules a focus on modelling behaviour as reactions to changes in the environment. However, whereas behaviourism restricts its attention to *descriptions* of behaviour, condition–action rules in production systems are used to *generate* behaviour.

The program for a thermostat implemented by means of a production system would look like this:

> *If the current temperature is C degrees*
> *and the target temperature is T degrees*
> *and C < T − 2°*
> *then **turn on** the heat.*

*If the current temperature is C degrees
and the target temperature is T degrees
and C > T + 2°
then **turn off** the heat.*

Production systems

Few psychologists subscribe today even to moderate versions of behaviourism. Most adhere instead to the cognitive science view that intelligent agents engage in some form of thinking that can usefully be understood as the application of computational procedures to mental representations of the world.

Paul Thagard (2005) states in his book *Mind: Introduction to Cognitive Science* that, among the various models of thinking investigated in Cognitive Science, production systems have "the most psychological applications" (page 51). Steven Pinker (1997) in *How the Mind Works* also uses production systems as his main example of a computational model of the mind (page 69). The most influential computational models of human thinking are probably the production system models Soar (Laird *et al.*, 1987) and ACT-R (Anderson and Lebiere, 1998).

A *production system* is a collection of *condition–action rules*, of the form:

If conditions then actions

which are incorporated in the thinking component of an agent's observation–thought–decision–action cycle. Condition–action rules (also called *production rules, if–then rules* or just plain *rules*) are similar to the behaviourist's descriptions of behaviour. However, because they are used by an agent *internally* to *generate* the agent's behaviour, their conclusions are often expressed in the *imperative* mood:

If conditions then do actions.

Production systems were invented as a mathematical model of computation by the logician, Emil Post (1943) in the 1920s, but first published in 1943. They were proposed as a computational model of human intelligence by the Artificial Intelligence researcher Alan Newell (1973). They have also been used for developing numerous *expert systems*, computer programs that simulate human expertise in such fields as medicine, finance, science and engineering.

The production system cycle

Production systems embed condition–action rules in an observation–thought–decision–action cycle:

> *Repeatedly,*
> *observe the world,*
> *think,*
> *decide what actions to perform,*
> *act.*

Thinking in production systems is similar to, but subtly different from, *forward reasoning* in logic. As in logic, if all of the conditions of a rule hold in a given state, then the rule is said to be *triggered* or *enabled*, and the conclusion is derived. However, whereas, in logic, forward reasoning derives a conclusion that is a logical consequence of the conditions, in production systems, the conclusion is only a *recommendation* to perform actions. This kind of thinking is often called *forward chaining*, which helps to distinguish it from genuine forward reasoning, although not everyone uses these terms in this way.

Although the conclusion of a production rule is only a recommendation to perform actions, it is common to express the actions as commands. If more than one rule is triggered in a given situation, and the actions of the rules are incompatible, then the agent needs to choose between them. This *decision* between conflicting recommendations is called *conflict resolution*. The rule or rules whose actions are chosen are said to be *fired*.

Production systems with no representation of the world

In the simplest case, an agent's mental state might consist solely of production rules, without any mental representation of the world. All of the conditions of a rule are verified simply by matching them against the agent's current observations. In such a case, it can be said that "the world is its own best model" (Brooks, 1991). If you want to find out about the world, don't think, just look!

Observing the current state of the world is a lot easier than trying to predict it from past observations and from assumptions about the persistence of past states of affairs. And it is a lot more reliable, because persistence assumptions can easily go wrong, especially when there are other agents around, changing the world to suit their own purposes.

What it's like to be a louse

To see what a production system without any representation of the world might be like, imagine that you are a wood louse and that your entire life's behaviour can be summed up in the following three rules:

> *If it's clear ahead, then move forward.*
> *If there's an obstacle ahead, then turn right.*
> *If I am tired, then stop.*

Because you are such a low form of life, you can sense only the fragment of the world that is directly in front of you. You can also sense when you are tired. Thus, your body is a part of the world, external to your mind. Like other external objects, your body generates observations, such as being tired or being hungry, which are attended to by your mind.

It doesn't matter where the rules came from, whether they evolved through natural selection, or whether they came from some Grand Designer. The important thing is, now that you have them, they regulate and govern your life.

Suppose, for the purpose of illustration, that you experience the following stream of observations:

> *clear ahead.*
> *clear ahead.*
> *obstacle ahead.*
> *clear ahead and tired.*

Matching the observations, in sequence, against the conditions of your rules results in the following interleaved sequence of observations and actions:

Observe: *clear ahead.*
Do: *move forward.*

Observe: *clear ahead.*
Do: *move forward.*

Observe: *obstacle ahead.*
Do: *turn right.*

Observe: *clear ahead and tired.*

At this point, your current observations trigger two different rules, and their corresponding actions conflict. You can't move forward and stop at the same time. Some method of conflict resolution is needed, to decide what to do.

Many different conflict resolution strategies are possible. But, in this as in many other cases, the conflict can be resolved simply by assigning different priorities to the different rules, and selecting the action generated by the rule with the highest priority. It is obvious that the third rule should have higher priority than the second. So the appropriate action is:

Do: *stop*.

An even simpler approach is to avoid conflict resolution altogether, by changing the rules, adding an extra condition *and you are not tired* to the first and second rules. A more complicated approach is to use decision theory, to compare the different options and to select the option that has the highest expected benefit. But, no matter how it is done in this case, the result is likely to be the same – better to rest when you are tired than to forge ahead regardless.

Once a louse has learned the rules, its internal state is fixed. Observations come and go and the louse performs the associated actions, as stimulus–response associations, without needing to record or remember them. The price for this simplicity is that a louse lives only in the here and now and has no idea of the great wide world around it. For a normal louse, this may be a small price to pay for enjoying the simple life.

Production systems with internal state

Although the simple life has its attractions, most people prefer a little more excitement. Some people even want to believe that their life has a purpose, whether or not they know what that purpose may be.

We will investigate the meaning of life for our imaginary louse in Chapter 9, but in the meantime we will have to be content with spicing up our production system model with an internal database that serves as an internal state. The database is a set of atomic sentences, which is like a relational database. Typically it is much smaller than a conventional database, and for this and for other, more psychological reasons it is often called a *working memory*.

The database can be used to simulate the external world, or to represent and manipulate some imaginary world. It is also commonly used as a temporary memory to store calculations to solve a temporary goal.

In a production system with an internal database, a rule is triggered when an atomic sentence that is an external or internal update of the database matches one of the conditions of the rule, and any additional conditions of the rule are verified as holding in the current state of the database.[1] If the rule is triggered in this way, then the actions of the rule are derived as candidates for execution. When all of the candidate actions have been determined, then conflict resolution is used to choose one or more actions for execution. If a chosen action is an external action, then it is

---

[1] More generally and to improve efficiency, partially triggered rules can be treated as new rules that can be further triggered by future updates.

performed on the external world. If it is an internal action, then it is performed as an internal update of the database.

What it's like to be a Mars explorer

To imagine what a production system with memory might be like, suppose that your life as a louse has expired; and, as a reward for your past efforts, you have been reincarnated as a robot sent on a mission to look for life on Mars.

Fortunately, your former life as a louse gives you a good idea how to get started. Moreover, because you are a robot, you never get tired and never have to rest. However, there are two new problems you have to deal with: How do you recognise life when you see it, and how do you avoid going around in circles?

For the first problem, your designers have equipped you with a life recognition module, which allows you to recognise signs of life, and with a transmitter to inform mission control of any discoveries. For the second problem, you have an internal database to remember whether you have been to a place before, so that you can avoid going to the same place again.

Of course, the problems facing a real-life robot are far more complex than that. They include very hard problems of constructing mental representations of observations and of converting mental representations of actions into physical motor controls. But to make the example tractible, we will ignore these interface problems and also simplify the associated knowledge representation issues.

Given these simplifications, a production system with memory, which is a refinement of the production system of a louse, might look something like this:

> *If the place ahead is clear*
> *and I haven't gone to the place before,*
> *then go to the place.*

> *If the place ahead is clear*
> *and I have gone to the place before,*
> *then turn right.*

> *If there's an obstacle ahead*
> *and it doesn't show signs of life,*
> *then turn right.*

> *If there's an obstacle ahead*
> *and it shows signs of life,*
> *then report it to mission control*
> *and turn right.*

To recognise whether you have been to a place before, you need to make a map of the terrain. You can do this, for example, by dividing the terrain into little squares and naming each square by a coordinate, (E, N), where E is the distance of the centre of the square East of the origin, N is its distance North of the origin, and the origin (0, 0) is the square where you start.

For this to work, each square should be the same size as the step you take when you move one step forward. Assuming that you have recorded the coordinates of your current location in the database, then you can use simple arithmetic to compute the coordinates of the square ahead of you and the square to the right of you, and therefore the coordinates of your next location.

Every time you go to a square, you record your visit in the database. Then, to find out whether you have gone to a place before, you just consult the database.

Suppose, for example, that you are at the origin, pointed in an Easterly direction. Suppose also that the following atomic sentences describe a part of the external world around you:

> *life at (2, 1)*
> *clear at (1, 0)*
> *clear at (2, 0)*
> *obstacle at (3, 0)*
> *obstacle at (2, −1)*
> *obstacle at (2, 1).*

Suppose also that you can see only one step ahead. So, when you start, the only thing you know about the world, in your internal database, is that your current location is (0, 0) and the only thing you can observe is that it is clear at (1, 0), which is the place immediately in front of you.

Assume also that, although it is your mission to look for life, you are the only thing that moves. So this description of the initial state of the world will also apply to all future states of the world that you will encounter.

With these assumptions, your behaviour is completely predetermined:

Initial database: *at (0, 0)*

Observe: *clear at (1, 0)*
Do: *move forward.*
Update database: delete *at (0, 0)*, add *at(1, 0)*, add *visited (0, 0)*

Observe: *clear at (2, 0)*
Do: *move forward.*
Update database: *delete at (1, 0)*, add *at (2, 0)*, add *visited (1, 0)*

Observe: *obstacle at (3, 0)*
Do: *turn right.*

Observe: *obstacle at (2, − 1).*
Do: *turn right.*

Observe: *clear at (1, 0).*
Do: *turn right.*

Observe: *obstacle ahead at (2, 1)* and *life at (2, 1).*
Do: *report life at (2, 1)* and *turn right*[2].

Notice that reporting your discovery of life to mission control is just another action, like moving forward or turning right. You have no idea that, for your designers, this is the ultimate goal of your existence.

Your designers have endowed you with a production system that achieves the goal of discovering life as an emergent property of your behaviour. Perhaps, for them, this goal is but a subgoal of some higher-level goal, such as satisfying their scientific curiosity. But for you, none of these goals or subgoals is apparent.

Condition–action rules with implicit goals

Condition–action rules that implement reactive behaviour are an attractive model of evolutionary theory. As in the theory of evolution, the ultimate goal of such *reactive rules* is to enable an agent to survive and prosper, and is *emergent* rather than explicit. For example, the two rules:

> *If there is an emergency then get help.*
> *If there is an emergency then run away.*

have the implicit goal of *dealing appropriately with the emergency,* which is a euphemism for trying to save yourself, and maybe trying to save others if you can.

Reactive rules are also a natural way to generate simpler kinds of reactive behaviour, with more modest emergent goals. Herbert Simon (1999) gives the example of a production system for solving algebraic equations in one unknown, for example for solving the equation $7X + 6 = 4X + 12$ with the unknown X.

1. *If the expression has the form $X = N$, where N is a number,*
   then halt and check by substituting N in the original equation.

---

[2] I leave it to the reader to work out what happens next, and I apologise for any complications in advance.

2. *If there is a term in X on the right hand side,*
   then subtract it from both sides and collect terms.
3. *If there is a numerical term on the left hand side,*
   then subtract it from both sides, and collect terms.
4. *If the equation has the form NX = M, N ≠ 0,*
   then divide both sides by N.

To solve the equation, both the initial equation and an extra copy of the equation are put into the initial database. The actions of the rules change the copy of the equation until it is in the right form for the application of rule 1, when the solution needs to be substituted into the original equation. The production system cycle executes the following steps:

Initial equation:	$7X + 6 = 4X + 12$
Use 2 to obtain:	$3X + 6 = 12$
Use 3 to obtain:	$3X = 6$
Use 4 to obtain:	$X = 2$
Use 1 to halt and check:	$7 \cdot 2 + 6 = 4 \cdot 2 + 12.$

Notice that there is no explicit representation of the top-level goal of solving the original equation. Nor is there any representation of the implicit intermediate subgoals of combining all occurrences of the variable into one occurrence and of isolating the variable. The first subgoal is the purpose of rule 2, and the second subgoal is the purpose of rules 3 and 4.

The top-level goal and its relationship with the intermediate subgoals could be made explicit by means of the conditional (Bundy *et al.*, 1979):

> *An equation with a single variable X is solved*
> *if all occurrences of X are combined into a single occurrence*
> *and the single occurrence of X is isolated.*

We will investigate the relationship between logical conditionals with explicit goals and production rules with emergent goals when we explore the meaning of life and dual process theories of thinking in Chapter 9. In that chapter, I will suggest that an agent has a higher level of consciousness when it has an explicit representation of its goals, and that it has a lower level of consciousness when its goals are only emergent.

But even emergent goals are better than none. The fact that an agent's behaviour has any goals at all, whether they be conscious or emergent, can be said to give the agent's life a meaning, in the sense that they give its life a purpose.

The use of production systems for forward reasoning

The natural correspondence between reactive condition–action rules and stimulus–response associations is probably production systems' biggest selling point. It may even be the evolutionary ancestor of all later forms of higher-level intelligence. If so, the next step in evolution might have been the extension from forward chaining with reactive rules to forward reasoning with conditionals.

Consider, for example, the following fragment of the family tree of Adam and Eve from the Book of Genesis:

> *Eve mother of Cain*
> *Eve mother of Abel*
> *Adam father of Cain*
> *Adam father of Abel*
> *Cain father of Enoch*
> *Enoch father of Irad*

Consider also the production rules:

> *If X mother of Y*
> *then* **add** *X ancestor of Y.*
>
> *If X father of Y*
> *then* **add** *X ancestor of Y.*
>
> *If X ancestor of Y*
> *and Y ancestor of Z*
> *then* **add** *X ancestor of Z.*

Suppose that the only conflict resolution that is performed is to avoid firing the same rule matching it with the same facts in the database more than once (called *refraction* in the production system literature). Then the initial database is successively updated, until no new facts can be added:

In the first iteration add: *Eve ancestor of Cain*
                                Eve ancestor of Abel
                                Adam ancestor of Cain
                                Adam ancestor of Abel
                                Cain ancestor of Enoch
                                Enoch ancestor of Irad

In the second iteration add: *Eve ancestor of Enoch*
                                Adam ancestor of Enoch
                                Cain ancestor of Irad

In the third iteration add: *Eve ancestor of Irad*
Adam ancestor of Irad

If the word *add* is omitted from the action part of the three production rules, then the rules are indistinguishable from logical conditionals, and forward chaining is indistinguishable from forward reasoning.

More generally, production systems can implement forward reasoning from an initial set of facts with any set of conditionals all of which satisfy the restriction that any variable in the conclusion of a conditional occurs somewhere in the conditions of the conditional. This restriction, called the *range-restriction*, is relatively easy to satisfy and avoids such conditionals as:

If pigs can fly then X is amazing
i.e. *If pigs can fly then everything is amazing*

To implement forward reasoning with production rules, it suffices to prefix the word *add* before every conclusion, to turn the conclusion into an action that updates the database.

The use of production systems for goal reduction

The step from reactive rules to forward reasoning with conditionals is an easy one. The next step, to goal reduction, is much harder. This is because, to represent goal reduction in production rule form, the working memory needs to contain, in addition to *"real" facts*, which represent the current state of a database, also *goal facts*, which represent some desired future state. Goal-manipulation actions need to add goal facts when goals are reduced to subgoals and to delete goal facts when they are solved. Goal reduction is implemented, not by backward reasoning as in logic programming, but by forward chaining with rules of the form:

If goal G and conditions C then add H as a subgoal.

Goal reduction in production rule form is an important feature both of cognitive models, such as Soar and ACT-R, and of many commercial expert systems.

In his *Introduction to Cognitive Science*, Thagard (2005) uses the ability of production systems to perform goal reduction to support his claim that "unlike logic, rule-based systems can also easily represent strategic information about what to do". He illustrates his claim with the following example (page 45):

If you want to go home and you have the bus fare,
then you can catch a bus.

Forward chaining with the rule reduces a goal (going home) to a subgoal (catching a bus).

But earlier in the book, we saw that goal reduction can also be performed by backward reasoning with conditionals. In the case of Thagard's example, with the conditional:

> *You go home if you have the bus fare and you catch a bus.*

Thus Thagard's argument against logic can be viewed instead as an argument for logic programming and Computational Logic, because they too can easily represent strategic information.

In fact, Thagard's argument can be turned against itself. How do you represent the fox's strategy for having an object by first getting near it and then picking it up? The production rule:

> *If you want an object and you are near the object,*
> *then you can pick the object up.*

assumes you are already near the object. It's not obvious how to formulate the more general strategy:

> *If you want an object*
> *then you can get near the object,*
> *and you can pick the object up.*

The actions in this general strategy are a sequence of a subgoal followed by an action. But production systems normally accommodate only actions that can be performed in the same iteration of a cycle.

To deal with problems of this kind, the production systems Soar and ACT-R employ a different structure for goals and subgoals than they do for ordinary facts. They store goals in a *stack*. When a goal is reduced to a subgoal, the new subgoal is put (or *pushed*) on top of the stack. When a goal is solved, it is taken off (or *popped*) from the top of the stack. Only the goal at the top of the stack can contribute to the triggering of a production rule.

The goal stack can be used to reduce the goal of having an object to the subgoals of getting yourself and the object near to one another and of picking the object up, for example in the following way:

> *If your goal (at the top of the goal stack) is to have an object*
> *and you are not near the object,*
> *then make your goal (pushing it on top of the stack) to be near the object.*

> *If your goal (at the top of the goal stack) is to have an object*
> *and you are near the object,*
> *then pick up the object.*

> *If your goal (at the top of the goal stack) is to have an object*
> *and you have the object*
> *then delete the goal (by popping it from the top of the stack).*

To represent the general strategy as a single rule, it is necessary either to represent it in logical form or to represent it in an agent programming language.

Many of the *agent programming languages* (see, for example, Dennis *et al.* (2008)) that have been developed in Artificial Intelligence can be viewed as extensions of production systems in which rules have the more general form of *reactive plans*:

> *If triggering condition and other conditions hold,*
> *then solve goals and perform actions.*

The conclusions of such reactive plans can be a collection of subgoals to be achieved and of actions to be performed over several agent cycles. The triggering condition can be either an observation or a goal. Thus, forward chaining with such rules can perform goal reduction, without the restriction of production systems that all the actions in the conclusion of a rule have to be performed in a single cycle.

The alternative to performing goal reduction by forward chaining, whether with simple production rules or with reactive plans, is to perform goal reduction by backward reasoning with logical conditionals. The advantage of the logical alternative is that it simultaneously represents both the goal-reduction procedure and the belief that justifies the procedure.

Logic versus production rules

Thus there are three kinds of production rules: reactive rules, forward reasoning rules and goal-reduction rules. It is only reactive rules that do not have an obvious logical counterpart. However, in the next chapter, we will see that reactive rules can be understood in logical terms as conditional goals. Forward reasoning rules can be understood as conditional beliefs used to reason forward, and goal-reduction rules as conditional beliefs used to reason backwards.

Thagard's textbook (2005, page 47) includes the claim that, in contrast with logic, "rules can be used to reason backward or forward". In fact, it would be more accurate to state that in contrast with production rules, logical conditionals can be used to reason backward or forward. Because conditions in production rules come first and actions come later, true production rules can be used only in the forward direction.

To be fair to Thagard, in most of his arguments against logic and in favour of rules, he is only reporting common misconceptions, failing to recognise the properties of logical conditionals and attributing their properties to production rules instead. What is most unfortunate is that these confusions have permeated Cognitive Science since the early 1970s.

However, production systems do have a critical feature that logic is missing – the production system cycle, which is the intellectual ancestor of the agent cycle. The agent cycle plays a critical role in the logic-based agent model of this book, linking an agent's thoughts in logical form to changes in the agent's surrounding environment.

Conclusions

The use of production systems to generate the behaviour of an intelligent agent, as seen in this chapter, can be pictured like this:

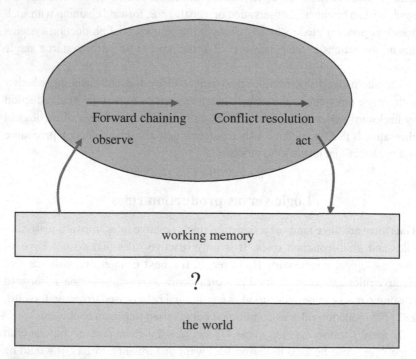

In the next chapter we will see how logic and production systems can be reconciled in a more general framework, which uses logic for an agent's thoughts, and uses an agent cycle to embed the agent in a semantic structure, which gives meaning to the agent's thoughts.

8
Maintenance goals as the driving force of life

What do the passenger on the London Underground, the fox, the wood louse, the Mars explorer and even the heating thermostat have in common? It certainly isn't the way they dress, the company they keep, or their table manners. It is the way that they are all embedded in a constantly changing world, which sometimes threatens their survival, but at other times provides them with opportunities to thrive and prosper.

To survive and prosper in such an environment, an agent needs to be aware of the changes taking place in the world around it, and to perform actions that change the world to suit its own purposes. No matter whether it is a human, wood louse, robot or heating thermostat, an agent's life is an endless cycle, in which it must:

> *repeatedly (or concurrently)*
> *observe the world,*
> *think,*
> *decide what actions to perform, and*
> *act.*

We can picture this relationship between the mind of an agent and the world like this:

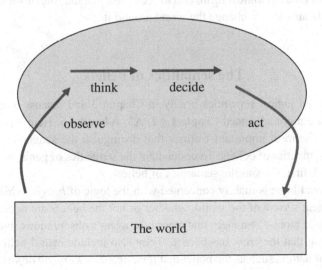

The observation–thought–decision–action cycle is common to all agents, no matter how primitive or how sophisticated. For some agents, thinking might involve little more than firing a collection of stimulus–response associations, without any representation of the world. For other agents, thinking might be a form of symbol processing, in which symbols in the mind represent objects and relationships in the world. For such symbol manipulating agents, the world is a semantic structure, which gives meaning to the agent's thoughts.

Although production systems perform thinking by manipulating symbolic expressions, they do not interpret expressions in terms of semantic structures. Instead, the production system cycle provides production systems with a so-called *operational semantics*, which is a mathematical characterisation of the transitions from one state of the production system cycle to the next. From a logical point of view, operational semantics is not a semantics at all.

In contrast with production systems, logic has a well-developed *semantics* understood in terms of the relationship between symbolic expressions and the objects those symbolic expressions represent. However, the semantics of traditional logic does not take adequate account of the dynamic interaction between symbolic representations and the environment in which those representations are embedded.

We will investigate the semantics of logical representations of the changing world in greater detail in Chapter 13. In this chapter, we sketch a preliminary framework that combines the dynamic interactions of the production system cycle with the semantics and inference mechanisms of Computational Logic. The first step in this direction is to interpret reactive condition–action rules as conditional goals in logical form, and to recognise that the role of such goals is to motivate an agent to change the world around it.

The semantics of beliefs

We discussed logical semantics briefly in Chapter 3 and discuss it in greater detail in the more advanced Chapters A2, A3, A4 and A6. Here we will deal with only the most important features that distinguish the semantics of goals from the semantics of beliefs. To understand the semantics of goals, we need to understand, first, the simpler semantics of beliefs.

Traditional logic is mainly concerned with the logic of *beliefs*, which represent an agent's view of the world, whether or not the beliefs are actually true. They include atomic sentences that record the agent's observations, such as the fox's seeing that the crow has cheese. They also include causal beliefs about the laws of nature, such as the belief that *if an agent picks up an object then the agent will possess the object*.

In addition to its beliefs about the directly observable world, an intelligent agent needs *theoretical beliefs* to organise and connect its other beliefs together. These include beliefs that identify objects as belonging to different theoretical *classes*, such as the classes of foxes, humans, animals, animates, agents, artefacts, and things. They typically also include beliefs that organise such classes into *hierarchies*, in which, for example, foxes and humans are animals, animals are agents, agents are animates, and animates and artefacts are things.

If an agent expresses its beliefs in the right form, then beliefs about objects belonging to classes higher in the hierarchy will apply with little extra effort to objects belonging to classes lower in the hierarchy. Thus the belief that *if an animal picks up an object then the animal will possess the object* also applies to all foxes and in particular to the fox in the story of the fox and the crow.

Theoretical beliefs can also include beliefs about unobservable entities, like ghosts, angels or electrons, and about unobservable relationships, such as haunting, blessing or sending out waves. Such beliefs complicate the semantics of logic, because their entities and relationships need not really exist in the agent's independently existing world.

But such complications arise even with classes of objects and with hierarchical relationships, which are also not directly observable. Indeed, even observable objects and relationships, as in the fox's observation that the crow has the cheese, are arguably constructed in part by the eye of the beholder. Thus, the easiest way to deal with all of these complications in one go is simply to identify the agent's external environment with the set of atomic sentences, which represents the world as the agent experiences it.

The semantics of goals

In contrast with an agent's beliefs, which represent the way the agent sees the world as it is, whether the agent likes it or not, an agent's *goals* represent the agent's view of the world as the agent would like it to be. There isn't much an agent can do about the past. So goals only affect actions that the agent can perform in the future.

The most obvious kind of goal is an *achievement goal*, to attain some desired future state of the world. The simplest kind of achievement goal is just an atomic action, such as *the fox picks up the cheese*. However, a more typical achievement goal is an observation sentence, such as *the fox has the cheese*, that the agent would like to hold in the future. Achievement goals can include actions and conjunctions of atomic sentences, such as *the fox has the cheese and the fox eats the cheese*. They can also include *existentially quantified* goals, which contain "unknowns" such as *there exists some instance of food, such that the fox has the food and the fox eats the food*. Achievement goals motivate an agent to generate a plan of actions, such as *the fox praises the crow, picks up the cheese and eats the cheese*, to change the world into future states in which the goals are true.

A less obvious kind of goal, but arguably one that is more fundamental, is a *maintenance goal*, which maintains the agent in a harmonious relationship with the changing state of the world. Achievement goals are typically derived from maintenance goals, as the result of the agent observing some change in the world around it.

For example, in the story of the fox and crow, the fox's goal of having the crow's cheese appears out of the blue. A more realistic version of the story would include the circumstance that triggered the goal. Perhaps the fox is behaving like a spoiled child, wanting to have anything she observes in the possession of another animal. Or perhaps she is just looking for her next meal. In either case, the fox's goal of having the cheese can be viewed as a goal of *achieving* some future state of the world, in response to *observing* a change in the world, which triggers a higher-level goal of *maintaining* some desired relationship with the world around her.

Suppose that we give the fox the benefit of doubt and assume that she wants to have the cheese simply because she is hungry, and not because she has a personality defect. This can be represented by the maintenance goal:

> *if I become hungry, then I have some food and I eat the food.*

The goal can be paraphrased, in the imperative:

> *if I become hungry, then get some food and eat the food.*

The imperative formulation resembles a condition–action rule, except the conclusion *get some food* is not a simple action. More generally, reactive condition–action rules can be understood as the special case of maintenance goals in which the conclusion is an action or a conjunction of actions, all of which are to be performed in the same iteration of the agent cycle.

It is common in natural languages to express goals, whether they be achievement goals, maintenance goals or constraints, imperatively as commands, in such forms as *do this, if this then do that* and *don't do that*. But in logic, it is simpler to express goals declaratively, with such expressions as *this will be the case, whenever this is the case then that will be the case* and *that will never be the case*.

The advantage of the declarative, logical representation of goals, compared with the imperative formulation, is that the same semantic notion of truth that relates an agent's beliefs to the world also applies to the relationship between the agent's goals and the world. The main difference being that beliefs represent sentences about the world that is outside the agent's control, whereas goals represent sentences about the world that the agent can try to control by performing actions to make them true.

To see how the fox's achievement goal *I have the cheese* is related to the maintenance goal, suppose that the fox's body tells her that she has just become hungry. Since her body is a part of the world, she becomes aware of her hunger by means of an observation:

Observation:　　　*I become hungry.*

The observation matches the condition of the maintenance goal and forward reasoning derives the conclusion of the maintenance goal as an achievement goal:

I have some food and I eat the food.

Thus, the real achievement goal is not specifically to have the crow's cheese, but more generally to have some instance of food. And having food is only half the story. The fox also needs to eat the food. As far as the top-level maintenance goal is concerned, having food without eating it is useless.

To connect the achievement goal with the rest of the story, the fox needs to have the taxonomic knowledge that cheese is a kind of food and that food is a kind of object. This knowledge can be represented in a number of different ways, and there are even specialised logics for this purpose, the details of which are unimportant here. Suffice it to say that, one way or another, this taxonomic knowledge is needed to instantiate the achievement goal, substituting the crow's *cheese* for the "unknown" existentially quantified variable *some food*.

The time factor

Our reconsideration of the story of the fox and crow is still an over-simplification, because it does not deal with the issue of time. It does not indicate how much time can elapse between becoming hungry and eating. Nor does it distinguish between different occurrences of becoming hungry at different times.

We have already seen briefly in earlier chapters that one way of dealing with time is by including time points in the mental language with such representations of the temporal relationship between cause and effect as:

an animal has an object at a time
if the animal is near the object at an earlier time

and the animal picks up the object at the earlier time
and nothing terminates the animal having the object between the two times.

In a similar way, the fox's maintenance goal with explicit temporal relationships can be represented like this:

if I become hungry at a time
then I have some food at a later time
and I eat the food at the later time.

Although the different times and temporal relationships are explicit, they can be made more precise with a little symbolic notation:

for every time T_1
if I become hungry at time T_1
then there exists a time T_2 and an object O such that O is food
and I have O at time T_2
and I eat O at time T_2
and $T_1 \leq T_2$.

Here the variable T_1 is *universally quantified with scope the entire goal*, and the variables T_2 and O are *existentially quantified with scope the conclusion of the goal*.

Although this representation does not put any limit on the amount of time that can elapse between the time T_1 of becoming hungry and the time T_2 of having food and eating, it does at least indicate their temporal order. It would be easy to add an extra condition to the conclusion, for example $T_2 \leq T_1 + 24$ hours, but it would be hard to quantify the limit exactly.

The alternative to adding an extra condition is to leave the decision about *when to do what* to the decision-making component of the agent cycle. This way, the decision is made in the broader context of the totality of the agent's current goals, balancing the urgency, utility and probability of achieving one goal against another. We shall investigate such decision making in Chapter 11 and return to the revised story of the fox and the crow in the section after next.

Maintenance goals as the driving force of life

The notion of maintenance goal arises, in one guise or another, in many different disciplines, often in opposition to the notion that the purpose of life, whether of an individual or of an organisation, consists of achievement goals.

At the lowest level, even below the level of condition–action rules, maintenance goals appear in the biological mechanism of *homeostasis*, which plants and animals use to maintain a stable relationship with their environment. For example, homeostasis controls our body's temperature by causing us to sweat when it's too hot, and to shiver when it's too cold. The body's homeostatic temperature control mechanism is like a maintenance goal, implemented in hardware rather than in software, responding to observations of the current temperature by generating actions to keep the body in balance with the changing environment.

More importantly for the topic of this book, an analogous notion appears also in Management Science, where it is associated with the so-called *soft systems methodology*, developed by Peter Checkland (2000) and inspired by Sir Geoffrey Vickers' notion of appreciative system. Vickers (1965) developed the notion of appreciative system as the result of his practical experience in management and administration in the British civil service, as a member of the National Coal Board and other public bodies.

In his work, Vickers acknowledged the influence of Simon's (1957, 1960) model of management, in which individuals and organisations set goals, consider alternative solutions and evaluate alternatives to make decisions. However, Vickers sought to transcend this goal-oriented view of management by supplementing it with a view that is more "appreciative" of the tight coupling between agents and their environment. As Checkland (2000) puts it, in an *appreciative system*:

> *"we all do the following:*
> *selectively perceive our world;*
> *make judgements about it,*
> *judgements of both fact (what is the case?) and*
> *value (is this good or bad, acceptable or unacceptable?);*
> *envisage acceptable forms of the many relationships*
> *we have to maintain over time; and*
> *act to balance those relationships in line with our judgements."*

Here there is an obvious similarity both with the agent cycle in general and with the focus on maintaining relationships between perceptions and actions. Judgements of value are a matter for the decision-making component of the agent cycle, which we investigate in Chapter 11.

Embedding goals and beliefs in the agent cycle

We return to the story of the fox and the crow. For simplicity, to focus on the way in which the fox's reasoning is integrated with the agent cycle, we ignore the factor of time, and ignore the alternative ways in which the fox can attempt to achieve the goal of having food. Suppose, therefore, that the fox has the following maintenance goal and beliefs:

Goal: *if I become hungry, then I have food and I eat the food.*
Beliefs: *an animal has an object*
if the animal is near the object
and the animal picks up the object.

I am near the cheese
if the crow has the cheese
and the crow sings.
the crow sings if I praise the crow.

cheese is a kind of food.
food is a kind of object.

For simplicity, we assume that the different components of the cycle – observing, thinking, deciding and acting – occur in sequence. In a real agent these individual components of the cycle might take place concurrently or even in parallel. To simulate concurrency, we will assume that the fox is such a rapid cycler that she has only enough time to perform one step of thinking in a single cycle.

We will also assume that the fox's attempts to perform an action can fail, and that in the next step of the cycle she gets feedback by observing whether her actions succeed or fail. We retell the story from the point where the fox becomes hungry.

The first iteration of the cycle

This is the classic case of an observation triggering a maintenance goal and deriving an achievement goal.

Observation: *I become hungry.*
Forward reasoning, achievement goal: *I have food and I eat the food.*
No candidate action.

The second iteration

The only thinking that the fox can do in this cycle is to reason backwards, to reduce the subgoal of having food to the subgoal of being near the food and picking it up. This reasoning involves the taxonomic reasoning of matching "food" with "object".

No observation.
Backward reasoning, new subgoals: *I am near food and I pick up the food and*
I eat the food.
No candidate action.

The third iteration

In this iteration of the cycle, we suppose that the fox observes *the crow has cheese*. The fox has the choice of continuing to reason backwards from its current subgoals or of reasoning forwards from its new observation. Generally, it is a good idea to give priority to reasoning with new observations, just in case there is an emergency that needs to be dealt with immediately or an opportunity that shouldn't be missed.

The observation matches one of the conditions of her belief *I am near the cheese if the crow has the cheese and the crow sings*. Because the belief is expressed in logical form, it can be used to reason forward or backward. Using it to reason forward, as in this case, it gives rise to a new belief.

Observation: *The crow has cheese.*
Forward reasoning, new belief: *I am near the cheese if the crow sings.*
No candidate action.

The fourth iteration

The fox matches the conclusion of the new belief with the subgoal *I am near food*, by instantiating the universally quantified variable *food* with *cheese*. This could be viewed as either forward or backward reasoning, or just marrying up the two, which is another case of the resolution rule presented in Chapter A5. No matter how you look at it, the effect is to reduce the goal of being near food to the subgoal of making the crow sing. This has the side-effect of finding out what the food is going to be if the new subgoals succeed.

No observation.
New subgoals: *the crow sings and I pick up the cheese and I eat the cheese.*
No candidate action.

The fifth iteration

The fox reduces the subgoal of making the crow sing to the subgoal of praising the crow. She now has a plan of actions, which she can start to execute. In this representation of actions without time, there is nothing to indicate the order in which the actions should be performed. So she cheats, knowing that in a representation with explicit time, it would be obvious that the new action *I praise the crow* should be performed first.

No observation.

Backward reasoning, new subgoals:	*I praise the crow and I pick up the cheese and I eat the cheese.*
Action:	*I praise the crow.*

The sixth iteration

The fox observes the result of the action she performed in the previous cycle. Assuming that the fox has not lost her voice, the observation confirms the success of her action, and solves the first of the three action subgoals, leaving the remaining two subgoals. The next of these two subgoals is also an action; and, given the intended order of the actions, there are no other candidate actions that she can perform at this time.

Observation:	*I praise the crow.*
Forward reasoning, remaining subgoals:	*I pick up the cheese and I eat the cheese.*
Action:	*I pick up the cheese.*

The seventh iteration

The fox observes the result of her action. However, this time, to make the story more interesting, assume that the action fails, either because the crow has not yet started singing, because the cheese has not yet reached the ground, or because the fox is physically inept. We also assume that the fox can try the same action again, provided that if there is a time limit on when the action needs to be performed, then that limit has not yet been reached.

Negative observation:	*I do not pick up the cheese.*
No thinking that can be shown without an explicit representation of time.	
Action:	*I pick up the cheese.*

The negative observation *I do not pick up the cheese* can be regarded as a negative response to the action *I pick up the cheese*, viewed as a query *do I pick up the cheese?* from the fox to the world.

In general, an agent's attempted actions can be regarded as queries posed to the world. In the simplest and ideal case, the world just responds in the affirmative, confirming that the action has succeeded. In the worst case, the world responds that the action has failed. But in the general case, the action may contain an existentially quantified variable representing an unknown, for example to indicate how far an action of moving forward one step actually succeeds. In such a case the world responds by instantiating the variable, giving *feedback* about the result of the action.

In our semantics, in which the world is described only by means of positive facts, a negative observation can be understood as a negative reply from the world to an attempted action or to an active observation by the agent.

The eighth iteration

The fox observes that the action was successful this time. The observation solves the associated action subgoal, leaving only the last action in the plan, which the fox decides to perform in this cycle.

Observation: *I pick up the cheese.*
Forward reasoning, remaining subgoal: *I eat the cheese.*
Action: *I eat the cheese.*

The ninth iteration

The observation of the successful performance of the action solves the last of the action subgoals. However, the maintenance goal remains, to be triggered on other, future occasions.

Observation: *I eat the cheese.*

The general pattern of reasoning in this example, spread out over several cycles and interleaved with other observations and actions, is this:

Observation: *An event happens.*
Forward reasoning: *The event matches a condition of*
                       a maintenance goal or belief.
Achievement goal: *Eventually, after a combination of forward and*
                       backward reasoning, an instance of the conclusion
                       of a maintenance goal is derived
                       as an achievement goal.
Backward reasoning: *Beliefs are used to reduce the achievement goal*
                       to actions.
Actions: *Action subgoals are selected for execution.*
Observation: *The agent observes whether the actions*
                       succeed or fail. Actions that fail are retried
                       if their time limit has not expired.

The simple pattern of reasoning needs to be made more elaborate, by monitoring not only whether the agent's actions succeed, but also whether its goals succeed. If its actions succeed, but its goals do not, then some of its beliefs, linking its actions to its goals, must be false. The agent can attempt both to diagnose the failure by identifying the false beliefs and to avoid future failures by correcting the faulty beliefs.

The general process of using confirming and refuting instances of beliefs to learn more correct beliefs is the basic technique of inductive logic programming (Muggleton and De Raedt, 1994). The integration of inductive logic programming into the agent cycle has been investigated by Dávila and Uzcátegui (2005), but is beyond the scope of this book.

The general pattern of reasoning that is exemplified by the story of the fox and the crow is not exceptional. A similar pattern arises in the London Underground example.

The London Underground revisited

Consider the following formulation of the London Underground example, ignoring other ways of dealing with emergencies and other ways of getting help:

Maintenance goal: *if there is an emergency then I get help.*
Beliefs: *a person gets help if the person alerts the driver.*
　　　　a person alerts the driver if the person presses the alarm signal button.
　　　　there is an emergency if there is a fire.
　　　　there is an emergency if one person attacks another.
　　　　there is an emergency if someone becomes suddenly ill.
　　　　there is an emergency if there is an accident.

Here the last four beliefs can be viewed as part of the definition of a hierarchy of classes of events. These definitions could be extended upwards, for example by classifying an emergency as a kind of threat that needs to be dealt with immediately. They could be extended sideways by adding other kinds of emergencies.

The hierarchy could also be extended downwards, for example by classifying different kinds of accidents. However, for the purpose of the present example, assume that we have additional beliefs, which do not classify fires, but help to recognise their manifestations. For simplicity, we represent these beliefs in the form *cause if effect*. We use this form, rather than the more fundamental causal formulation *effect if cause*, because it simplifies the kind of reasoning needed. We will discuss the reasoning, called *abduction*, needed for the causal formulation in Chapter 10. Moreover, we will also discuss the relationship between the two formulations when we discuss the treatment of conditionals as biconditionals in Chapter 15.

Additional beliefs: *there is a fire if there are flames.*
                        there is a fire if there is smoke.

This decomposition of the problem of recognising fire could be carried on indefinitely. But we would soon find it impossible to describe all the necessary lower-level concepts in recognisable, linguistic terms. Eventually, there must come a point at which there is a lowest level, which is irreducible to lower-level concepts. This is the level at which the agent's sensory system transforms the sensations it receives from the world into observations that can be represented as concepts in symbolic terms.

Suppose, for the sake of the example, that the concepts of flames and smoke are the lowest-level concepts directly observable in the environment. Suppose, moreover, that you are travelling on the Underground and you observe smoke. Without going into all of the detail we went into for the fox and crow example, your reasoning, possibly spread across several iterations of the agent cycle, will look like this:

Observation:	*there is smoke.*
Forward reasoning, new belief:	*there is a fire.*
Forward reasoning, new belief:	*there is an emergency.*
Forward reasoning, achievement goal:	*I get help!*
Backward reasoning, subgoal:	*I alert the driver!*
Backward reasoning, action:	*I press the alarm signal button!*

We can picture this combination of forward and backward reasoning like this:

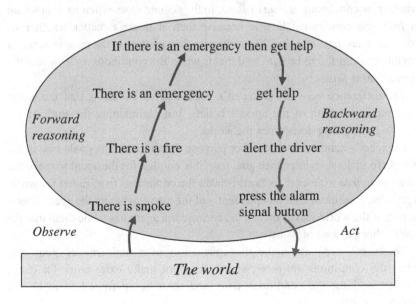

The action of pressing the alarm signal button, like the observation of an emergency, can be reduced to lower-level terms; for example, by first moving your finger to the button and then pushing the button with your finger. Moving your finger to the button can also be reduced, in turn, to still lower-level subgoals, like first moving your arm to the vicinity of the button and then fine-tuning the movement of your finger to the button. But eventually, there has to be a point where your body takes over from your mind and performs the actions directly on its own.

All of this thinking takes time, during which you may have to deal with other observations and perform other actions. Scheduling actions so that everything is dealt with in a timely manner is a task for the decision-making component of the agent cycle. We have kept the examples in this chapter deliberately simple, so that no such decisions need to be made. However, we will address the problem of making decisions in Chapter 11.

The semantics of maintenance goals reconsidered

The same definition of truth applies to both conditional goals and conditional beliefs. In general a conditional, whether a goal or a belief, is *true* if and only if either its conditions are *false* or its conclusion is *true*. In the first case, when its conditions are *false*, the conditional is *true* because then it doesn't matter whether its conclusion is *true* or *false*. In the second case, when its conclusion is *true*, the conditional is *true* because then it doesn't matter whether its conditions are *true* or *false*. The only case that matters is the case in which a conditional can fail to be *true*, and that is when the conditions are *true* and the conclusion is *false*.

The difference between an agent's goals and its beliefs is that the world determines the truth of the agent's beliefs, but maintaining the truth of the agent's goals partly determines the world.

An agent's actions serve no other purpose than to make its goals *true* in the world. To make a maintenance goal *true*, it is enough for the agent to make the conclusion *true* whenever the world makes the conditions *true*. Either the world makes the conditions *true* independently of the agent, whether the agent likes it or not; or the world makes them *true*, because the agent has made them *true* for some other purpose of its own.

The agent need not make the conclusion of a maintenance goal *true* when the conditions are *false*; and it need not make extra work for itself, by first making the conditions *true*, and then being forced to make the conclusion *true*.

However, there is another case in which an agent can make a maintenance goal *true*, which although it is not strictly necessary can nonetheless be very useful. It is the case in which an agent makes the conditions *false*, to *prevent* them from becoming *true*, to avoid the need to make the conclusion *true* in the future. For example, although an agent can make *true* the goal *if there is an emergency then I get help* simply by waiting for an emergency and then getting help, it can also make the goal *true* by preventing the emergency instead.

We will see how Computational Logic deals with preventative maintenance in Chapter A6. In the meanwhile, we note that, if production systems are viewed in logical terms, then they make condition–action rules *true* only by making their conclusions *true* when the world makes their conditions *true*. They cannot make condition–action rules *true* by preventing their conditions from becoming *true*.

Prohibitions

Prevention can be viewed as a voluntary form of *prohibition*. Given the obligation of making a maintenance goal *true*, an agent has a choice: Either make the conclusion *true* when the conditions become *true*, or make the conditions *false*, preventing the conditions from becoming *true*. With genuine prohibitions there is no choice: Make the conditions *false*.

A prohibition can be regarded as a special kind of maintenance goal whose conclusion is literally *false*. For example:

> *if you steal then false.*

i.e.   *Do not steal.*

> *if you are drinking alcohol in a bar and are under eighteen then false.*

i.e.   *Do not drink alcohol in a bar if you are under eighteen.*

> *if you are liable to a penalty for performing an action*
> *and you cannot afford the penalty and you perform the action*
> *then false.*

i.e.   *Do not perform an action*
> *if you are liable to a penalty for performing the action*
> *and you cannot afford the penalty.*

The advantage of regarding prohibitions as a special kind of maintenance goal is that the same semantics and the same inference rules that apply to maintenance goals in general also apply to prohibitions in particular.

The semantics of maintenance goals applies to prohibitions, because the only way to make a conditional *true* if its conclusion is *false* is to make the conditions *false*.

We will see later that reasoning forwards with a maintenance goal can be triggered not only by an observation, but also by a hypothetical candidate action. Similarly, the consideration of a candidate action can trigger forward reasoning with a prohibition. Backward reasoning can then attempt to determine whether the other conditions of the prohibition are *true*. If they are, then one step of forward reasoning derives the conclusion *false*. The only way to make the prohibition *true*, therefore, is to make the conditions of the prohibition *false*, by making the candidate action *false* and thereby eliminating it from further consideration. For example:

> *if you are considering stealing, then banish it from your thoughts.*

> *if you are tempted to drink alcohol in a bar*
> *and are under eighteen, then don't.*

> *if you are thinking of performing an action*
> *and you are liable to a penalty for performing the action*
> *and you cannot afford the penalty, then do not perform the action.*

Constraints

Prohibitions are constraints on the actions you can perform. But there can also be constraints on what you are willing to believe. Constraints of this second kind are familiar in the context of computer databases, where they maintain the integrity of the database, and for this reason are called *integrity constraints*.

For example, a family database might contain such integrity constraints as:

> *if X is the mother of Y and X is the father of Z then false.*
i.e. *No one is both a mother and a father.*

> *if X is an ancestor of X then false.*
i.e. *No one is their own ancestor.*

Integrity constraints are used to reject an update of the database that makes an integrity constraint *false*. For example, the second of the two integrity constraints above, would reject the following update to the database given by:

Update: *Enoch father of Adam*
Database: *Eve mother of Cain*
                 Eve mother of Abel
                 Adam father of Cain
                 Adam father of Abel
                 Cain father of Enoch

> *Enoch father of Irad*
> *X ancestor of Y if X mother of Y*
> *X ancestor of Y if X father of Y*
> *X ancestor of Z if X ancestor of Y and Y ancestor of Z.*

The pattern of reasoning to check the integrity of the update is the same as the pattern for assimilating observations:

Update:	*Enoch father of Adam*
Forward reasoning:	*Enoch ancestor of Adam*
Forward reasoning:	*X ancestor of Adam if X ancestor of Enoch*
Backward reasoning:	*X ancestor of Adam*
	if X ancestor of Y and Y ancestor of Enoch
Backward reasoning:	*X ancestor of Adam*
	if X ancestor of Y and Y father of Enoch
Backward reasoning:	*X ancestor of Adam if X ancestor of Cain*
Backward:	*X ancestor of Adam if X father of Cain*
Backward reasoning:	*Adam ancestor of Adam*
Forward reasoning:	*false.*

In a conventional database, the update would be rejected, because it implies the impossible conclusion *false*. But in Quine's web of belief, any of the goals or beliefs involved in the derivation of *false* could be deemed the culprit, and could be rejected or revised instead.

But belief and goal revision are complicated processes, not to be undertaken lightly. Fortunately, in many cases, full-scale revision is unnecessary because it is obvious from the start which goals and beliefs are regarded with suspicion and which are deemed to be beyond any doubt. In the case of database updates, the integrity constraints are treated as given, and old data has higher priority than new data. So if new data violates an integrity constraint, it is the new data that takes the blame. In other applications, such as in learning new beliefs, in which the beliefs are under suspicion, the observations have higher priority than other beliefs, and belief revision is used to refine the beliefs.

In subsequent chapters we will see that constraints play an important role in eliminating candidate explanations of observations (abduction), and in eliminating candidate actions (prohibition). In these applications, it is even more obvious than in the case of database updates that it is the candidate explanation or action that is on trial, and which is the sole potential culprit to be rejected if *falsity* is derived.

Summary

The examples in this chapter illustrate how logic can be used in the context of an agent's observation–thought–decision–action cycle. Placed in this context, logic is used for the higher levels of thought – both to reason forwards from observations, triggering maintenance goals and deriving achievement goals, and to reason backwards to reduce achievement goals to actions.

Below the logical level, sensory and perceptual processes transform raw sensations into observations, and motor processes transform conceptual representations of actions into raw physical activity. The entire process can be pictured like this:

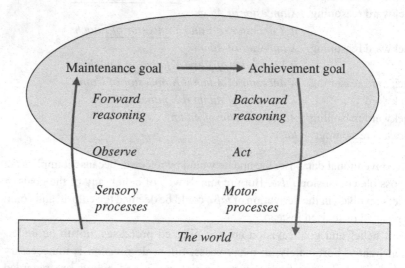

We have seen that forward reasoning with maintenance goals generalises condition–action rules, achievement goals generalise the actions of condition–action rules, and backward reasoning with beliefs generates plans of action. In later chapters, we will see how backward reasoning can also be used to explain observations (abduction) and how forward reasoning can also be used to infer consequences of both candidate explanations of observations and candidate actions. We will also see how this use of forward reasoning from candidate explanations and actions helps to inform the next, decision-making stage in the cycle, so that different candidates can be compared, and better informed decisions can be made.

But first, in the next chapter, we will see that much of this sophisticated reasoning can often be compiled into more efficient, lower-level stimulus–response associations.

9

The meaning of life

It'ls bad enough to be a Mars explorer and not to know that your purpose in life is to find life on Mars. But it's a lot worse to be a wood louse and have nothing more important to do with your life than just follow the meaningless rules:

Goals: *if it's clear ahead, then I move forward.*
if there's an obstacle ahead, then I turn right.
if I am tired, then I stop.

In fact, it's even worse than meaningless. Without food the louse will die, and without children the louse's genes will disappear. What is the point of just wandering around if the louse doesn't bother to eat and make babies?

Part of the problem is that the louse's body isn't giving it the right signals – not making it hungry when it is running out of energy, and not making it desire a mate when it should be having children. It also needs to be able to recognise food and eat, and to recognise potential mates and propagate.

So where does the louse go from here? If it got here by natural evolution, then it has nowhere to go and is on the road to extinction.

But if it owes its life to some Grand Designer, then it can plead with her to start all over again, this time working from the top down. The Grand Designer would need to rethink the louse's top-level goals, decide how to reduce them to subgoals and derive a new, more effective specification of the louse's input–output behaviour.

Suppose the Grand Designer identifies these as the louse's top-level goals:

Top-level goals: *the louse stays alive for as long as possible and*
the louse has as many children as possible.

Of course, a critic might well ask: What purpose do these goals serve, and why these goals and not others? Perhaps staying alive is just a subgoal of having children. And perhaps having children is just one way of promoting the survival of one's genes. But eventually the critic would have to stop. Otherwise he could continue asking such questions forever.

To reduce the louse's top-level goals to subgoals, the designer needs to use her beliefs about the world, including her beliefs about the louse's bodily capabilities. Moreover, she can build upon her earlier design, in which the louse moved around aimlessly, and give its movements a purpose. She could use such beliefs as:

Beliefs: *the louse stays alive for as long as possible,*
if whenever it is hungry then it looks for food
and when there is food ahead it eats it,
and whenever it is tired then it rests,
and whenever it is threatened with attack then it defends itself.

the louse has as many children as possible,
if whenever it desires a mate then it looks for a mate and
when there is a mate ahead it tries to make babies.

the louse looks for an object,
if whenever it is clear ahead then it moves forward,
and whenever there is an obstacle ahead and it isn't the object
    then it turns right
and when the object is ahead then it stops.

the louse defends itself if it runs away.

food is an object.
a mate is an object.

If the louse were as intelligent as the designer, then the designer could just hand these beliefs and the top-level goal directly over to the louse itself. The louse could then reason forwards and backwards, as the need arises, and would be confident of achieving its goals, provided the designer's beliefs are actually true.

But the louse possesses neither the designer's obvious physical attractions, nor her superior intellect and higher education. The designer, therefore, not only has to identify the louse's requirements, but she has to derive an input–output representation, which can be implemented in the louse, using its limited physical and mental capabilities.

One way for the designer to do her job is to do the necessary reasoning for the louse in advance. She can begin by reasoning backwards from the louse's top-level goals, to generate the next, lower level of subgoals:

Subgoals: *whenever the louse is hungry then it looks for food and*
       when there is food ahead it eats it, and
       whenever the louse is tired then it rests, and

whenever the louse is threatened with attack then it defends
    itself and
whenever the louse desires a mate then it looks for a mate and
when there is a mate ahead it tries to make babies.

The English words "whenever" and "when" are different ways of saying "if", but they carry an additional, temporal dimension.[1] It would be a distraction to deal with such temporal issues here. For that reason, it is useful to reformulate the subgoals in more conventional logical terms. At the same time, we can take advantage of the reformulation to eliminate an ambiguity associated with the scope of the words "and when":

Subgoals: *if the louse is hungry then it looks for food, and*
        if the louse is hungry and there is food ahead then it eats it, and
        if the louse is tired then it rests, and
        if the louse is threatened with attack then it defends itself, and
        if the louse desires a mate then it looks for a mate, and
        if the louse desires a mate and there is a mate ahead
        then it tries to make babies.

Unfortunately, the designer's work is not yet done. Some of the conclusions of the subgoals include other goals (like looking for food, defending itself, and looking for a mate) that need to be reduced to still lower-level subgoals.[2] Fortunately, for the designer, this is easy work. It takes just a little further backward reasoning and some logical simplification[3] to derive a specification that a behaviourist would be proud of:

New goals: *if the louse is hungry and it is clear ahead*
        then the louse moves forward.

        if the louse is hungry and there is an obstacle ahead and it isn't food
        then the louse turns right.

        if the louse is hungry and there is food ahead
        then the louse stops and it eats the food.

        if the louse is tired then the louse rests.

        if the louse is threatened with attack then the louse runs away.

        if the louse desires a mate and it is clear ahead
        then the louse moves forward.

[1] It is interesting that both the temporal and logical interpretations of the ambiguous English word "then" are meaningful here.

[2] For simplicity, we assume that running away, resting and trying to make babies are all actions that the louse can execute directly without reducing them to lower-level subgoals.

[3] The necessary simplification is to replace sentences of the form *if A, then if B then C* by logically equivalent sentences of the form *if A and B then C*.

*if the louse desires a mate and there is an obstacle ahead and it
isn't a mate then the louse turns right.*

*if the louse desires a mate and there is an obstacle ahead and it is
a mate then the louse stops and it tries to make babies.*

The new goals specify the louse's input–output behaviour and can be implemented directly as a production system without memory. However, the new goals
are potentially inconsistent. If the louse desires a mate and is hungry at the same
time, then it may find itself in a situation, for example, where it has to both stop
and eat and also turn right and look for a mate simultaneously. To avoid such
inconsistencies, the louse would need to perform conflict resolution.

But if it's too much to expect the louse to reason logically, it's probably also
too much to expect the louse to perform conflict resolution. And it's certainly far
too much to expect it to apply decision theory to weigh the relative advantages
of satisfying its hunger compared with those of satisfying its longing for a mate.
The simplest solution is for the designer to make these decisions for the louse,
and to build them into the specification:

*if the louse is hungry and **is not threatened with attack** and
it is clear ahead then the louse moves forward.*

*if the louse is hungry and **is not threatened with attack** and
there is an obstacle ahead and it isn't food and **it doesn't desire a mate**
then the louse turns right.*

*if the louse is hungry and **is not threatened with attack** and
there is food ahead then the louse stops and eats the food.*

*if the louse is tired and **is not threatened with attack** and
is not hungry and **does not desire a mate** then the louse rests.*

if the louse is threatened with attack then the louse runs away.

*if the louse desires a mate and **is not threatened with attack** and
it is clear ahead then the louse moves forward.*

*if the louse desires a mate and **is not threatened with attack** and
is not hungry and there is an obstacle ahead and it isn't a mate
then the louse turns right.*

*if the louse desires a mate and **is not threatened with attack** and
there is a mate ahead then the louse stops and tries to make babies.*

***if the louse desires a mate and is hungry and
is not threatened with attack** and*

> *there is an obstacle ahead and **it isn't a mate and it isn't food***
> *then the louse turns right.*

The new specification is a collection of input–output associations that give highest priority to reacting to an attack, lowest priority to resting when tired, and equal priority to mating and eating. Now the only situation in which a conflict can arise is if there is a mate and food ahead at the same time. Well, you can't always worry about everything. Even a wood louse deserves a modicum of free will, even if it means nothing more than making a random choice.

The mind/body problem

In general, a designer's job ends when she has constructed a declarative description of her object's input–output behaviour. How that behaviour is implemented inside the object is not her concern.

In computer science, this decoupling of an object's design from its implementation is called *encapsulation*. The implementation is encapsulated inside the object. Objects can interact with other objects, taking only their input–output behaviour into account.

The notion of encapsulation partially vindicates the behaviourist's point of view. Not only is it impossible in many cases to determine what goes on inside another object, but for many purposes it is also unnecessary and even undesirable.

Our louse is no exception. It would be easy, given the input–output specification, to implement the louse's behaviour using a primitive production system without memory and without conflict resolution. But does the louse need to have a mind at all – to represent concepts such as hunger and food and to derive symbolic representations of its actions? Does the louse really need to carry around all this mental baggage, when the necessary, instinctive behaviour can be hardwired, as a collection of input–output associations, directly into the louse's body instead?[4]

Similarly, as we saw in Chapter 7, a designer might specify a thermostat in symbolic terms. But it doesn't follow that the thermostat needs to manipulate symbolic expressions to generate its behaviour. Most people would be perfectly

---

[4] This argument has been made, among others, by Rodney Brooks at MIT, who has implemented several generations of mindless, louse-like robots, which display impressively intelligent behaviour.

happy if the design were implemented with a simple mechanical or electronic device.

In the same way that a thermostat's behaviour can be viewed externally in logical, symbolic terms, without implying that the thermostat itself manipulates symbolic expressions, our louse's behaviour can also be implemented as a collection of instinctive input–output associations in a body without a mind.

Dual process theories of intuitive and deliberative thinking

In our imaginary example, the Grand Designer has a high-level awareness of the louse's goals and has beliefs that explain how the louse's behaviour helps the louse to achieve its goals. But the louse has only low-level, instinctive input–output associations, without being aware of their purpose.

But people are different. Although much of our human behaviour is intuitive, instinctive and sometimes even mindless, we can often step back from our intuitive judgements, consciously deliberate about their implicit goals, and control our behaviour to better achieve those goals. It is as though we could be both a louse and a louse designer at the same time.

This combination of intuitive and deliberative thinking is the focus of dual process theories of human thinking. As Kahneman and Frederick (2002) put it, the intuitive, subconscious level "quickly proposes intuitive answers to judgement problems as they arise", while the deliberative, conscious level "monitors the quality of these proposals, which it may endorse, correct, or override".

In Computational Logic, dual process theories have both a computational and logical interpretation. The computational interpretation is that, when an agent is deliberative, its behaviour is controlled by a high-level program, which manipulates symbols that have meaningful interpretations in the environment. But when the agent is intuitive, its behaviour is generated by a low-level program or physical device, whose structure is largely determined by the physical characteristics of the agent's body.

The logical interpretation of dual process theories is that, when an agent is deliberative, its behaviour is generated by reasoning with high-level goals and beliefs. When the agent is intuitive, its behaviour is determined by low-level input–output associations, even if these associations can also be represented in logical form.

Two kinds of thinking on the Underground

The London Underground example illustrates the two kinds of thinking and the relationship between them. The high-level representation contains an explicit representation of the goal, and the supporting beliefs:

Goal: *if there is an emergency then I get help.*
Beliefs: *a person gets help if the person alerts the driver.*
          a person alerts the driver if the person presses the alarm signal button.
          there is an emergency if there is a fire.
          there is an emergency if one person attacks another.
          there is an emergency if someone becomes seriously ill.
          there is an emergency if there is an accident.
          there is a fire if there are flames.
          there is a fire if there is smoke.

A passenger can use the high-level goal and the beliefs explicitly, reasoning forward from observations to recognise there is an emergency and to derive the goal of getting help, and then reasoning backward, to get help by pressing the alarm signal button.

However, the same behaviour can be generated more efficiently, with less thought, by using a low-level representation in the form of input–output associations or condition–action rules. This representation can also be expressed in the logical form of maintenance goals, which need only one step of forward reasoning to generate output actions from input observations.

Goals: *if there are flames then I press the alarm signal button.*
         if there is smoke then I press the alarm signal button.
         if one person attacks another then I press the alarm signal button.
         if someone becomes seriously ill then I press the alarm signal button.
         if there is an accident then I press the alarm signal button.

The low-level representation can be derived from the high-level representation by doing the necessary forward and backward reasoning in advance, before the need arises.

The low-level representation is nearly as low as a representation can go, while still remaining in logical form. However, it is possible to go lower, if the associations are implemented by direct physical connections between the relevant parts of the agent's sensory and motor systems. This is like implementing software in hardware.

A computational interpretation of intuitive and deliberative thinking

In computing, different levels of representation have different advantages and are complementary. Low-level representations are more efficient. But high-level representations are more flexible, easier to develop and easier to change.

In the London Underground example, the low-level representation lacks the awareness, which is explicit in the high-level representation, of the goal of getting help, which is the purpose of pressing the alarm signal button. If something goes wrong with the low-level representation, for example if the button doesn't work or the driver doesn't get help, then the passenger might not realise there is a problem. Moreover, if the environment changes, and there are new kinds of emergencies, or newer and better ways of dealing with emergencies, then it is harder to modify the low-level representation to adapt to the changes.

In computing, the high-level representation is typically developed first, sometimes not even as a program but as an analysis of the program requirements. This high-level representation is then *transformed*, either manually or by means of another program called a *compiler*, into a low-level, more efficiently executable representation.

The reverse process is also possible. Low-level programs can sometimes be *decompiled* into equivalent high-level programs. This is useful if the low-level program needs to be changed, perhaps because the environment has changed or because the program has developed a fault. The high-level representation can then be modified and *recompiled* into a new, improved, lower-level form.

However, this reverse process is not always possible. Legacy systems, developed directly in low-level languages and modified over a period of many years, may not have enough structure to identify their goals precisely and to decompile them into higher-level form. But even then it may be possible to decompile them partially and to approximate them with higher-level programs. This process of rational reconstruction can help to improve the maintenance of the legacy system, even when wholesale reimplementation is not possible.

The relationship between intuitive and deliberative thinking

This relationship between high-level and low-level programs in computing has similarities with the relationship between deliberative and intuitive thinking in people.

Compiling a high-level program into a lower-level program in computing is similar to the migration from deliberative to intuitive thinking that takes place, for example, when a person learns to use a keyboard, play a musical instrument or drive a car. In computing, compiling a high-level program or specification is normally done by reasoning in advance, before the more efficient program is implemented. But in human thinking, it is more common to collapse an explicit high-level representation into a lower-level shortcut after an extended period of repeated use.

Decompiling a low-level program into a higher-level program is similar to the process of reflecting on subconscious knowledge and representing it in conscious terms – for example, when a linguist constructs a formal grammar for a natural language. Whereas a native speaker of the language might know the grammar only tacitly and subconsciously, the linguist formulates an explicit model of the grammar consciously and deliberatively. Non-native speakers can learn the explicit grammar, and with sufficient practice eventually compile the grammar into more efficient and spontaneous form.

Conclusions

Computational Logic is a wide-spectrum language of thought, which can represent both high-level goals and beliefs, as well as low-level stimulus–response associations. An intelligent agent can use the high-level representation when time allows, and the low-level representation when time is limited. It can also use both representations simultaneously.

An agent may have inherited its stimulus–response associations at birth, and finely tuned them to its own personal experiences. If so, then it can reasonably rely upon them when new situations are similar to situations that the agent and its designer or ancestors have successfully dealt with in the past.

An intelligent agent, on the other hand, might also be able to reflect upon its behaviour and formulate an understanding of the consequences of its actions. The agent can use this higher-level understanding, to help it better achieve its fundamental goals, especially in new situations that are unlike situations that have arisen in the past.

In the more advanced Chapter A5, I show how the resolution rule of inference can be used to perform not only forward and backward reasoning when they are needed in the current situation, but also similar kinds of reasoning in advance. This kind of reasoning in advance can be viewed as compiling high-level representations of goals and beliefs into more efficient, lower-level form.

The ability to combine the two levels of representation combines their individual strengths and compensates for their individual weaknesses.

10

Abduction

Most changes in the world pass us by without notice. Our sensory organs and perceptual apparatus filter them out, so they do not clutter our thoughts with irrelevancies. Other changes enter our minds as observations. We reason forward from them to deduce their consequences, and we react to them if necessary. Most of these observations are routine, and our reactions are spontaneous. Many of them do not even make it into our conscious thoughts.

But some observations are not routine: the loud bang in the middle of the night, the pool of blood on the kitchen floor, the blackbird feathers in the pie. They demand explanation. They could have been caused by unobserved events, which might have other, perhaps more serious consequences. The loud bang could be the firing of a gun. The pool of blood could have come from the victim of the shooting. The blackbird feathers in the pie could be an inept attempt to hide the evidence.

Even routine observations can benefit from explanation: Why do the Sun, the Moon and the stars rise in the East and set in the West? Why does the door stick? Why do the apples drop before they are ready to eat? Explaining routine observations helps us to discover new connections between otherwise unrelated phenomena, predict the future and reconstruct the past.

An agent might explain its observations by using its existing beliefs or by using new hypothetical beliefs. Both kinds of explanation deductively imply the observations, because if the explanations are true, then the observations are true. Forward reasoning is a natural way to justify explanations after they have been found, but backward reasoning is normally a much better way of actually finding them. As Sherlock Holmes explained to Dr. Watson, in *A Study in Scarlet*:

> "I have already explained to you that what is out of the common is usually a guide rather than a hindrance. In solving a problem of this sort, the grand thing is to be able to reason backward. That is a very useful accomplishment, and a very easy one,

but people do not practise it much. In the everyday affairs of life it is more useful to reason forward, and so the other comes to be neglected. There are fifty who can reason synthetically for one who can reason analytically."

"I confess," said I, "that I do not quite follow you."

"I hardly expected that you would. Let me see if I can make it clearer. Most people, if you describe a train of events to them, will tell you what the result would be. They can put those events together in their minds, and argue from them that something will come to pass. There are few people, however, who, if you told them a result, would be able to evolve from their own inner consciousness what the steps were which led up to that result. This power is what I mean when I talk of reasoning backward, or analytically."

Backward reasoning can be used to find explanations, whether the resulting explanations use existing beliefs or generate new hypothetical beliefs. Forward reasoning, in contrast, makes sense only when deducing consequences from existing beliefs or hypotheses. To use forward reasoning to explain an observation, you have to make a guess in the dark, generate a hypothesis, and then check whether or not the hypothesis has any relevance to the observation. With backward reasoning, the hypothesis is generated automatically and guaranteed to be relevant.

But the main problem with explaining an observation is, not so much the problem of generating relevant explanations, but the problem of deciding which is the *best explanation*, given that there can be many alternative, candidate explanations for the same observation. We will see later that the problem of determining the best explanation is similar to the problem of determining the best plan for achieving a goal.

Hypothetical beliefs come in two forms: in the form of *general rules* (or conditionals) and in the form of *specific facts*. Hypotheses in the form of general rules represent connections between several observations; and the process of generating hypotheses in the form of rules is known as *induction*. Generating hypotheses by induction is hard, and includes the case of generating a scientific theory, like the laws of celestial motion. We shall return to the problem of induction briefly in the concluding chapter of this book.

Hypotheses in the form of facts, on the other hand, represent possible underlying causes of observations; and the process of generating them is known as *abduction*. Typically, a hypothesis generated by abduction is triggered by the desire to explain one or more particular observations. The more observations the hypothesis explains, the better the explanation. Similarly, in deciding between different plans of action, the more goals a plan achieves, the better.

Abduction is possible only for an agent who has an open mind and is willing to entertain alternative hypotheses. It is not possible for a *close-minded agent*, who thinks he knows it all. The simplest way to have an open mind, but to keep the candidate hypotheses within manageable bounds, is to restrict them to open predicates, to which selective closed-world assumptions and negation as failure do not apply.

The term *abduction* was introduced by the logician Charles Sanders Peirce (1931). He illustrated the difference between deduction, induction and abduction with the following example:

Deduction: *All the beans from this bag are white.*
            These beans are from this bag.
            Therefore   *These beans are white.*
Induction: *These beans are from this bag.*
            These beans are white.
            Therefore   *All the beans from this bag are white.*
Abduction: *All the beans from this bag are white.*
            These beans are white.
            Therefore   *These beans are from this bag.*

Generating abductive hypotheses and deciding between them includes the classic case in which Sherlock Holmes solves a crime by first identifying all the hypothetical suspects and then eliminating them one by one, until only one suspect remains. To put it in his own words (from *The Adventure of the Beryl Coronet*): "It is an old maxim of mine that when you have excluded the impossible, whatever remains, however improbably, must be the truth."

Sherlock Holmes described his reasoning technique as deduction. But *deduction* in logic leads from known facts or observations to inescapable conclusions. If the beliefs used to deduce the conclusions are true, then the conclusions must also be true. Abduction, on the other hand, can lead from true observations and other beliefs to false hypotheses. For this reason, abductive inference is said to be *fallible* or *defeasible*. We will see in Chapter 15 that the distinction between deduction and abduction is blurred when conditionals are interpreted as biconditionals in disguise.

The grass is wet

The time-worn example of abduction in Artificial Intelligence is to explain the observation that *the grass is wet* when you get up one morning. Of course, there are many possible explanations, but in this part of the world the most likely alternatives are either that *it rained* or that *the sprinkler was on*. The easiest way to find these explanations is by reasoning backwards from the

observation, treated as a goal,[1] with causal connections represented in the form
effect if cause:

Beliefs: *the grass is wet if it rained.*
                 the grass is wet if the sprinkler was on.

Here *the grass is wet* is a closed predicate, and *it rained* and *the sprinkler was on*
are open predicates:

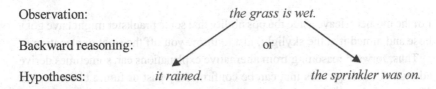

Observation: *the grass is wet.*

Backward reasoning: or

Hypotheses: *it rained.*   *the sprinkler was on.*

Instead of failing to solve the goal, because there is no direct evidence that
either of the two subgoals hold, abduction by backward reasoning identifies
the two possible causes as alternative hypothetical explanations of the
observation.

It would be possible just to leave it at that: Either *it rained* or *the sprinkler
was on*. But to be on the safe side, it may pay to spend a little more
mental energy and pursue the logical consequences of the alternatives. If
it rained last night, then the clothes on the clothes line outside will be wet,
and you won't be able to do the ironing you planned for this morning. If the
sprinkler was on, then your water bill is going to go through the roof, and you
had better disconnect the sprinkler in case it decides to turn itself on again
tonight.

Suppose you are too lazy or too clever to do the obvious thing and just go
outside and check the clothes on the clothes line or check the state of the
sprinkler. Instead, you might just sit in your living room armchair and reason
as follows: If *it rained* last night, then there will be drops of water on the living
room skylight. There are drops of water on the skylight. So it is likely that it
rained last night, because the assumption that it rained explains two independent
observations, compared with the assumption that the sprinkler was on, which
explains only one. The combination of backward and forward reasoning
involved in this example can be pictured like this:

---

[1] Notice that treating observations as goals extends the notion of goal, beyond representing the
world as the agent would like it to be in the future, to explaining the world as the agent actually
sees it. This is because the two kinds of reasoning, finding actions to achieve a goal and finding
hypotheses to explain an observation, can both be viewed as special cases of the more abstract
problem of finding assumptions to deductively derive conclusions. See, for example, Kakas *et al.*,
(1998).

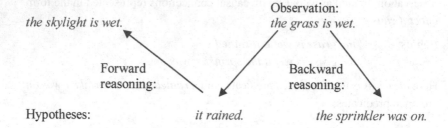

For the moment, leave aside the possibility that some prankster might have got a hose and aimed it at the skylight, just to throw you off the right explanation.

Thus, forward reasoning from alternative explanations can sometimes derive additional consequences that can be confirmed by past or future observations. The greater the number of such additional observations a hypothesis explains, the better the explanation. We will see in the next chapter that forward reasoning from alternative plans of action can also help to decide between alternative plans. The greater the number of additional goals a plan achieves, the better the plan.

The London Underground revisited again

In the previous chapters, we represented the relationships between fire, smoke and flames in the form *cause if effect*. This form made it easy to assimilate the observation of smoke and to conclude by forward reasoning that there is an emergency. It would have been more natural to express the relationship in the form *effect if cause*:

> *there are flames if there is a fire.*
> *there is smoke if there is a fire.*

However, with this representation, given the observation *there is smoke*, it is impossible to derive *there is an emergency* by using deduction alone. It is necessary instead to first use abduction, to determine that *there is a fire* as the explanation of the observation, and then use forward reasoning as before.

This comparison between the two ways of representing the connection between cause and effect might remind you of the discussion in Chapter 2 about the two ways of representing the connection between being red and looking red. In that example, we also argued that it is more natural to represent alternative causes of looking red in the *effect if cause* form with separate conditionals:

> *an object looks red if it is red.*
> *an object looks red if it is illuminated by a red light.*

Similarly, it is more natural to represent the alternative causes of smoke by separate conditionals in *effect if cause* form:

> *there is smoke if there is a fire.*
> *there is smoke if there is teargas.*

We will see later in Chapter 15 that it is possible to derive, from the assumption that these are the only conditions under which the conclusion holds, the two alternative *cause if effect* conditionals:

> *there is a fire if there is smoke and it is not the case that there is teargas.*
> *there is teargas if there is smoke and it is not the case that there is a fire.*

In classical logic, both of these conditionals are logically equivalent to a conditional with a disjunctive conclusion:

> *there is a fire or there is teargas if there is smoke.*

In Computational Logic with negative conditions interpreted as negation as failure, we obtain an asymmetric approximation to the disjunction, with one of the two alternatives holding by default. In this example, because fire is a more common cause of smoke than teargas, the first of the two *cause if effect* conditionals can be used to derive fire as the cause of smoke by default. This avoids the computationally expensive effort of trying to determine the best explanation, and amounts to the use of a simple and quick heuristic instead.

The two alternative ways of representing the relationship between cause and effect have different advantages and disadvantages. The *effect if cause* representation is higher-level, in the sense that its syntax is closer to the causal structure that it represents. However, it requires more complex abductive reasoning. The *cause if effect* representation is lower-level and more efficient. It requires only deductive reasoning, and makes it easy to build in a preference for one explanation over another. This relationship between the two levels of representation is similar to other such relationships that we have seen elsewhere in the book. However, in this chapter we focus on the higher-level abductive representation, bearing in mind that it can also be implemented purely deductively, as we will see again in greater detail in Chapter 15.

What counts as a reasonable explanation?

Not every set of abductive hypotheses that deductively implies an observation is a reasonable explanation of the observation. To be a reasonable explanation, the hypotheses:

- should be *relevant* to the observation, and should not include arbitrary hypotheses that have no bearing on the observation and
- should be *consistent* with the agent's existing beliefs.

We touched upon the relevance requirement earlier. It is automatically satisfied by reasoning backwards from the observation. Backward reasoning ensures that every hypothesis generated in an explanation is ultimately connected to the observation by a chain of links in the connection graph of beliefs. The relevance requirement is weaker than the requirement that explanations be minimal. The *minimality* requirement insists that no subset of the explanation is also an explanation. For example:

Beliefs:	*the floor is wet if it rained and the window was open.*
	the floor is wet if it rained and there is a hole in the roof.
	there is a hole in the roof.
Observation:	*the floor is wet.*
Relevant explanation:	*it rained and the window was open.*
Minimal explanation:	*it rained.*
Irrelevant explanation:	*it rained and the dog was barking.*

Minimality is often cited as a desirable, or even necessary property of abductive explanations; but ensuring that an explanation is minimal can be computationally infeasible. Relevance, on the other hand, comes for free with backward reasoning, and in most cases is an acceptable approximation to minimality. Both relevance and minimality are a form of Ockham's razor.

The consistency requirement excludes impossible explanations, such as the explanation *it rained*, if there were clothes outside and they didn't get wet. Ensuring consistency is complicated in the general case. However, in many cases it can be facilitated by representing negative concepts in positive form, and by using constraints to monitor that contrary predicates do not hold simultaneously. For example, the negative concept *not wet* can be represented by the positive concept *dry*, and the relationship between *wet* and *dry* can be expressed by means of the constraint:

	if a thing is dry and the thing is wet then false.
i.e.	*nothing is both dry and wet.*

In such cases, consistency reduces to the requirement that a hypothesis does not deductively imply the conclusion *false*, and a natural way to enforce the requirement is to reason forward from a hypothesis and eliminate it if it implies *false*. For example:

Beliefs:	*the clothes outside are dry.*
	the clothes outside are wet if it rained.
Hypothesis:	*it rained.*
Forward reasoning:	*the clothes outside are wet.*
Forward reasoning:	*if the clothes outside are dry then false.*
Forward reasoning:	*false.*

The derivation of *false* eliminates the hypothesis that *it rained* as a candidate explanation of the observation that *the grass is wet*.

Contraries and strong negation

As we saw in Chapter 5, many concepts occur as pairs of *contrary* positive concepts, like *wet* and *dry*, *tall* and *short*, *big* and *small*, *good* and *bad*. Often these contraries are expressed as negations of one another, as in *not wet* instead of *dry* and *not dry* instead of *wet*. This use of negation is sometimes called *strong negation*. Viewed as a form of negation, it has the *truth value gap property* that there can be instances of a predicate that are neither *true* nor *false*. For example, if my clothes are merely damp, I might consider them as being neither wet nor dry.

The use of pairs of contrary predicates with truth gaps is a natural way to represent vague concepts. Positive instances of the concept can be represented by one predicate of the pair, and negative instances of the concept by the other predicate. Instances that are neither clearly positive nor clearly negative can simply be left undetermined.

Thus, reasoning with strong negation in the form of positive contraries requires no extension of the inference rules of Computational Logic, if for every pair of contrary predicates, we have constraints of the form:

if predicate and contrary-predicate then false.

What counts as a best explanation?

Restricting explanations to hypotheses that are relevant and consistent is not good enough. In many situations, there will be several such relevant and consistent explanations. In some cases, where none of the alternatives has any important, foreseeable consequences, it may be unnecessary to choose between them. But in other cases, where an explanation does have such consequences, it can be a good idea to determine whether the explanation is actually true, so that preparations can be made to deal with those consequences. If the consequences are beneficial, then they can be exploited: and if they are harmful, then it might be possible to counteract them before they do too much damage.

For example, for most people most of the time, the observation that *the grass is wet* is hardly worth explaining. Whether *it rained* or *the sprinkler was on* is likely to be of little significance, especially if the sprinkler doesn't belong to you and the grass needs watering anyway. In comparison, some of the alternative explanations of an observation that *the floor is wet* do have important consequences. If the wet floor is due to a hole in the roof, then the roof will have to be repaired before it gets much worse. If it is due to leaking plumbing, then you need to deal with the problem before you have a flood on your hands.

> Global warming is a more topical example. If observed rises in world temperature are primarily due to carbon emissions, then at the rate we are going global warming will soon make much of our planet uninhabitable, and we had better dramatically reduce our emissions before it is too late. But if they are primarily due to natural climatic processes, then we might as well just adjust to climate change and its consequences and enjoy them while we can.
>
> Nothing in life is certain, and that goes as much for explaining observations as it does for everything else. One way to judge the likelihood of an explanation is to consult expert opinion. For example, according to the IPCC Fourth Assessment Report: Climate Change 2007, most of the observed increase in global temperatures since the mid-twentieth century is more than 90% likely to be due to the increase in manmade greenhouse gas concentrations. Therefore, weighing the importance of the consequences by the probabilities of their causes and choosing the most likely explanation with the most significant consequences, we should assume that the causes of climate change are human greenhouse gas emissions, and act accordingly.
>
> Another way to judge the likelihood of an explanation is to use statistical information about the relative past frequency of different causes. For example, you don't need to be a car mechanic to realise that, if your car doesn't start, it must be due to a fuel problem, an electrical problem, or a mechanical problem. But you need at least a little experience to realise that electrical problems are more common than fuel and mechanical problems. So everything else being equal, it is a good strategy to check whether there is an electrical problem first. You can do this, for example, by reasoning forward from the hypothesis that there is an electrical problem caused by the battery, and conclude that if the battery is at fault then the lights will not work. So if you try the lights and they don't work, then the problem is most likely due to a faulty battery, because the more observations a hypothesis explains the more likely it is to be true.

These two criteria for helping to decide between competing explanations, their relative likelihood and their utility as judged by the number and importance of their consequences, are virtually identical to the criteria that are most helpful in deciding between different courses of action to achieve a higher-level goal. We will explore these criteria in greater detail in the next chapter.

Conclusions

Abduction builds upon traditional logic and is a defining feature of Computational Logic. Like default reasoning, it addresses a problem that has been one of the greatest obstacles to the use of logic in everyday life, the problem that we need to make judgements and to act upon those judgements in situations where our knowledge about the world is incomplete.

Abduction and default reasoning are related by their common use of assumptions to augment beliefs. In abduction, we augment our beliefs with assumptions concerning instances of open predicates. In default reasoning, we augment them with assumptions that an instance of the contrary of a predicate cannot be shown. In both cases, these assumptions are defeasible, and can be withdrawn if later observations provide information to the contrary. This relationship between abduction and default reasoning was first investigated by Poole *et al.* (1987).

The problem of identifying the best explanation has many important features in common with the problem of deciding between different courses of action. Similar criteria involving judgements of probability and utility apply to both problems. We will look at these criteria in the next chapter and at the technical underpinnings of abductive logic programming in Chapter A6.

11

The Prisoner's Dilemma

Suppose, in your desperation to get rich as quickly as possible, you consider the various alternatives, infer their likely consequences and decide that the best alternative is to rob the local bank. You recruit your best friend, John, well known for his meticulous attention to detail, to help you plan and carry out the crime. Thanks to your joint efforts, you succeed in breaking into the bank in the middle of the night, opening the safe and making your get-away with a cool million pounds (approximately 1.65 million dollars – and falling – at the time of writing) in the boot (trunk) of your car.

Unfortunately, years of poverty and neglect have left your car in a state of general disrepair, and you are stopped by the police for driving at night with only one headlight. In the course of a routine investigation, they discover the suitcase with the cool million pounds in the boot. You plead ignorance of any wrong doing, but they arrest you both anyway on the suspicion of robbery.

Without witnesses and without a confession, the police can convict you and your friend only of the lesser offence of possessing stolen property, which carries a penalty of one year in jail. However, if one of you turns witness against the other, and the other does not, then the first will be released free of charge, and the second will take all of the blame and be sentenced to six years in jail. If you both turn witness, then you will share the blame and will be sentenced to three years in jail each.

This is an example of the classical Prisoner's Dilemma, studied in decision theory and game theory. In decision theory, the general problem of deciding between alternative actions is often represented as a decision table, in which the rows represent actions, the columns represent the state of the world and the entries represent the resulting outcome. In this case, your decision table looks like this:

Action	State of the world *John turns witness*	*John refuses*
I turn witness	*I get 3 years in jail*	*I get 0 years in jail*
I refuse	*I get 6 years in jail*	*I get 1 year in jail*

If you and John are offered the same deal and have a chance to consult before you decide, then you will soon realise that the best option is for you both to refuse to turn witness against the other. To prevent this, the police interrogate you in separate cells. Thus you have to decide what to do without knowing what John will do.

According to classical decision theory, you should choose the action that has highest expected utility, in this case the action that minimises the number of years you expect to spend in jail. We will see how to do this later in the chapter.

The logic of the Prisoner's Dilemma

The Prisoner's Dilemma has a natural representation in terms of goals and beliefs:

Goal: *if an agent requests me to perform an action,*
          then I respond to the request to perform the action.

Beliefs: *I respond to a request to perform an action if I perform the action.*
          I respond to a request to perform an action
          if I refuse to perform the action.

          I get 3 years in jail if I turn witness and john turns witness.
          I get 0 years in jail if I turn witness and john refuses to turn witness.
          I get 6 years in jail if I refuse to turn witness and john turns witness.
          I get 1 year in jail if I refuse to turn witness
          and john refuses to turn witness.

According to our agent model, the maintenance goal is triggered by the observation:

Observation: *the police request me to turn witness.*
Forward reasoning,[1] achievement goal:
          I respond to the request to turn witness.

---

[1] To make the connection between the observation and the condition of the goal, it is necessary to unify *the police* with *an agent* and *turn witness* with *perform an action*. In a computer implementation, this unification would have to be done mechanically. For this purpose, it would be necessary to recognise *turn witness* as shorthand for *perform turn witness*.

Backward reasoning, one candidate action:

> *I turn witness.*

Forward reasoning, consequences:

> *I get 3 years in jail if john turns witness.*
> *I get 0 years in jail if john refuses to turn witness.*

Backward reasoning, another candidate action:

> *I refuse to turn witness.*

Forward reasoning, consequences:

> *I get 6 years in jail if john turns witness.*
> *I get 1 years in jail if john refuses to turn witness.*

Here the consequences (or outcome) of your candidate actions depend upon whether or not John turns witness against you. Unfortunately, you need to decide what to do without knowing what John will do.

In classical logic, it would be possible to reason as follows:

Candidate action:	*I turn witness.*
Disjunctive constraint:	*john turns witness or*
	john refuses to turn witness.
Disjunctive consequence:	*I get 3 years in jail or I get 0 years in jail.*

Candidate action:	*I refuse to turn witness.*
Disjunctive constraint:	*john turns witness or*
	john refuses to turn witness.
Disjunctive consequence:	*I get 6 years in jail or I get 1 years in jail.*

Intuitively, the disjunctive consequence of the first candidate action seems better than the disjunctive consequence of the second alternative, and in theory it might be possible to evaluate the disjunctive consequences, compare them and use the result of the comparison to help choose between the alternative candidates.

However, the disjunctive constraint is a crude way to express uncertainty. It cannot represent degrees of uncertainty. For example, because John is your friend, you might believe:

> *john turns witness with probability 10%.*
> *john refuses to turn witness with probability 90%.*

These probabilities can be propagated from the conditions to the conclusions of beliefs. For example:

> *if I turn witness*
> *and john turns witness with probability 10%*
> *then I get 3 years in jail with probability 10%.*

Decision theory provides a principled way of propagating uncertainty and of combining judgements of probability with judgements of utility to determine the expected utility of an action. According to the norms of decision theory, given a collection of alternative candidate actions, an agent should choose an action that has the best expected utility.

Before seeing how to compute the expected utility of an action, and investigating its application to the Prisoner's Dilemma, we will take a short break and look at the more mundane problem of deciding whether or not to take an umbrella when you leave home.

Should you carry an umbrella?

The problem can be represented in a decision table:

Action	State of the world *It rains*	*It doesn't rain*
I take an umbrella	*I stay dry* *I carry an umbrella*	*I stay dry* *I carry an umbrella*
I leave without an umbrella	*I get wet*	*I stay dry*

We can represent the problem by the (simplified) goals and beliefs:

Goal: *if I go outside, then I take an umbrella*
          or I leave without an umbrella.

Beliefs: *I go outside.*
          I carry an umbrella if I take the umbrella.
          I stay dry if I take the umbrella.
          I stay dry if it doesn't rain.
          I get wet if I leave without an umbrella and it rains.

Notice that the representation in terms of beliefs is more informative than the decision table representation, because it indicates more precisely the conditions on which the outcome of an action depends. For example, it indicates that staying dry depends only on taking an umbrella and not on whether or not it rains.

You can control whether or not you take an umbrella, but you cannot control the weather. To decide between the alternative actions that you can control, you should infer their possible consequences, and choose the action with highest overall expected utility.

Suppose you judge that the value of staying dry is greater than the inconvenience of taking an umbrella. Then intuitively you should decide to take the umbrella, if you estimate that the probability of rain is high. But, you should decide to leave without the umbrella, if you estimate that the probability of rain is low. These intuitions are justified and made more precise by the mathematics of decision theory.

Applying decision theory to taking an umbrella

According to decision theory, you can compute the overall expected utility of an action by weighing the utility of each possible outcome of the action by its probability, and then sum all of the weighted utilities. In mathematical terms:

> *the expected utility* of an action is $p_1u_1 + p_2u_2 + \cdots + p_nu_n$
> if the action has n alternative outcomes with associated
> *utilities* $u_1, u_2, \ldots, u_n$ and respective *probabilities* $p_1, p_2, \ldots, p_n$.

You should then choose the action with greatest expected utility.

In the case of deciding whether to take an umbrella, suppose you judge:

> the *benefit* of staying dry is worth 2 candy bars,
> the *cost* of carrying an umbrella is worth -1 candy bar,
> the *cost* of getting wet is worth -8 candy bars,
> the *probability* that it will rain is P, and therefore
> the *probability* that it will not rain is $(1 - P)$.

These judgements of utilities and probabilities can be added to the decision table:

Action	State of the world		Expected utility
	It rains with probability P	*It doesn't rain with probability (1–P)*	$P \times utility_1 +$ $(1-P) \times utility_2$
I take an umbrella	*I stay dry* *I carry an umbrella with utility$_1$ =* $2-1=1$	*I stay dry* *I carry an umbrella with utility$_2$ =* $2-1=1$	$P + (1-P) = 1$
I leave without an umbrella	*I get wet* *with utility$_1$ = -8*	*I stay dry* *with utility$_2$ = 2*	$-8P + 2(1-P) =$ $-10P + 2$

If the expected utilities of the alternative actions are the same, then it makes no difference, measured in candy bars, whether you take an umbrella or not. This is the case when:

$$-10P + 2 = 1$$

i.e. $P = 0.1$

Therefore, if the probability of rain is greater than 10%, then you should take an umbrella; and if it is less than 10%, then you should leave your umbrella at home.

The use of decision theory is a *normative* ideal. In real life, we tend to approximate this ideal, by compiling routine decisions directly into goals and beliefs. For example:

Goals: *if I go outside and it looks likely to rain,*
then I take an umbrella.
if I go outside and it looks unlikely to rain,
then I leave without an umbrella.

Beliefs: *it looks likely to rain if there are dark clouds in the sky.*
it looks likely to rain if it is forecast to rain.
it looks unlikely to rain if there are no clouds in the sky.
it looks unlikely to rain if it is forecast not to rain.

More generally:

if I am leaving a place and I have a thing at the place
and the thing would be useful while I am away from the place
and the value of the thing outweighs the trouble of taking the thing,
then I take the thing with me.

if I am leaving a place and I have a thing at the place
and the thing would be useful while I am away from the place
and the trouble of taking the thing outweighs the value of the thing,
then I leave the thing at the place.

the value of an umbrella outweighs the trouble of taking the umbrella
if it looks likely to rain.

the trouble of taking an umbrella outweighs the value of the umbrella
if it looks unlikely to rain.
etc.

A psychologist might prefer to view such goals and beliefs as pragmatic reasoning schemes or Darwinian algorithms. But, as we have been arguing throughout this book, both of these views are compatible with the view that *thinking* is the application of *general-purpose* logical rules of inference to *domain-specific knowledge* (goals and beliefs) expressed in logical form.

Solving the Prisoner's Dilemma

The Prisoner's Dilemma and the problem of deciding whether to take an umbrella are both instances of the same general pattern of cause and effect:

> *a particular outcome happens if I do a certain action*
> *and the world is in a particular state.*

Similarly:

> *I will be rich if I buy a lottery ticket and my number is chosen.*
> *I will be famous if I write a book and it receives critical acclaim.*
> *It will rain tomorrow if I do a rain dance and the gods are pleased.*

In all of these cases, you can control your own actions, but you cannot completely control the actions of others or the state of the world. At best, you might be able to judge the exact probability that the world will be in a particular state. At worst, you might just assume that the odds of its being or not being in the state are simply equal.

However, suppose that in the case of the Prisoner's Dilemma, you decide to do a little high school algebra. Let:

> the *utility* of your getting N years in jail be $-N$.
> the *probability* that John turns witness be P.

Therefore the *probability* that John refuses to turn witness is $(1 - P)$.

These utilities and probabilities can be added to the decision table:

Action	State of the world *John turns witness with probability P*	*John refuses with probability (1–P)*	Expected utility $P \times utility_1 +$ $(1-P) \times utility_2$
I turn witness	*I get 3 years with utility$_1$ =–3*	*I get 0 years with utility$_2$ = 0*	$-3P$
I refuse	*I get 6 years with utility$_1$ =–6*	*I get 1 year with utility$_2$ =–1*	$-6P-(1-P) =$ $-5P-1$

But the expected utility $-3P$ of turning witness is greater than the expected utility $-5P-1$ of refusing to turn witness, for all values of P between 0 and 1. So no matter what the probability P that John turns witness against you, you are always better off turning witness against him.

Unfortunately, if John has the same beliefs, goals and utilities as you, then he will similarly decide to turn witness against you, in which case both of you will get a certain 3 years in jail. You would have been better off if both of you had ignored decision theory, taken a chance and refused to turn witness against the other, in which case you would both have got only 1 year in jail.

But there is a different moral you could draw from the story: that the fault lies, not with decision theory, but with your own selfish judgement of utility. You have placed no value at all on the consequences of your actions for the time that John will spend in jail.

Suppose, for example, that you assign equal value to the time that both of you will spend in jail. The corresponding new judgements of utility can be incorporated into a revised decision table:

Action	State of the world		Expected utility
	John turns witness with probability P	*John refuses with probability (1–P)*	$P \times utility_1 +$ $(1-P) \times utility_2$
I turn witness	I get 3 years John gets 3 years with $utility_1 = -6$	I get 0 years John gets 6 years with $utility_2 = -6$	$-6P - 6(1-P) = -6$
I refuse	I get 6 years John gets 0 years with $utility_1 = -6$	I get 1 year John gets 1 year with $utility_2 = -2$	$-6P - 2(1-P) =$ $-4P - 2$

But $-6 \geq -4P -2$, for all values of P between 0 and 1. Therefore, no matter what the probability P that John turns witness against you, there is never any advantage in your turning witness against him. Moreover, if John has the same beliefs, goals and utilities as you, then he will similarly decide not to turn witness against you, in which case you will both get a certain 1 year in jail.

But it is probably unrealistic to expect you to value equally both what happens to John and what happens to yourself. To be more realistic, suppose instead that you value what happens to John only half as much as you value what happens to yourself:

Action	State of the world		Expected utility
	John turns witness with probability P	*John refuses with probability (1–P)*	$P \times utility_1 +$ $(1-P) \times utility_2$
I turn witness	I get 3 years John gets 3 years with $utility_1 = -4.5$	I get 0 years John gets 6 years with $utility_2 = -3$	$-4.5P - 3(1-P) =$ $-1.5P - 3$
I refuse	I get 6 years John gets 0 years with $utility_1 = -6$	I get 1 year John gets 1 years with $utility_2 = -1.5$	$-6P - 1.5(1-P) =$ $-4.5P - 1.5$

The expected utilities of the two alternatives are the same when:

$$-1.5P - 3 = -4.5P - 1.5$$

i.e. $3P = 1.5$

i.e. $P = 0.50$

Therefore, if you judge that the probability of John turning witness is less than 50%, then you should not turn witness. But if you judge that the probability is greater than 50%, then you should turn witness. Tit for tat.

Just as in the case of deciding whether to take an umbrella when you leave home, these calculations are a normative ideal. But in real life, we more normally compile our decisions into rules (or heuristics), which approximate the decision-theoretic ideal, but which can be applied more simply and more efficiently. For example:

Goals: *if an agent requests me to perform an action,*
           and the action does not harm another person
           then I perform the action.

           if an agent requests me to perform an action,
           and the action harms another person
           then I refuse to perform the action.

These rules are not very subtle, but clearly they can be refined, both by adding extra rules to deal with other cases, and by adding extra conditions to accommodate extra qualifications.

Smart choices

But decision theory and heuristics are not the only possibilities. In fact, in their different ways, they both miss seeing the bigger picture. Decision theory deals only with independently given alternative candidate actions, evaluating their likely consequences, but ignoring where the alternatives came from and the purposes that they serve. Heuristics sidestep the fundamental issues by employing little more than higher-level stimulus–response associations.

The smarter way to make decisions is to step back, and pay due attention to your higher-level goals and to any outside circumstances that may have triggered the need to make a decision:

• Identify the higher-level goal (purpose, motivation, problem or objective) of the decision you need to make. Is this goal an implicit property of heuristics triggered by events in the environment? Or is it an explicit, higher-level achievement goal; or a subgoal (or means) towards a yet higher-level goal (or fundamental objective).

- Assuming that you can identify the top-level goal and any subgoals along the way, consider the alternative ways of solving these goals. Have you adequately considered all of the relevant alternatives? Or have you constrained yourself unnecessarily by considering only the first alternatives that entered your mind? Do you have enough knowledge (or beliefs) of the problem domain to generate the "best" alternatives?
- Explore the consequences (or outcomes) of the alternatives, and their impacts. Evaluate these consequences for the extent to which they achieve, not only the goals that may have motivated the alternatives, but also any other goals that might be achieved opportunistically along the way. Check whether the alternatives violate any constraints, or whether they have any other negative consequences that you should avoid.
- Assess the uncertainties associated with the consequences. Are you indulging in wishful thinking, or taking any unnecessary risks?
- Compare the alternatives, by combining your evaluation of their consequences with your assessment of their uncertainty. Use this comparison, not only to identify your final decision, but also to guide you efficiently in your search.
- Identify the other linked subgoals that need to be solved to achieve your top-level goals. Make sure that the decision is compatible with the smart solution of these other subgoals. Give preference to decisions that facilitate achieving future subgoals and that keep future options open for as long as possible.

If these guidelines look familiar, it is because they are based on the issues that recur throughout this book. But if they sound a little unfamiliar, it is because I have paraphrased them in the manner of Hammond *et al.*'s (1999) *Smart Choices – A practical guide to making better decisions.*

The guidelines in the *Smart Choices* book are based on solid research in decision science and on extensive practical experience. They appeal to logic and common sense, but of the familiar, informal variety. In this book, we deal with similar issues, but we place them within a Computational Logic and Artificial Intelligence setting.

Conclusions

The use of decision theory, heuristics and smart choices are three different ways of making decisions.

Decision theory is a powerful, normative tool. But it needs knowledge about utility and probability, and time to calculate and compare expected utilities, which is typically not available in most commonly occurring situations. Moreover, it neglects the motivations of actions, and the structure of those motivations in a hierarchy of goals and subgoals, and of alternative ways of reducing goals to subgoals.

Instead of decision theory, most people probably use heuristics to guide their decision making. Heuristics deal efficiently with the most commonly occurring cases, and often they approximate the decisions that would be taken using a decision-theoretic analysis. But heuristics are subject to biases of all kinds, and often lead to bad choices, sometimes when we are making the most important decisions in our lives.

In situations where it is important to make as good a decision as possible, we need to monitor our heuristic responses, and to analyse their role within the full hierarchy of our goals and subgoals. We need to question the implicit goals of our intuitive reactions, determine the alternative ways of achieving those goals, explore their possible consequences and make a smart choice.

But no matter how we make our decisions, we cannot avoid the uncertainty of their outcomes. As we have seen in this chapter and elsewhere throughout this book, the outcomes of our actions typically depend upon the uncertain state of the world:

> *a particular outcome happens if I do a certain action*
> *and the world is in a particular state.*

Because the world is such an uncertain place, and because our knowledge of the world is so incomplete, it is impossible to judge these outcomes without uncertainty.

The approach to uncertainty taken in this book is based upon the approach developed by David Poole (1997), in which probability is associated with conditions of conditionals rather than with conditionals as a whole. This approach fits well with other applications of probability, for example in helping to choose between different abductive explanations of an observation. Integrating probability and logic is one of the most active areas of research in Artificial Intelligence today. The collection of papers in De Raedt *et al.* (2008) contains an overview of recent work in this field.

12

Motivations matter

In the Prisoner's Dilemma, the need to choose between different actions is generated by the need to solve an achievement goal, obtained as the result of a request from the police to turn witness against your friend. The achievement goal, triggered by the external event, is the *motivation* of the action you eventually choose.

But in classical decision theory, the motivation of actions is unspecified. Moreover, you are expected to evaluate the alternatives by considering only their likely consequences.

Conflict resolution in production systems shares with decision theory a similar need to decide between mutually exclusive actions. However, whereas in decision theory the deciding factor is the likely consequences of the actions, in production systems the decision is normally compiled into much simpler considerations. In production systems, actions are derived explicitly by means of condition–action rules, whose motivations (or goals) are typically implicit (or emergent).

In contrast with both decision theory and production systems, in which motivations are missing or implicit, in classical planning systems in AI motivation is the main concern. In classical planning, plans of action are motivated (or intended) by higher-level achievement goals; but, in contrast with decision theory, the unintended consequences of actions are commonly ignored. The different ways in which actions are evaluated in different paradigms are summarised in the following table:

Evaluation of actions	Production systems	Decision theory	Classical planning	Computational Logic
Motivations	No	No	Yes	Yes
Consequences	No	Yes	No	Yes

In Computational Logic, actions are motivated by achievement goals, which are generated by maintenance goals, which are triggered by observations of changes in the world. Deciding which alternative actions to execute is informed by evaluating the likely consequences of the actions, including the achievement goals, which motivated the actions to begin with. This decision can be assisted by employing the techniques of decision theory, or it can be compiled into more pragmatically useful goals and beliefs, in which the evaluation of motivations and consequences is emergent rather than explicit.

Moral considerations

Decision theory guides an agent's actions towards the optimal achievement of the agent's personal goals. These personal goals might be concerned solely with the agent's own selfish interests, or they might include the interests of other agents. As we saw in the Prisoner's Dilemma, the interests of an individual agent can sometimes be better served if the agent also values the interests of other agents. Arguably, the encouragement of personal goals that include the interests of other agents is the basis of human intuitions about morality.

Although morality is one of the main concerns of religion, psychological studies have shown that people of widely diverse cultural and religious backgrounds share similar moral intuitions (Hauser *et al.*, 2007). Moreover, these studies show that many of these intuitions depend upon distinguishing between the motivations and the consequences of actions. In particular, they support the principle of double effect.

The principle of *double effect* holds that an action with bad consequences may be morally acceptable if the action was motivated by a good end, provided the bad consequences were not intended as a means to achieve the good end. But an action is not morally acceptable if it was motivated by a bad end or if it involved the use of a bad means to a good end, even if its good consequences might outweigh its bad consequences.

The principle of double effect has been used, for example, to justify bombing a military facility in wartime even if there is a potential danger to innocent civilians. But it condemns bombing a civilian target to terrorise the enemy.

The principle of double effect is opposed to *consequentialism*, which, like decision theory, is concerned only with the consequences of actions. According to consequentialism, there is no moral distinction between killing innocent civilians as a side-effect of destroying a military facility and killing them as a deliberate act of terrorism.

The principle of double effect also plays a normative role in law. For example, it accounts for the distinction between murder, in which the death of a person is directly intended, and manslaughter, in which it is foreseeable as a possible side-effect of a less bad, but still blameworthy intention.

Thus the principle of double effect plays a descriptive role in understanding moral intuitions and a normative role in law. Mikhail (2007) explains this dual role with the suggestion that, although individuals seem to be unaware of the principles that guide their moral intuitions, "the judgments can be explained by assuming that these individuals are intuitive lawyers who implicitly recognize the relevance of ends, means, side effects and *prima facie* wrongs, such as battery, to the analysis of legal and moral problems".

The challenge is to explain these intuitions, which cannot be explained by decision theory alone.

The runaway trolley

The most famous psychological experiment concerning intuitions about double effect is the *trolley problem*. There are two main variants:

Passenger: A runaway trolley is about to run over and kill five people. The driver has fainted. You are a passenger on the train and you can press a button that will turn the train onto a sidetrack, saving the five people, but killing one man who is standing on the sidetrack. Is it morally permissible to press the button?

Footbridge: A runaway trolley is about to run over and kill five people. You are a bystander standing on a footbridge over the track. The only way to stop the train and save the five people is to throw a heavy object in front of the train. The only heavy object available is a large man standing next to you. Is it morally permissible to throw the man onto the track?

In an experiment (Hauser *et al.*, 2007) on the Internet with approximately 5000 voluntary subjects, 85% judged that it is permissible for the passenger to push the button, but only 12% judged that it is permissible for the bystander to throw the man. The difference between the two cases is explained by the principle of double effect. In the case of the passenger pressing the button, the person on the sidetrack is killed as a consequence of the action of pushing the button, which is a subgoal of saving five people. The action of pushing the button is not bad in and of itself. So most people regard the action as morally permissible.

However, in the case of the bystander throwing the heavy man onto the track, the action of throwing the man onto the track is morally bad itself, even though it helps to achieve the morally good goal of saving five people.

According to consequentialism, both cases have the same moral standing; and according to *utilitarianism*, which holds that it is best to do what most benefits the greatest number of people, both cases are morally justifiable and preferable to doing nothing.

Assuming that people subconciously apply the principle of double effect in judging the morality of actions may explain intuitive judgements in trolley problems and the like. But that doesn't explain why people use the principle of double effect rather than straightforward decision theory. I will propose such an explanation – namely that motivations matter – after we first investigate a logical representation of the runaway trolley problem.

The logic of the runaway trolley

The following representation is specialised for the runaway trolley problem. As with other examples in this book, the representation could also be expressed more generally to separate out general-purpose beliefs from the special beliefs needed for the problem at hand. However, the specialised representation has the advantage that it allows us to ignore distracting details.

Beliefs:
  a person is killed if the person is in danger of being killed by a train
  and no one saves the person from being killed by the train.

  an agent kills a person
  if the agent throws the person in front of a train.

  a person is in danger of being killed by a train
  if the person is on a railtrack
  and a train is speeding along the railtrack
  and the person is unable to escape from the railtrack.

  an agent saves a person from being killed by a train
  if the agent stops the train or the agent diverts the train.

  an agent stops a train
  if the agent places a heavy object in front of the train.

  an agent places a heavy object in front of the train
  if the heavy object is next to the agent
  and the train is on a railtrack

and the agent is within throwing distance of the object to the railtrack
and the agent throws the object in front of the train.

an agent diverts a train
if there is a sidetrack ahead of the train
and an agent is on the train
and the agent pushes the sidetrack button.

a train is speeding along a sidetrack
if the train is speeding along a track
and there is a sidetrack ahead of the train
and an agent pushes the sidetrack button.

In a more precise formulation, using the event calculus for example, it would be stated that the act of pushing the sidetrack button terminates the state of the train speeding along its current track and initiates a state in which the train is speeding along the sidetrack.

The current situation:　　*five people are on the maintrack.*
　　　　　　　　　　　　　one person is on the sidetrack.
　　　　　　　　　　　　　a train is speeding along the maintrack.
　　　　　　　　　　　　　the sidetrack is ahead of the train.
　　　　　　　　　　　　　the five people are unable to escape from the maintrack.
　　　　　　　　　　　　　the one person is unable to escape from the sidetrack.

　　　　　　　　　　　　　mary is on the train.
　　　　　　　　　　　　　john is next to bob.
　　　　　　　　　　　　　john is a heavy object.
　　　　　　　　　　　　　bob is within throwing distance of john to the maintrack.

There is nothing in these beliefs to motivate anyone to do anything. To motivate Bob, John or Mary, they need a motivating goal. As with other examples in this book, the motivating goal is an achievement goal derived from a maintenance goal, triggered by an observation of the environment. In this case, the maintenance goal and associated supporting beliefs might be:

Goal:　*if a person is in danger of being killed by a train*
　　　　then you respond to the danger of the person being killed by the train.
Beliefs:　*you respond to the danger of a person being killed by the train*
　　　　if you ignore the danger.

　　　　you respond to the danger of a person being killed by the train
　　　　if you save the person from being killed by the train.

Given that all three agents have knowledge of the current situation, and assuming for simplicity that they treat the five people on the maintrack as a single person, then the three agents would similarly conclude:

Forward reasoning: *five people are in danger of being killed by the train.*
Achievement goal: *you respond to the danger of*
                        the five people being killed by the train.
Alternative subgoal: *you ignore the danger.*
Alternative subgoal: *you save the five people from being killed by the train.*

Mary can save the five people by diverting the train, by pushing the sidetrack button. Bob can save the five people by stopping the train, by placing a heavy object in front of the train, by throwing John in front of the train. Fortunately for Bob, John cannot similarly save the five people by throwing Bob in front of the train, because he has no reason to believe that Bob is a heavy object. Also, conveniently for John, we have ignored the possibility that he can save the five people simply by throwing himself in front of the train of his own volition. Therefore, only Mary and Bob have to choose between the two alternative subgoals.

Mary has to decide whether to save the five people by pushing the sidetrack button. Given the urgency of the situation, she may or may not have the time to contemplate all the possible consequences of the action. If she does have enough time and enough composure, then she will conclude that the one person on the sidetrack will be killed by the train if no one saves the person. But saving five people for sure compared with the near certainty of one person being killed is better than doing nothing.

If Mary does not have the time to think through the consequences, then she may simply judge that saving five people is better than doing nothing, in which case she will simply push the button, whatever the consequences. In either case, her behaviour is morally justified, because her intentions are good, and any possible bad side-effects are both unintended and outweighed by the benefits.

Bob, on the other hand, has to decide whether to save the five people by throwing John in front of the train. Assuming that Bob has enough time to generate this plan, he may well have enough time to realise that if he throws John in front of the train, then not only will John be killed as a consequence, but he will kill John as a means to the end.

Of course, Bob could use decision theory, to decide whether it is worth it: Five people saved compared with one person killed. The calculation argues in favour of killing John. But if Bob concludes that as a consequence of killing John he might be committing a crime, then the calculation isn't so easy.

In cases like these, decision making is a lot easier if there are clear and simple rules (or constraints) that can be followed, like:

if an agent kills a person
and the person is not threatening another person's life
then false.

If Bob has no such rule, then he may decide to throw John onto the track, with the good higher-level intention of saving five people. Nonetheless, we may judge that his action is morally unacceptable. Our judgement would be justified by concern about Bob's lack of moral constraint. Although his lack of constraint might lead to an overall good consequence on this occasion, it could lead to very bad consequences on other occasions.

If Bob does have such a constraint, but still decides to throw John onto the track, it must be because he has enough time to generate the plan, but not enough time to trigger and exercise the constraint. Or so a lawyer might argue, if the case ever came to a court of law.

The computational case for moral constraints

You could argue for moral constraints on religious grounds. But you can also argue for them on the computational grounds that there are many situations in which people don't have the time or knowledge to make optimal decisions in accordance with the norms of decision theory. Even if they did, it would be unreasonable to expect everyone to adhere to the purely utilitarian principle that their own personal interests, or the interests of their family and friends, are worth no more than the interests of their worse enemy or greatest rival.

If everyone used decision theory without any constraints, there would be chaos. Some people would use the freedom to employ arbitrary utility measures to suit their own interests and to trample over the interests of others. To protect against the antisocial consequences of the exercise of such unbridled self-interests, societies impose constraints on the behaviour of individuals. But to be effective, these constraints need to be simple and easy to apply, even when time and knowledge are in short supply.

In our representation of the trolley problem, the constraint was a qualified version of the sixth commandment, *thou shalt not kill*, and the only way to kill a person was to throw the person in front of a train. This was an oversimplification. It employs a very specific definition of killing a person, which conveniently applies to Bob, but not to Mary. It could be argued that an alternative, more realistic definition, like:

an agent kills a person
if the agent performs an action and the action causes the person's death.

would apply to both Bob and Mary, depending on how causality is defined. Certainly throwing a person in front of a train causes the death of the person. But does pushing the sidetrack button also cause the death of the person on the sidetrack?

Philosophers and legal scholars have struggled with dilemmas of this kind for centuries. There has to be an easier solution. Otherwise the exercise of constraints would require solving difficult problems of causality, and it would be impossible to apply constraints in practice.

There is an easier solution. Replace the condition that the action *causes* the person's death by the computationally much simpler condition that the action causes the person's death directly by *initiating* it in one step:

> *an agent kills a person*
> *if the agent performs an action*
> *and the action **initiates** the person's death.*

In most cases, determining whether an action initiates a person's death takes only one step of deductive inference, which every agent of full age and capacity should be able to perform. The inference can be made even simpler by compiling the definition of killing into the constraint:

> *if an agent performs an action*
> *and the action **initiates** a person's death*
> *and the person is not threatening another person's life*
> *then false.*

In contrast, determining whether an action *causes* a person's death may require an unbounded number of inferences through an arbitrarily long chain of actions. The greater the number of inferences, the less reasonable it is to expect an agent to be able to perform them.

The use of simple constraints on actions that *initiate* bad consequences makes the exercise of constraints much easier, but does not solve all of the problems that can arise. There will always be hard cases where the direct effect of an agent's actions also depends on the state of the world – for example if a person's death is initiated by an agent driving too fast and the car going out of control.

Hard cases like these are the livelihood of the legal profession, and are beyond the scope of this book. But, before we leave this topic, there is an even bigger problem with constraints.

What to do about violations?

The problem with constraints is that people violate them. They violate them, and either they get away with it or they pay the penalty: Don't press the alarm signal button improperly. But if you do, then be prepared to pay a £50 fine.

Logically it doesn't make sense. Formulating a constraint as a conditional with conclusion *false*, is supposed to prevent the conditions of the constraint from becoming *true*. It doesn't make sense to have additional constraints that apply only when the conclusion *false* has been derived.

This problem has been studied in philosophical logic in the form of Chisholm's paradox (Chisholm, 1963). The paradox is usually formulated in some form of deontic logic, but it can be also formulated in terms of constraints. Here is an informal statement of the paradox:

> It ought to be that Jones goes to assist his neighbors.
> It ought to be that if Jones goes, then he tells them he is coming.
> If Jones doesn't go, then he ought not tell them he is coming.
> Jones doesn't go.

In standard deontic logic, these statements imply the paradoxical conclusions:

> Jones ought to tell them he is coming.
> Jones ought not to tell them he is coming.

Almost all deontic logics are modal logics, in which *ought* is a logical connective with the same logical status as *and*, *or*, *if* and *not*. But in abductive logic programming (ALP), which is the basis of the Computational Logic that we use in this book, obligations and prohibitions are represented by means of integrity constraints, which include maintenance goals and constraints. Here is a representation of the paradox in ALP terms:

Goals: *jones goes.*
        if jones goes then jones tells.
        if jones stays and jones tells then false.
        if jones stays and jones goes then false.
Belief: *jones stays.*

The first sentence is an achievement goal. In a more complete version of the story it might have been derived by means of a maintenance goal, such as *if a person needs help and jones can help then jones goes.*

The second sentence is neither a maintenance goal nor a conventional constraint, but is nonetheless a typical integrity constraint. Viewed in database terms, it imposes the restriction that whenever the database contains a record that *jones goes* then it also contains a record that *jones tells*. Viewed in ALP/ planning terms, it imposes the restriction that any plan that includes the action *jones goes* also includes the action *jones tells*.

The third and fourth sentences are contraints. The fourth sentence expresses that *staying* is the contrary of *going*, and the third sentence constrains Jones from both staying (not going) and telling.

The fifth sentence expresses that Jones doesn't go as a positive atomic fact. Not only does the collection of five sentences together imply the conclusion *false*, but the first, fourth and fifth sentences alone imply *false*. In other words, Jones ought to go, but doesn't. In the ALP representation the second and third sentences serve no function at all.

Constraints and violations of constraints are similar to rules and exceptions. The primary constraint is like a general rule, and remedial constraints that deal with violations are like exceptions. We have seen that, in the case of ordinary rules and exceptions, inconsistency can be avoided by adding an explicit condition to the general rule stating that no exception applies. We can try to solve the paradox of constraints and their violation similarly. In Jones' case, for example, we can add to the primary constraint an extra condition, for example that *jones is not irresponsible*:

> *if a person needs help and jones can help*
> *and jones is not irresponsible then jones goes.*

Several solutions of this kind have been developed and explored, both in the context of defeasible deontic logic (Nute, 1997) and in repairing violations of integrity constraints in databases (Bertossi and Chomicki, 2003). They also arise more generally in computing, for example when a program malfunctions and corrective measures need to be applied. The existence of practical solutions to these problems in computing suggests that similar solutions exist in a more logical setting. However, the investigation of these solutions is yet another problem that is beyond the scope of this book.

Conclusions

The Prisoner's Dilemma shows that it pays for an agent to value the interests of other agents, and to include those interests in its judgements of the utility of its actions. More generally, the Prisoner's Dilemma and similar examples show that an agent's decisions can be judged not only for their consequences for the agent alone, but for the good of society as a whole. Such concern for the general good of society seems to be the basis of human intuitions about morality.

In the Prisoner's Dilemma, moral values can be catered for relatively simply by including the interests of other agents in judgements of utility. And according to consequentialism and utilitarianism, these judgements are sufficient to determine the moral status of an agent's decisions in general. However, according to the proponents of the principle of double effect, they do not fully account for human moral intuitions, nor for the normative role of distinctions between ends, means and side-effects in the field of law.

Psychological studies of moral intuitions about trolley problems show that people instinctively judge an agent's actions both for their motivations and for their consequences. We have seen that Computational Logic provides a model of agency in which such moral intuitions can be explained. The model shows that, in situations where knowledge and time are limited, an agent may not be able to judge and compare the expected utilities of all the relevant consequences of its alternative candidate actions. In cases such as these, the agent can use constraints to avoid actions that are deemed to be morally unacceptable.

The application of Computational Logic to Computational Morality in general and to the trolley problem in particular has been investigated by Luis Pereira (Pereira and Saptawijaya, 2007, 2009). Although in this chapter we have used Computational Logic to justify moral intuitions concerning the principle of double effect, it does not follow that Computational Logic is restricted to modelling or justifying only one moral theory, or to modelling only one analysis of trolley problems. Its conceptual framework of goals, subgoals, constraints and consequences is morally neutral and can be used for many purposes, for better or for worse.

13

The changing world

In mathematics, semantic structures are *static* and truth is eternal. But for an intelligent agent embedded in the real world, semantic structures are *dynamic* and the only constant is change.

Perhaps the simplest way to understand change is to view actions and other events as causing a change of state from one static world structure to the next. For example:

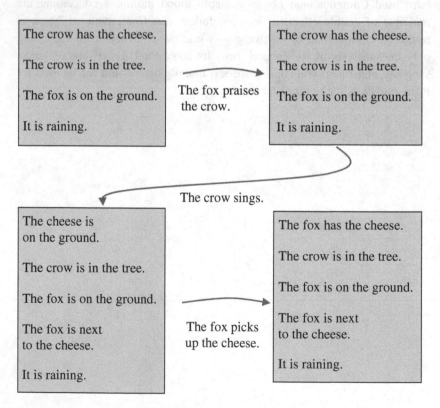

This view of change is formalised in the *possible world semantics* of modal logic. In *modal logic*, sentences are given a truth value relative to a static

166

possible world embedded in a collection of possible worlds linked with one another by an accessibility relation.

In modal logics of time, one possible world is directly *accessible* from another if it can be reached from the other by one state-transforming event. Syntactic expressions such as "in the past", "in the future", "after", "since" and "until" are treated as *modal operators*, which are logical connectives, like "and", "or", "if", "not" and "all".

The truth value of sentences containing modal operators is defined, as for ordinary classical logic, in terms of the truth values of simpler sentences. However, whereas in classical logic truth is relative to one interpretation (or possible world), truth in modal logic is relative to one possible world in a collection of possible worlds. For example:

> A sentence of the form *in the future P* is *true*
> in a possible world *W* in a collection of worlds *C*
> if there is possible world *W'* in *C*
> that can be reached from *W* by a sequence of state-transforming events
> and the sentence *P* is *true* in *W'*.

For example, in modal logic, it is possible to express the sentence

> *In the future the crow has the cheese*.

This sentence is *true* in the possible world at the beginning of the story of the fox and the crow and *false* in the possible world at the end of the story (assuming there are no possible worlds after the story ends).

One objection to the modal logic approach is that its *ontology* (the things that exist) is too conservative, which makes knowledge representation unacceptably difficult. The alternative is to increase the expressive power of the language by treating events and states of the world as individuals. To treat something as an individual, as though it exists, is to *reify* it; and the process itself is called *reification*.

The advantage of reification is that it makes talking about things a lot easier. The disadvantage is that it makes some people very upset. It's alright to talk about material objects, like the fox, the crow and the cheese, as individuals. But it's something else to talk about states of the world and other similarly abstract objects as though they too were ordinary individuals.

The situation calculus

The *situation calculus* shares with modal logic the same view of change as transforming one state of the world into another, but it reifies actions and states (or situations) as individuals. In effect, it treats the accessibility relation of modal logic as a first-class relation, along with other relations, like *the fox has the cheese*, among ordinary material objects.

For example, in the situation calculus, in the story of the fox and the crow, there is only one relevant semantic structure and it contains, in addition to ordinary individuals, individuals that are actions and individuals that are global states. It is possible to express such sentences as:

> *the crow has the cheese in the state at the beginning of the story.*
> *the crow has the cheese in the state*
> *after the fox picks up the cheese,*
> *after the crow sings,*
> *after the fox praises the crow,*
> *after the state at the beginning of the story.*

The first of these two sentences is *true*. But the second sentence is *false*.

Reifying actions and states as individuals makes it possible to represent and reason about the effect of actions on states of the world. If we also reify "facts", then this representation can be formulated as two situation calculus axioms:

> *a fact holds in the state after an action,*
> *if the action initiates the fact*
> *and the action is possible in the state just before the action.*

> *a fact holds in a state after an action,*
> *if the fact held in the state just before the action*
> *and the action is possible in the state just before the action*
> *and the action does not terminate the fact.*

Our original version of the story of the fox and the crow can be reformulated in situation calculus terms, by defining the appropriate *initiates*, *terminates* and *is possible* predicates. For this purpose, it is convenient to treat the action of the crow singing also as a fact:

> *an action in which an animal picks up an object*
> *initiates a fact that the animal has the object.*
> *an action in which an animal picks up an object*
> *is possible in a state in which the animal is near the object.*

> *an action in which I praise the crow*
> *initiates a fact that the crow sings.*
> *an action in which I praise the crow*
> *is possible in any state.*

> *an action in which the crow sings*
> *initiates a fact that I am near the cheese.*

> *an action in which the crow sings*
>   *terminates a fact that the crow has the cheese.*
> *an action in which the crow sings*
>   *is possible in any state.*

In theory, an agent, such as the fox, could include such axioms among its beliefs, to plan its actions, infer their consequences, and infer the consequences of other agents' actions. In practice, however, the use of the second situation calculus axiom (called *the frame axiom*) is computationally explosive. This problem, called *the frame problem*, is often taken to be an inherent problem with the use of logic to reason about change.

The frame problem is not very noticeable with the goal of determining whether or not the crow has the cheese at the end of the story. Two applications of backward reasoning with the frame axiom reduce the goal to a conjunction of subgoals, one of which is to show that the action of singing does not terminate the "fact" that the crow has the cheese. But because the action of singing does terminate the fact, the subgoal is *false*, and therefore the initial goal is also *false*.

However, the frame problem is more obvious with the goal of determining whether or not it is raining at the end of the story, on the assumption that it was raining at the beginning of the story. Whether used forward or backward, the frame axiom needs to be used as many times as there are actions in the story, to show that it was raining in every state between the beginning and end of the story. This kind of thinking is not so difficult in the imaginary world of the fox and the crow, but it is clearly impossible for a real agent living in the real world.

Arguably, it is not logic that is the source of the problem, but the situation calculus view of change, which the situation calculus shares with the possible world semantics of modal logic. In both cases, an action is treated as changing the entire global state of the world. As a result, to show that a fact that holds in a given state of the world continues to hold until it is terminated, it is necessary to know and reason about all the other actions that take place throughout the entire world in the meantime.

An event-oriented approach to change

The alternative is to abandon the global view of actions as transforming one state of the world into another, and replace it with a more local view that actions and other events can occur simultaneously and independently in different parts of the world.

In the event calculus, *events* include both ordinary actions, which are performed by agents, and other events, like the cheese landing on the ground, which can be understood metaphorically as actions that are performed by inanimate objects.

For simplicity, we can assume that events occur instantaneously. For this purpose, an event that has duration can be decomposed into an instantaneous event that starts it, followed by a state of continuous change, followed by an instantaneous event that ends it. Thus the cheese falling to the ground can be decomposed into an instantaneous event in which the cheese starts to fall, which initiates the state of the cheese actually falling, followed by an instantaneous event in which the cheese lands, which terminates the state of falling.

Events initiate and terminate relationships among individuals. These relationships, together with the time periods for which they hold, can be regarded as *atomic states* of affairs. We can picture such an atomic state and the events that initiate and terminate it like this:

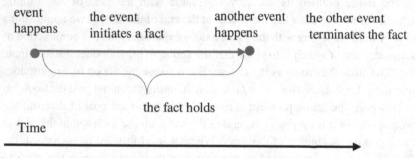

In the story of the fox and the crow, this picture looks like this:

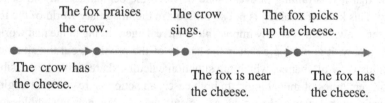

Here the crow's singing is treated as an action/event that is caused by the action/event of praising the crow. This causal relationship can be viewed as yet another instance of the general pattern:

> *a particular outcome happens if I do a certain action*
> *and the world is in a particular state.*

In this case, the actions/events in the relationship are associated with the times of their occurrence:

> *the crow sings at time T' if I praise the crow at time T*
> *and the crow reacts to the praise between times T and T'.*

The condition *the crow reacts to the praise between times T and T'* is an open predicate, which can be assumed, either to explain an observation of the crow breaking out in song at some time T' or as part of a plan for the fox to have the cheese.

A simplified calculus of events

The event calculus represents the relationship between events and the properties they initiate and terminate by means of the following axiom and constraint:

Axiom: *a fact holds at a time,*
    if an event happens at an earlier time
    and the event initiates the fact
    and there is no other event
      that happens between the two times and
      that terminates the fact.

Constraint: *if an event happens at a time*
    and the event is not possible at the time then false.

Equivalently: *if an event happens at a time*
    then the event is possible at the time.

The event calculus constraint is analogous to the situation calculus condition that *an action is possible in a state*. The constraint is necessary for planning. Without it, an agent could generate unexecutable plans containing actions whose preconditions do not hold at the time of execution.

In many cases, the execution of an action terminates a precondition. For example, to give an object away, the agent must have the object. For this reason, to make the constraint work correctly, the event calculus employs the convention that a fact holds after the event that initiates it, but at the time of the event that terminates it. So, for example, if Mary gives an apple to John, then Mary must have the apple at the time that she gives it (constraint), but John has the apple afterwards (axiom).

To apply the event calculus in practice, it needs to be augmented, like the situation calculus, with additional axioms defining initiation, termination, possibility and temporal order. Thus, the event calculus treats the predicates *a fact holds at a time, an event initiates a fact, an event terminates a fact, an event is possible at a time* and the predicates for *temporal ordering* as closed predicates. But it treats the predicate *an event happens at a time* as an open predicate.

The event calculus for predicting consequences of events

The open predicate *an event happens at a time* can be given directly as an observation, generated by abduction to explain observed facts, or generated as a candidate action in a plan to solve an achievement goal. Here is an example of the first of these three cases, given similar definitions of initiation, termination and possibility as in the situation calculus example, but using the event calculus representation of events:

> *the fox praises the crow at time 3.*
> *the crow sings at time 5.*
> *the fox picks up the cheese at time 8.*

We also need to represent the fact that the crow has the cheese at the beginning of the story. This can be done in several different ways, but the simplest is just to assume an additional event, such as:

> *the crow picks up the cheese at time 0.*

Reasoning backwards to determine whether or not the crow has the cheese at the end of the story, say at time *9*, the event calculus axiom generates the following sequence of goals and subgoals:

Initial goal: *the crow has the cheese at time 9.*

Subgoals: *an event happens at time T and T < 9 and*
            the event initiates the fact that the crow has the cheese and
            there is no other event that happens between T and 9 and
            the other event terminates the fact that the crow has the cheese.

Subgoals: *the crow picks up the cheese at time T and T < 9 and*
            there is no other event that happens between T and 9 and
            the other event terminates the fact that the crow has the cheese.

Subgoals: *there is no other event that happens between 0 and 9 and*
            the other event terminates the fact that the crow has the cheese.

Naf: *an event happens at time T' and T' is between 0 and 9 and*
       the event terminates the fact that the crow has the cheese.
       Subgoals: *the crow sings at time T' and T' is between 0 and 9.*
       Subgoals: *5 is between 0 and 9.*
       Success: *yes!*

Failure: *no!*

The conclusion that the crow does not have the cheese follows from negation as failure and the fact that, given the order in which the subgoals are selected, there are no other ways of solving the initial goal. Of course, this conclusion depends upon the closed-world assumption, that there are no other events that take place before time *9* that initiate the crow having the cheese. On the other hand, there is nothing to rule out the possibility that the crow could regain possession of the cheese at some time after *9*, for example by praising the fox.

Notice that the efficiency of the search for a solution is highly sensitive to the order in which subgoals are selected. Given the order of selection in the proof presented above, there are no other branches in the search space; and the search is very efficient. However other selection strategies, for example selecting the subgoal *an event happens at time T* first, would be very inefficient. The efficiency of the search can be further improved by storing and accessing events in order of occurrence, so that only the most relevant events are considered.

The event calculus and the frame problem

Taken together, the subgoal selection and event storage strategies help the event calculus to overcome many, but not necessarily all of the inefficiencies of the frame problem. Other inefficiencies are avoided as a result of the event calculus localised view of change.

Suppose, for example, that we add that it was raining at the beginning of the story, by assuming an additional event, such as *it starts raining at time − 1*, where:

> *an event in which it starts raining initates a fact that it is raining.*
> *an event in which it stops raining terminates a fact that it is raining.*

We can simplify the problem of determining whether or not *it is raining at time 9* by solving the subgoals *an event initiates a fact* and *an event terminates a fact* of the event calculus axiom in advance, generating the specialised axiom:

> *it is raining at a time,*
> *if it starts raining at an earlier time*
> *and it does not stop raining between the two times.*

Reasoning backwards with the specialised axiom generates the following sequence of goals and subgoals:

Initial goal: *it is raining at time 9.*

Subgoals: *it starts raining at time T and T < 9 and*
               and it does not stop raining between T and 9.

Subgoals: *it does not stop raining between −1 and 9.*

               Naf: *it stops raining at time T' and T' is between −1 and 9.*
               Failure: *no!*

Success: *yes!*

Notice that, unlike the solution of the same problem in the situation calculus, the length of the solution does not depend on the number of states, actions or events between the time *−1* at which it starts raining and the time *9* under consideration. In the event calculus, the length depends only on the number of relevant rain initiating and terminating events, and their time of occurrence.

The event calculus for plan generation

The event calculus constraint is not needed when the event calculus axiom is used to predict the consequences of observed events. But it can be used to monitor observed events. If an observation violates the constraint, then the agent needs to choose between rejecting the observation as an illusion, and rejecting a belief that is incompatible with the observation.

However, the constraint is needed when the event calculus axiom is used to generate candidate events to explain observations or to generate candidate actions to solve achievement goals.

Here is the beginning of a solution of the fox's achievement goal of having the crow's cheese. In this solution only the initial event *the crow picks up the cheese at time 0* is given:

Initial goal: *the fox has the cheese at time T.*

Subgoals: *an event happens at time T' and T' < T and*
         the event initiates the fact that the fox has the cheese and
         there is no other event that happens between T' and T and
         the other event terminates the fact that the fox has the cheese.

Subgoals: *the fox picks up the cheese at time T' and T' < T and*
         there is no other event that happens between T' and T and
         the other event terminates the fact that the fox has the cheese.

Without the event calculus constraint, this is as far as the fox needs to go to solve the goal. The fox can simply pick up the cheese at any time, provided she doesn't do anything to terminate having the cheese in between times. Although this solution may seem incomplete, it actually satisfies all of the formal conditions for a solution in the proof procedure of the additional Chapter A6.

However, the solution is genuinely incomplete when the constraint is taken into account. When the constraint is considered, the candidate action *the fox picks up the cheese at time T'* triggers the constraint and generates the further achievement goal:

Further goal: *the fox picks up the cheese is possible at time T'.*
Using the relevant definition of *possibility*:
         an animal picks up an object is possible at a time
         if the animal is near the object at the time.
backward reasoning reduces this further goal to:
Subgoal: *the fox is near the cheese at time T'.*

This subgoal is the same kind of achievement goal that we started with, but it is one step closer to a complete plan.

Reasoning in this way, alternating between the use of the event calculus axiom and the event calculus constraint, the fox can soon generate a complete plan to achieve her initial goal. In addition to the relevant actions, the plan includes subgoals that prevent the fox from performing any other actions that might interfere with the plan. It also contains an explicit assumption that the crow will react to the fox's praise by singing.

The solution looks more complicated than it is. Some of the apparent complexity can be eliminated by compiling the constraint into the event calculus axiom itself:

Compiled axiom: *a fact holds at a time,*
> *if an event happens at an earlier time*
> *and the event initiates the fact*
> **and the event is possible at the earlier time**
> *and there is no other event*
>> *that happens between the two times and*
>> *that terminates the fact.*

Even more of the complexity can be eliminated by solving the subgoals *an event initiates a fact* and *an event is possible at a time* in advance, generating specialised axioms for the special case under consideration. For example:

> *an animal has an object at a time,*
> *if the animal picks up the object at an earlier time*
> *and the animal is near the object at the earlier time*
> *and there is no other event*
>> *that happens between the two times and*
>> *the event terminates the fact that the animal has the object.*

This compiled form of the event calculus is closer to the representation of the story of the fox and the crow in Chapters 3 and 4. But it is less flexible for predicting the consequences of observed events, where the use of the constraint is unnecessary.

Notice that explaining an observation that the fox has the cheese is similar to generating a plan for the fox to have the cheese. This is because planning and explaining observations are formally identical.

Partially ordered time

Whereas the possible world semantics and the situation calculus both associate global states with facts, actions and other events, the event calculus associates time points. In the examples we have seen so far, these time points are numbers, with the property that all facts and events are ordered linearly on the same time line. However, the times of unrelated events do not need to be linearly ordered, as pictured in the example:

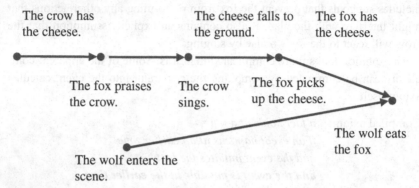

To represent such partially ordered events, we need a different way of naming time points, and of determining when one time point comes before another. For example:

 the crow picks up the cheese at time$_{crow\text{-}pickup}$.
 the fox praises the crow at time$_{praise}$.
 the crow sings at time$_{sing}$.
 the fox picks up the cheese at time$_{fox\text{-}pickup}$.
 the wolf enters the scene at time$_{enter}$.
 the wolf eats the fox at time$_{eat}$.
 time$_{crow\text{-}pickup}$ < time$_{praise}$ < time$_{sing}$ < time$_{fox\text{-}pickup}$ < time$_{eat}$
 time$_{enter}$ < time$_{eat}$
 $T_1 < T_3$ *if* $T_1 < T_2$ *and* $T_2 < T_3$

The event calculus works equally well with such different representations of time.

Keeping track of time

The representation of time by numbers, dates and/or clock time serves two functions. It not only linearly orders time points, but it also measures the duration between time points. This ability to judge duration is necessary for the proper functioning of the agent cycle. For example, if you are hungry, then you need to get food and eat it before you collapse from lack of strength. If a car is rushing towards you, then you need to run out of the way before you get run over. If you have a 9:00 appointment at work, then you need to get out of bed, wash, eat, dress, journey to work and arrive before 9:00.

To get everything done in time, you need an internal clock, both to timestamp observations and to compare the current time with the deadlines of any internally derived future actions. This creates yet more work for the agent cycle:

> *repeatedly (or concurrently):*
> *observe the world, record any observations,*
> *together with the time of their observation,*
> *think,*
> *decide what actions to perform, choosing only actions*
> *that have not exceeded their deadline, and*
> *act.*

Consider, for example, the fox's response to an observation that she is hungry. She needs to estimate how long she can go without eating before it is too late:

> *if I am hungry at time T_{hungry}*
> *and I will collapse at a later time $T_{collapse}$ if I don't eat*
> *then I have food at a time T_{food}*
> *and I eat the food at the time T_{food}*
> *and T_{food} is between T_{hungry} and $T_{collapse}$.*

She also needs to be able to deal with any attack from the local hunters:

> *if the hunters attack me at time T_{attack}*
> *and they will catch me at a later time T_{catch} if I don't run away*
> *then I run away from the hunters at a time T_{run}*
> *and T_{run} is between T_{attack} and T_{catch}.*

Suppose, the fox is both hungry and under attack at the same time. Then the fox needs to do a quick mental calculation, to estimate both how much time she has to find food and how much time she has to run away. She needs to judge the probability and utilities of the two different actions, and schedule them to maximise their overall expected utility. If the fox has done her calculations well and is lucky with the way subsequent events unfold, then she will have enough time both to satisfy her hunger and to escape from attack. If not, then either she will die of starvation or she will die from the hunt.

But this kind of reasoning is a normative ideal, which is perhaps better suited to a robot than an intelligent biological being. It would be easier simply to give higher priority to escaping from attack than to satisfying hunger, using heuristic "rules of thumb" that might look more like this:

> *if I am hungry at time T_{hungry}*
> *then I have food at a time T_{food}*
> *and I eat the food at the time T_{food}*
> *and T_{food} is as soon as possible after T_{hungry}.*

> *if someone attacks me at time T_{attack}*
> *then I run away from the attackers at a time T_{run}*
> *and T_{run} is immediately after T_{attack}.*

Then if you are both hungry and attacked at the same time, say time 0 arbitrarily, your goals would look like this:

> *I have food at a time T_{food}*
> *I eat the food at the time T_{food}*
> *I run away from the hunters at a time T_{run}*
> *and T_{run} is immediately after time 0*
> *and T_{food} is as soon as possible after 0.*

It would then be an easy matter for you to determine not only that T_{run} should be before T_{food} but that T_{run} should be the next moment in time.

It would be the same if you were attacked after you became hungry, but before you succeeded in obtaining food. You would run away immediately, and resume looking for food only after (and if) you have escaped from attack.

Rules of thumb give a quick and easy decision, which is not always optimal. If you were running away from attack and you noticed a piece of cheese on the ground, a normative calculation might determine that you have enough time both to pick up the cheese and to resume running and escape from attack. Rules of thumb, which are designed to deal with the most commonly occurring cases, are less likely to recognise this possibility.

Our agent model is neutral with respect to the way decisions are made. It is compatible, in particular, with the use of decision theory, the use of heuristic rules of thumb and any combination of the two.

Historical background and additional reading

The event calculus (Kowalski and Sergot, 1986) was inspired in large part by the situation calculus developed by McCarthy and Hayes (1969). The use of temporal storage of events to alleviate the frame problem in the event calculus is discussed in Kowalski (1992). A more radical approach to the frame problem, which manipulates a destructively updated working memory, is described in Kowalski and Sadri (2010). The frame problem is the subject of Murray Shanahan's (1997) *Solving the Frame Problem*.

The use of the event calculus for knowledge representation and reasoning in Artificial Intelligence is one of the main topics in Erik Mueller's (2006) *Commonsense Reasoning*. The application of the event calculus to the analysis of tense and aspect in natural language from the vantage point of Cognitive Science is the topic of van Lambalgen and Hamm's (2005) *The Proper Treatment of Events*.

14

Logic and objects

What is the difference between the fox and the crow, on the one hand, and the cheese, on the other? Of course, the fox and the crow are animate, and the cheese is inanimate. Animate things include agents, which observe changes in the world and perform their own changes on the world. Inanimate things are entirely passive.

But if you were an Extreme Behaviourist, you might think differently. You might think that the fox, the crow and the cheese are all simply *objects*, distinguishable from one another only by their different input–output behaviours:

> *if the fox sees the crow and the crow has food in its mouth,*
> *then the fox praises the crow.*

> *if the fox praises the crow,*
> *then the crow sings.*

> *if the crow has food in its beak and the crow sings,*
> *then the food falls to the ground.*

> *if the food is next to the fox,*
> *then the fox picks up the food.*

Extreme Behaviourism was all the rage in Psychology in the mid-twentieth century. A more moderate form of behaviourism has been the rage in Computing for approximately the past 30 years, in the form of *Object-Orientation*.

It's easy to make fun of yesterday's Extreme Behaviourists. But it's not so easy to dismiss today's Object-Orientated Computer Scientists and Software Engineers. Object-Orientation (OO) today dominates every aspect of computing: from modelling the system environment, through specifying the system requirements, to designing and implementing the software and hardware.

Advocates of OO argue that it provides a natural way of looking at the world, helping to decompose large systems into manageable components, making them easier to develop and maintain. These claims of naturalness place it in direct competition with logic in general and Computational Logic (CL) in particular.

For a while in the 1980s, it looked as though some form of Computational Logic might come to occupy the central role in computing that OO occupies today. If we can understand why OO won the competition between them, then we might gain a better understanding of the prospects of CL, not only for computing, but for human reasoning as well.

Objects as individuals

In the object-oriented way of looking at things, the world consists of objects, which interact with one another through their externally manifest input–output behaviour. OO turns the relationship between an agent and the world, as viewed in conventional logic:

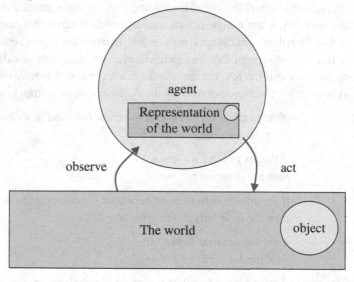

outside in:

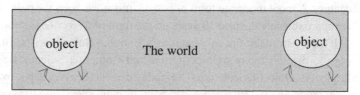

An agent's observations turn into messages received from other objects, and its actions turn into messages sent to other objects. The world becomes absorbed into the network of interacting objects, or becomes a separate object like any other object.

Encapsulation

An object consists of a *local state*, which is a collection of current *values* of the object's *attributes*, and a collection of *methods*, which the object uses to respond to messages or to compute values of its attributes. Both of these are *encapsulated* within the object, hidden from other objects.

Encapsulation of an object's methods is an inherent property of the natural world, because no object can tell for sure what goes on inside another object. In theory, if you could get inside another object, you might discover that it is just like you. Every object – bear, tree, river, mountain or stone – might have a spirit, which is its internal mental state. Contrariwise, you might discover that no object, other than yourself, has any internal state at all.

Encapsulation of methods is a useful property for constructing artificial worlds. It reduces the complexity of combining individual objects into complex systems of objects, because the engineer needs to take into account only the external behaviour of the components. Furthermore, should one of the components of a functioning system become defective or obsolete, it can be replaced by a new component that has the same external behaviour, without affecting the behaviour of the system overall.

OO is more moderate than behaviourism. In addition to combining existing encapsulated objects, the engineer can create new objects by initialising the values of their attributes and implementing their methods.

Methods

The common OO languages used for implementing methods are typically procedural languages with a syntax inherited from pre-OO programming languages and without the declarative semantics of logic-based knowledge representation languages.

However, even when OO methods are implemented in procedural programming languages, it is natural to express their specifications in logical form. These specifications often have the form of condition–action rules in declarative mood:

> *if an object receives a message of the form S from object O*
> *then the object sends a message of the form R to object P.*

For example:

> *if the fox receives a message that the crow has food in its mouth,*
> *then the fox sends a message of praise to the crow.*

> *if the crow receives a message of praise from the fox,*
> *then the crow sends a message of song.*

> *if the crow has food in its mouth*
> *and the food receives a message of song from the crow*
> *then the food sends a message of falling to the ground.*

> *if the food sends a message that it is next to the fox,*
> *then the fox sends a message that she picks up the cheese.*

The encapsulated methods by means of which these specifications are implemented can be programmed in different ways. They can be implemented, in particular, as we will discuss later and as should already be apparent, by programs expressed in logical form.

Classes

OO makes it easy for the engineer to create new objects by instantiating more general classes of objects.

For example, an engineer might create a new fox by creating a new instance of the general class of all foxes. The class of foxes as a whole might have general methods for dealing with such messages as the sight of another animal having food and the appearance of food within its grasp. It might also have typical values for such attributes as the colour of its fur and the shape of its tail. The new fox would inherit these methods and values of attributes with little or no modification, possibly with the addition of certain special methods and attributes unique to itself.

Classes are organised in taxonomic hierarchies. So for example, the class of all foxes might inherit most of its methods and attributes from the class of all animals. The class of all animals might inherit them, in turn, from the class of all animate beings; the class of all animate beings might inherit them from the class of all material objects; and the class of all material objects might inherit them from the class of all things.

Reconciling logic and objects

There is an obvious way to reconcile logic and objects: simply by using Computational Logic to implement the methods associated with objects and classes. An implementation of this logical kind might combine maintenance goals, which respond to observations of incoming messages, with beliefs, which reduce goals to subgoals, including actions of sending outgoing messages. For example:

Goal: *if I receive message of form S from object O then G.*
Beliefs: *G if conditions and I send message of form R to object P.*

Using CL to implement OO methods can benefit OO by providing it with higher-level knowledge representation and problem-solving capabilities.

Conversely, using OO encapsulation and inheritance techniques can benefit CL by providing a framework for combining individual logic-based agents into multi-agent communities. Individual agents can share their knowledge and problem-solving resources with other agents in the same community.

In such a community of agents, complex problems can be decomposed into simpler subproblems, and their solution can be distributed to different agents, specialising in different problem domains. No single agent needs to know it all, or to solve every problem on its own.

Similarly, a complex connection graph of goals and beliefs might be distributed among several agents. Relatively self-contained subgraphs with sparse links to other subgraphs can be associated with individual agents. The links between the subgraphs can serve as communication channels between the agents, sending requests for help in solving subgoals and receiving solutions and other information in return.

Message-passing or shared environment?

In computing, there are two main alternative approaches to combining agents into multi-agent systems: the communicating agents approach, in which agents interact directly by communicating messages, and the shared environment approach, in which agents interact indirectly through the medium of a global database. Computational Logic is compatible with both approaches, and suggests a natural way of combining them.

CL supports the communicating message approach, when agents are interpreted as subgraphs of a connection graph, and messages are interpreted as links between subgraphs. But it supports the shared environment approach, when the environment is viewed as a semantic structure that gives meaning to an agent's thoughts. In CL, these two views are compatible and combined.

The simplest way to combine and reconcile the two approaches in CL is to use message passing as an internal mechanism to link subgraphs of the connection graph of a single agent's mind, and to use the environment as an external medium to coordinate the agent's interactions with other agents. Viewed in this way, the main contribution of OO is the way in which it structures knowledge and goals into manageable, semi-independent, encapsulated, modular and hierarchically organised components.

Semantic networks as a variant of Object-Orientation

There are a number of other computing paradigms that structure knowledge in similar object-oriented terms. Among the most notable of these are *semantic networks*, which represent the world as a web of relationships among individuals. For example, a semantic network representing the initial state of the story of the fox and the crow might look like this:

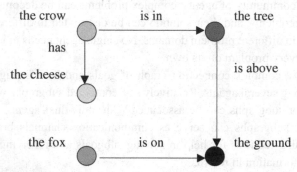

Here circles (or nodes) represent individuals (or objects), and arcs represent binary relationships between pairs of individuals. The representation can be extended to non-binary relationships.

Semantic network representations are object-oriented, in the sense that they store all the facts about an individual in a single place, namely surrounding the node that represents the individual. These facts are represented by the arcs connected to that node and by the other nodes to which those arcs are also connected.

However, in contrast with orthodox OO, relationships are represented only once, but are connected to all the individuals that participate in the relationship. Moreover, they are visible to the outside world, and not merely encapsulated inside objects.

Semantic networks have also been used to represent dynamic information, by reifying events. For example:

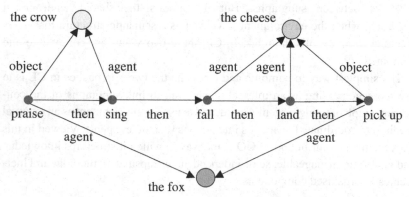

In this network, the terms *object* and *agent* are only loosely associated with our notions of object and agent.

Semantic networks have also been used to represent hierarchies of classes. For example:

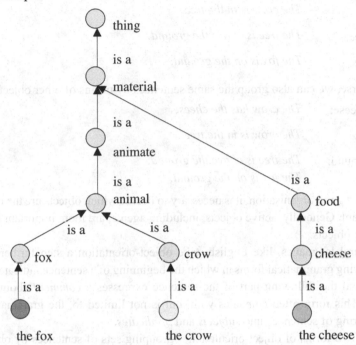

Semantic networks are like the semantic structures of Chapter A2, which are just sets of atomic sentences. In fact, semantic network connections of the form:

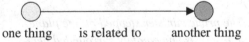

one thing   is related to   another thing

are simply graphical representations of atomic sentences of the form *one thing is related to another thing*.

Object-oriented structuring of natural language

Semantic networks are a graphical way of picturing object-oriented structuring of information. OO structuring can also be applied to natural language.

We noted earlier in Chapter 1 that sentences expressed in logical form are context-independent and can be written in any order, but some sequences of sentences are much easier to understand than others. Grouping sentences into collections of sentences about objects is another way to make sentences easier to understand.

For example, we can group the atomic sentences describing the beginning of the story of the fox and the crow into collections of sentences about the objects in the story:

The crow: *The crow has the cheese.*
                   The crow is in the tree.

The tree: *The tree is above the ground.*

The fox: *The fox is on the ground.*

Of course, we can also group the same sentences by means of other objects:

The cheese: *The crow has the cheese.*

The tree: *The crow is in the tree.*

The ground: *The tree is above the ground.*
                   The fox is on the ground.

To find a good organisation, it is necessary to decide which objects are the most important. Generally, active objects, including agents, are more important than passive objects.

Natural languages, like English, take object-orientation a step further, by employing grammatical forms in which the beginning of a sentence indicates its *topic* and the following part of the sentence expresses a *comment* about the topic. This form often coincides with, but is not limited to, the grammatical structuring of sentences into *subjects* and *predicates*.

The two forms of object-orientation – grouping sets of sentences by object and structuring individual sentences by object – are often combined in practice. Consider, for example, the pair of English sentences from Brown and Yule (1983, page 130):

> *The prime minister stepped off the plane.*
> *Journalists immediately surrounded her.*

Both sentences are formulated in the active voice, which conforms to the guidelines for good practice advocated in all manuals of English style.

The two sentences refer to three objects, the prime minister (referred to as "her" in the second sentence), journalists and the plane. The prime minister is the only object in common between the two sentences. So, the prime minister is the object that groups the two sentences together. However, the topic changes from the prime minister in the first sentence to the journalists in the second.

Now consider the following logically equivalent pair of sentences:

> *The prime minister stepped off the plane.*
> *She was immediately surrounded by journalists.*

Here, the two sentences have the same topic. However, the second sentence is now expressed in the passive voice. Despite this fact and despite its going against a naïve interpretation of the guidelines of good writing style, most people find this second pair of sentences easier to understand. This seems to suggest that people have a strong preference for organising their thoughts in object-oriented form, which is stronger than their preference for the active over the passive voice.

Object-orientation is not the only way of structuring and ordering sentences. In both of the two pairs of sentences above, the sentences are ordered by the temporal sequence of events.

Now consider the following sequence of sentences:

> *The fox praised the crow.*
> *The crow sang a song.*
> *The cheese fell to the ground.*
> *The fox picked up the cheese.*

Here the sentences are ordered by temporal sequence. Individual sentences are structured, not by object, but by agent, as reflected in the use of the active voice.

Conclusions

In the same way that there are many systems of logic, there are many forms of object-orientation. In extreme forms of OO, there is no distinction between active and passive objects, and all interaction between objects is reduced to sending and receiving messages.

Extreme OO takes equality of objects too far. Instead of treating all objects as equal, it would be more natural to distinguish between active and passive objects. Active objects, which have encapsulated methods, are like agents, which have internal goals and beliefs. Passive objects, which have no internal structure, simply participate in external relationships with other objects.

Extreme OO also takes the message-passing metaphor too far. Instead of forcing all interactions between objects to be messages, it would be more natural to distinguish between messages sent from one active object to another and messages that are really observations or actions.

The real value of object-orientation lies in moderate forms of OO in which objects are encapsulated, modular collections of relatively self-contained knowledge, most of which is inherited from more general classes.

The example of natural languages like English shows that logic and OO have different areas of concern. Logic is concerned with representing knowledge, whereas OO is concerned with structuring knowledge representations. It would be interesting to see how OO notions of stucturing might apply to the collection of sentences that make up this book.

15

Biconditionals

As we saw in Chapter 5, negation as failure has a natural meta-logical (or autoepistemic) semantics, which interprets the phrase *cannot be shown* literally, as an expression in the meta-language or in autoepistemic logic. But historically the first and arguably the simplest semantics is the *completion semantics* (Clark, 1978), which treats conditionals as biconditionals in disguise.

Both the meta-logical and the completion semantics treat an agent's beliefs as specifying the *only* conditions under which a conclusion holds. But whereas the meta-logical semantics interprets the term *only* in the meta-language, biconditionals in the completion semantics interpret the same term, *only*, in the object language.

Suppose, for example, that we have complete information about whether or not Mary will go to the party, and the *only* belief we have is:

> *mary will go if john will go.*

Then it follows that: *mary will go only if john will go.*The meta-logical interpretation of negation as failure interprets this use of *only if* in the meta-language:

> *"mary will go if john will go"*
> *is the only way of showing "mary will go".*

However, the orthodox interpretation of *only if* in traditional logic interprets *only if* in the object-language, understanding sentences of the form:

> *conclusion only if conditions*

as object-language conditionals of the form:

> *conditions if conclusion.*

Thus given a single conditional:

> *conclusion if conditions*

188

together with an assumption that the conditional describes the *only* conditions under which the conclusion holds, traditional logic interprets the conditional as the object-language *biconditional*:

> *conclusion if and only if conditions.*

More generally, in the propositional case (where there are no variables), traditional logic interprets the assumption that the conditionals:

> *conclusion if conditions₁*
>
> . . .
>
> *conclusion if conditionsₙ*

are the *only* ways of establishing the given *conclusion* as the *biconditional*:

> *conclusion if and only if conditions₁ or . . . or conditionsₙ.*

Written in this form, the conditions of the biconditional can be regarded as giving a *definition* of the *conclusion*.

If the conditional is a simple fact, then the biconditional is equivalent to a definition of the form:

> *conclusion if and only if true.*

If an *atomic predicate* is the conclusion of no conditional, then it is equivalent to a definition of the form:

> *atomic predicate if and only if false.*

Or equivalently: *it is not the case that atomic predicate.*

This is also equivalent to the constraint:

Constraint: *if atomic predicate then false.*

The biconditional form is more complicated in the non-propositional case. For example, suppose that we have complete information about who will go to the party, and that the *only* beliefs we have are:

> *mary will go if john will go.*
> *john will go if bob will not go.*

Then the biconditional form of the beliefs is:

> *a person will go*
> *if and only if the person is identical to mary and john will go*
> *or the person is identical to john and bob will not go.*

For simplicity, we ignore the non-propositional case in the rest of the book.

Reasoning with biconditionals used as equivalences

The object-level interpretation of *only if* was originally used by Clark (1978) as a semantics for negation as **finite** failure. But it can also be used in its own right as a basis for an object-level proof procedure, in which biconditionals are used as *equivalences*, to replace atomic formulas that match their conclusions by their defining conditions (Fung and Kowalski, 1997). Using biconditionals in this way is a form of backward reasoning, which behaves almost exactly like backward reasoning with normal conditionals. Moreover, when applied to an atomic formula inside negation, it behaves almost exactly like negation as failure. In fact, in everyday informal reasoning, it can be hard to distinguish between ordinary backward reasoning and reasoning with equivalences.

Suppose, for example, that we want to determine whether or not *mary will go* to the party, but this time using biconditionals to represent the assumption that the conditionals are the only ways of showing their conclusions:

> *mary will go if and only if john will go.*
> *john will go if and only if it is not the case that bob will go.*
> *bob will go if and only if false.*

Initial goal:	*mary will go.*
Equivalent subgoal:	*john will go.*
Equivalent subgoal:	*it is not the case that <u>bob will go</u>.*
Equivalent subgoal:	*it is not the case that false.*
Equivalent subgoal:	*true.*

Suppose Bob changes his mind:

> *mary will go if and only if john will go.*
> *john will go if and only if it is not the case that bob will go.*
> *bob will go if and only if true.*

Initial goal:	*mary will go.*
Equivalent subgoal:	*john will go.*
Equivalent subgoal:	*it is not the case that <u>bob will go</u>.*
Equivalent subgoal:	*it is not the case that true.*
Equivalent subgoal:	*false.*

Now suppose Bob is out of the picture, and we try to show *mary will not go* with the beliefs:

> *mary will go if and only if john will go.*
> *john will go if and only if mary will go.*

Initial goal: *it is not the case that mary will go.*
Equivalent subgoal: *it is not the case that john will go.*
Equivalent subgoal: *it is not the case that mary will go.*
Equivalent subgoal: *it is not the case that john will go.*
ad infinitum: . . .

It is impossible to show that *mary will not go* and impossible to show that *mary will go*. Similarly for John.

This last result is different from the one we obtained with the same example when we understood *it is not the case that* as *it cannot be shown*, using negation as failure in Chapter 5. There the result was that *mary will not go*, because it cannot be shown that *mary will go*. This shows that default reasoning with biconditionals is a form of *negation as **finite** failure*.

Using biconditionals to simulate autoepistemic failure

Reconsider the belief that a person is innocent unless proven guilty. Let's see what happens if we replace the meta-level negation *it cannot be shown* by the object-level negation *it is not the case that* and replace conditionals by biconditionals:[1]

a person is innocent of a crime
if and only if the person is accused of the crime
and it is not the case that the person committed the crime.

a person committed an act
if and only if another person witnessed the person commit the act.

bob is accused of robbing the bank if and only if true.

In addition, we need to represent a form of the closed-world assumption for predicates that do not occur either as facts or as the conclusions of conditionals, for example to represent the initial situation in which no one has seen Bob commit the crime. This can be expressed as a negative fact in biconditional form or as a constraint:[2]

---

[1] This discussion glosses over a number of details. For example, if Bob is the only person accused of committing a crime, then this could be represented by *a person is accused of committing a crime if and only if the person is identical to bob and the crime is robbing the bank*, where *is identical to* is a kind of equality (defined by *X is identical to X*).

[2] There are arguments for both representations. However, in practice, the two representations behave similarly. The biconditional representation uses backward reasoning to replace an atom by

> *a person witnessed bob commit robbing the bank if and only if false.*
>
> or   *if a person witnessed bob commit robbing the bank then false.*

To solve a goal, such as showing that *bob is innocent of robbing the bank*, it suffices to repeatedly replace atomic formulas by their definitions, performing obvious simplifications associated with *true* and *false*. In the case of showing that *bob is innocent of robbing the bank*, this form of backward reasoning generates the following transformation of the initial goal into a sequence of equivalent expressions, representing subgoals. Atomic formulae that are replaced by their definitions are underlined:

Initial goal:	*bob is innocent of robbing the bank.*
Equivalent subgoal:	*bob is accused of robbing the bank and*
	it is not the case that
	bob committed robbing the bank.
Equivalent subgoal:	*it is not the case that*
	bob committed robbing the bank.
Equivalent subgoal:	*it is not the case that another person*
	witnessed bob commit robbing the bank.
Equivalent subgoal:	*it is not the case that false.*
Equivalent subgoal:	*true.*

This solves the initial goal, because it is equivalent to *true*. Although reasoning explicitly with *true* and *false* may seem a little awkward, it mirrors the kind of reasoning that takes place implicitly when reasoning with meta-level conditions of the form *it cannot be shown*.

Reasoning with biconditionals in this way is defeasible, because if we now replace the assumption that no one witnessed Bob commmit robbing the bank by:

> *john witnessed bob commit robbing the bank if and only if true.*

then the previous conclusion is withdrawn:

Initial goal:	*bob is innocent of robbing the bank.*
Equivalent subgoal:	*bob is accused of robbing the bank and*
	it is not the case that
	bob committed robbing the bank.
Equivalent subgoal:	*it is not the case that*
	bob committed robbing the bank.
Equivalent subgoal:	*it is not the case that another person*
	witnessed bob commit robbing the bank.

---

its definition *false*. The constraint representation uses forward reasoning from the atom to derive *false* and to conjoin *false* to the atom. In both cases, logical simplification (of the kind described in Chapter A6) transforms the atom and its conjuncts to *false*.

Equivalent subgoal: *it is not the case that true.*
Equivalent subgoal: *false.*

Remarkably, not only do both proofs mirror the search for proofs using negation as failure, but they simulate the autoepistemic character of negation as failure. This is because any conclusion derived using the biconditional representation has an implicit global autoepistemic assumption that the conclusion holds *as far as I know.*

Abduction or deduction?

Similarly to the way in which reasoning with biconditionals provides an alternative way of performing default reasoning, it also provides an alternative way of explaining observations by deduction rather than by abduction. For example, to explain the observation that *the grass is wet*, it uses biconditionals as equivalences to replace closed predicates by their definitions, leaving open predicates as potential hypotheses:

Belief: *the grass is wet if and only if it rained*
                                               or the sprinkler was on.
Observation and initial goal: *the grass is wet.*
Equivalent subgoal: *it rained or the sprinkler was on.*

Here the predicate *the grass is wet* is closed, whereas the predicates *it rained* and *the sprinkler was on* are both open and serve as hypotheses to explain the observation.

Note that, using deduction with biconditionals, the disjunction *or* is expressed in the object language. In contrast, using abduction with conditionals, the same disjunction would be expressed in the meta-language by saying that *the grass is wet* because *it rained or the grass is wet* because *the sprinkler was on.*

In the same way that forward reasoning can be used to deduce consequences of hypotheses derived by abduction, forward reasoning can also be used to deduce consequences of hypotheses derived by means of biconditionals. For example, if *it rained* last night, then the clothes outside will be wet. If you check the clothes, and observe they are dry, then you can eliminate the possibility that it rained (using the fact that *wet* and *dry* are contraries). This reasoning can be expressed more precisely in the following way:

Beliefs: *the grass is wet if and only if it rained or the sprinkler was on.*
               the clothes outside are wet if and only if it rained.
               the clothes outside are dry if and only if true.
Constraint: *if the clothes outside are dry and the clothes outside are wet then*
               false.

Here we represent the fact that *wet* and *dry* are contraries as a *constraint*, which we write (and use) in the same way as maintenance goals, but with conclusion *false*.

Observation and initial goal: *the grass is wet.*
Equivalently (by backward reasoning):   *it rained* **or** *the sprinkler was on.*
Equivalently (by forward reasoning):
        (it rained **and** *the clothes outside are wet) or the sprinkler was on.*
Equivalently (by forward reasoning):
        (it rained **and** *the clothes outside are wet*
        and *(if the clothes outside are dry then false)) or the sprinkler was on.*
Equivalently (by backward reasoning):
        (it rained **and** *the clothes outside are wet* **and** *false)*
        or the sprinkler was on.
Equivalently: *false or the sprinkler was on.*
Equivalently: *the sprinkler was on.*

Here the atom is underlined if it is replaced by its definition using backward reasoning, or if it is used for forward reasoning.

Deriving *cause if effect* from *effect if cause*

Interpreting a conditional *conclusion if conditions* as a biconditional *conclusion if and only if conditions* in disguise explains why it is so easy to confuse the conditional with its converse *conditions if conclusion*. It also explains the relationship between the more natural *effect if cause* representation of causality and the more efficient *cause if effect* representation.

For example, given an assumed complete *effect if cause* representation of the alternative causes of smoke:

>   *there is smoke if there is a fire.*
>   *there is smoke if there is teargas.*

the completion semantics interprets the representation as a biconditional:

>   *there is smoke if and only if there is a fire or there is teargas.*

One half of the biconditional is the original pair of conditionals. The other half of the biconditional is the converse of the original pair of conditionals, and is a conditional with a disjunctive conclusion:

>   *there is a fire or there is teargas if there is smoke.*

Conditionals with disjunctive conclusions are not very informative. If we had statistical information about the relative frequency of different causes of smoke, we could be more informative. For example:

> *there is a fire with 99.9% probability if there is smoke.*
> *there is teargas with 0.1% probability if there is smoke.*

This would be analogous to associating probabilities with the alternative hypotheses in the more natural *effect if cause* representation.

But we can obtain a similar effect if we rewrite the conditional having a disjunctive conclusion as a logically equivalent conditional with an atomic conclusion and a negative condition:

> *there is a fire if there is smoke*
> *and it is not the case that there is teargas.*

This conditional derives fire as the cause of smoke by default, avoiding both the completely uninformative disjunctive conclusion and the overly informative probabilistic conclusion.

Again, we have a case of different levels of representation. The *effect if cause* representation is higher-level. But it needs abduction to explain observations, and such criteria as relative likelihood and explanatory power to help decide between alternative hypotheses. The *cause if effect* representation is lower-level. It gives similar results, but it does so more efficiently, using deduction instead of abduction.

Truth versus proof in arithmetic

The two interpretations of negation as failure, the two ways of understanding explanations, and the two ways of representing the relationship between cause and effect are related to the difference between truth and proof in arithmetic.

Arguably, the meta-logical interpretation of negation as failure, the abductive understanding of explanations, and the representation of cause and effect in the form *effect if cause* are all more fundamental than their object-level, deductive and *cause if effect* alternatives. Similarly, truth in arithmetic is more fundamental than proof.

For simplicity in mathematical logic, the natural numbers are represented by repeatedly adding 1 to the number 0, so that $X+1$ is the number immediately after X. For example, the numbers 0, 1, 2, 3, ... come out looking like:

$$0, 0+1, (0+1)+1, ((0+1)+1)+1, \ldots$$

With this representation, arithmetic is just the set of all the properties of addition and multiplication, defined by the conditionals:

$$0 + Y = Y. \qquad (X+1) + Y = (Z+1) \text{ if } X + Y = Z.$$
$$0 \times X = 0. \qquad (X+1) \times Y = V \text{ if } X \times Y = U \text{ and } U + Y = V.$$

A more precise and more formal representation is given in the additional Chapter A2, where $X+1$ is represented by the successor function $s(X)$.

Forward reasoning with these conditionals generates the addition and multiplication tables for all the natural numbers. Backward reasoning reduces addition and multiplication problems to similar problems for smaller numbers. For example, here is a computation by backward reasoning, reducing the multiplication problem 1×3 to the simpler subproblems of multiplying 0×3 and adding 3 to the result:

Initial goal:	$(0+1) \times (((0+1)+1)+1) = V$
Subgoals:	$0 \times (((0+1)+1)+1) = U \text{ and } U + (((0+1)+1)+1) = V$
Subgoal:	$0 + (((0+1)+1)+1) = V$
which succeeds with:	$V = (((0+1)+1)+1)$, i.e. $V = 3$.

The addition and multiplication tables generated by forward reasoning have a number of intuitive properties. For example, the order in which two numbers are multiplied doesn't matter:

$$X \times Y = Y \times X$$

The intuition that such (universally quantified) properties are true is due to the fact that they are true of the set of all atomic facts that can be derived from the definitions of addition and multiplication. This notion of truth is more fundamental than any notion of proof in arithmetic.

However, the notion of truth in arithmetic is non-constructive, in the same way that negation as potentially infinite failure is non-constructive. In the case of negation as failure, showing that the negation of a sentence is true requires recognising infinite failure. In the case of arithmetic, showing that a universally quantified sentence is true requires showing that potentially infinitely many instances of the sentence are true.

In many, but not all cases, truth can be captured by proof. In the case of negation as failure, the completion semantics, replacing conditionals by biconditionals, captures finite failure. Moreover, with the addition of axioms of induction, the completion semantics can also capture cases where infinite failure is due to a regular loop.

Similarly, many properties of arithmetic can be proved by finite means, using the biconditional representations of addition and multiplication augmented with axioms of induction. In fact, this representation is equivalent to the standard set of axioms of arithmetic, called Peano arithmetic. The analogy between the Peano axioms and the completion and induction axioms used to prove properties of logic programs was investigated by Clark and Tärnlund (1978).

But in arithmetic, as we know from Gödel's incompleteness theorem, there exist true sentences (or properties of arithmetic) that cannot be proved by any finite means. Similarly for logic programs and other conditionals, there exist true negative sentences that hold by infinite failure that cannot be proved using the completion, even augmented with axioms of induction or sophisticated forms of loop detection.

The incompleteness theorem for arithmetic is arguably the most important result of mathematical logic in the twentieth century. The analogy with negation as failure shows that the theorem has similar importance for the relationship between truth and proof in human reasoning more generally.

Conclusions

There are two ways to understand conditional beliefs. One way is to understand them as representing the semantic structure of all the atomic facts that can be derived from them by means of forward reasoning. This semantic structure is the minimal model of the conditionals, which determines the truth (or falsity) of all other sentences expressed in the same language. The other way to understand conditional beliefs is as biconditionals in disguise.

The first way, which is explored in the additional Chapters A2, A3, A4 and A6, is arguably more fundamental. It specifies the notion of truth against which all methods of proof need to be judged for soundness and completeness. The second way is the standard way of trying to prove such true sentences. It is sound, but incomplete, even augmented with axioms of induction.

Thus both ways of understanding conditionals have their place. The first way identifies the goal, which is to determine the truth. The second way seeks to achieve the goal constructively by finite means.

However, it is not always easy to tell the two approaches apart. For example, the ALP procedure of the additional Chapter A6, which is designed to generate and determine truth in minimal models, is a modification of the IFF proof procedure for showing logical consequence by reasoning with biconditionals.

16

Computational Logic and the selection task

In Chapter 2, we saw that psychological studies of the selection task have been used to attack the view that human thinking involves logical reasoning, and to support the claim that thinking uses specialised algorithms instead. I argued that these attacks fail to appreciate the relationship between logic and algorithms, as expressed by the equation:

specialised algorithm =
specialised knowledge + general-purpose reasoning.

Specialised knowledge can be expressed in logical form, and general-purpose reasoning can be understood largely in terms of forward and backward reasoning embedded in an observe–think–decide–act agent cycle.

I also argued that many of the studies that are critical of the value of logic in human thinking fail to distinguish between the problem of understanding natural-language sentences and the problem of reasoning with logical forms. This distinction and the relationship between them can also be expressed by an equation:

natural language understanding =
translation into logical form + logical reasoning.

We saw that even natural-language sentences already in seemingly logical form need to be interpreted, in order to determine, for example, whether they are missing any conditions, or whether they might be the converse of their intended meaning. Because of the need to perform this interpretation, readers typically use their own background goals and beliefs, to help them identify the intended logical form of the natural-language problem statement.

However, even after taking these problems of representation and interpretation into account, there remains the problem of reasoning with the resulting logical forms. This problem is the topic of this chapter.

An abstract form of the selection task

Assume that an agent has been told that a sentence having the logical form:

if P then Q

ought to be true, but might be false. Assume, moreover, that *P* and *Q* are open predicates that are directly observable. The abstract form of the selection task is to determine how the agent should respond to various observations of the truth values of these predicates.

I will argue that this is a natural way of presenting the selection task to an agent in the context of the agent cycle. Because the agent believes that the conditional ought to be true, it is natural for the agent to use the conditional to assimilate observations by deriving their consequences. But because the agent believes that the conditional might be false, it is also natural for the agent to actively observe whether consequences that ought to be true if the conditional is true are actually true.

In our agent model, the agent's response depends upon whether the agent interprets the conditional as a goal or as a belief. If the agent interprets it as a goal, then the possibility that the goal might be false means that the state of the world may not conform to the goal. But if the agent interprets it as a belief, then the possibility that the belief might be false means that the belief may not conform to the state of the world.

But classical logic does not distinguish between goals and beliefs. According to classical logic, the correct responses are:

From an observation of *P* deduce *Q*.   *(modus ponens)*
From an observation of *not Q* deduce *not P*.   *(modus tollens)*

However, in psychological studies of some variants of the selection task, including the original card version, most people:

From an observation of *P* deduce *Q*. *(modus ponens)*
From an observation of *Q* deduce *P*. *(affirmation of the consequent)*

They correctly perform *modus ponens*, but they commit the fallacy of *affirmation of the consequent*, and they fail to perform *modus tollens*. In theory, there is one additional response they could make:

From an observation of *not P* to deduce *not Q*. *(denial of the antecedent)*

However, most people make this inference only rarely.

The challenge is to explain why most people reason correctly in some cases, and seemingly incorrectly in other cases. Part of the problem, of course, is that the psychological tests assume that subjects have a clear concept of deductive inference. But we have seen that even Sherlock Holmes had trouble distinguishing deduction from abduction. And we have also seen that there is good reason for this trouble, because abduction can be performed by deduction if conditionals are understood as biconditionals. This explains why most subjects commit the deductive fallacy of *affirmation of the consequent*, which is not a fallacy at all, when these considerations are taken into account.

I will argue that, given the above abstract form of the selection task:

- *Modus ponens* is easy, no matter whether the conditional is interpreted as a goal or as a belief, because in both cases, forward reasoning derives *Q* from an observation of *P*.
- *Affirmation of the consequent* is a correct inference if the conditional is interpreted as the *only* belief that implies its conclusion. It is justified either by abduction if *only* is interpreted in the meta-language, and by the biconditional formulation of the conditional if *only* is interpreted in the object language. However, it is not justified if the conditional is interpreted as a goal.
- *Modus tollens* is hard if the conditional is interpreted as a belief, mostly because it is necessary to connect a positive observation *Q'* with the negation *not Q* of the conclusion of the conditional *if P then Q*. In many cases, this connection needs to be made through an unstated background constraint *if Q and Q' then false*.

  In such cases, *modus tollens* is easier if the conditional is interpreted as a goal, because then it is natural to reason in advance of obervations and to compile the conditional and the constraint into the form *if P and Q' then false*. Represented in this form, the conditional can easily derive *if P then false*, i.e. *not P* from the observation *Q'*.
- *Denial of the antecedent* is a theoretical possibility if the conditional is interpreted as the *only* conditional implying its conclusion, but is made harder by the need to derive the negative conclusion *not P* from a positive observation *P'*. Arguably, the need both to interpret the conditional as the *only* conditional and to derive a negative conclusion makes *denial of the antecedent* harder and therefore less likely.

A more accurate representation of the selection task

The abstract form of the conditional *if P then Q* is only an approximation to the conditionals in the psychological experiments. It would be more accurate to represent them in the form:

if X has value u for property p then X has value v for property q.

For example:

> *if a card X has letter d on the letter side*
> *then the card X has number 3 on the number side.*

> *if a person X is drinking alcohol in a bar*
> *then the person X has age at least eighteen years old.*

In many cases, the properties *p* and *q* have only a single value for a given value of *X*.[1] For example, a card has only one letter on the letter side of the card, and only one number on the number side of the card. In the case of the property *q*, this can be expressed as an integrity constraint:

> *if X has value V for property q and X has value W for property q*
> *then V is identical to W.*

where the predicate *is identical to* is defined by the clause:

> *X is identical to X.*

For example:

> *if a card X has number N on the number side*
> *and the card X has number M on the number side*
> *then N is identical to M.*

We will see that we need such integrity constraints – or something like them – to derive negative conclusions from positive observations. A similar constraint holds for the age of a person:

> *if a person X has age at least eighteen years old*
> *and the person X has age under eighteen years old*
> *then false.*

These integrity constraints are similar to the constraints:

> *if predicate and contrary-predicate then false.*

that we used to reason with negation when performing abduction, and which we treated as a species of goal.

We now consider in greater detail the case in which the conditional is interpreted as a belief, and afterwards the case in which the conditional is interpreted as a goal.

---

[1] In mathematics this means that the relationship *X has value V for property q* is a functional relationship, which is normally written $q(X) = V$, where *q* is now a function symbol.

The conditional interpreted as a belief

If an agent understands the conditional as a belief, and has reasons to doubt the belief, then the agent can test the belief by checking its consequences. If these consequences are not already derivable from other beliefs, and if they are observable, then the agent can attempt to observe the consequences to confirm or refute the belief. For example, in the card version of the selection task, if the agent observes what is on one side of a card and concludes what should or should not be on the other side of the card, then the agent can turn the card over to actively observe whether the conclusion is actually *true*.

The situation is similar to the one in which an observation can be explained by a hypothesis. The agent can test the hypothesis by checking its consequences. Observing that a consequence is *true* adds to the weight of evidence in favour of the hypothesis. But observing that a consequence is *false* refutes the hypothesis once and for all, and excludes it from further consideration.

Thus, if the validity of a conditional belief is in doubt, then forward reasoning from a *true* observation to consequences of the belief and observing that a consequence is *true* increases confidence in the belief. But in the case of a conditional belief with universally quantified variables, a *true* consequence does not validate the belief, because other instances of the belief may be *false*. On the other hand, the observation of a single *false* consequence refutes the belief forever. In concrete versions of the selection task, it is usual to formulate the instructions to encourage observations of consequences that can falsify the conditional, and to discourage observations that can only confirm that an instance of the conditional is *true*.

Modus ponens

In Computational Logic, conditional beliefs are used to reason both backwards and forwards. In particular, given a (passive) observation of a positive predicate P, forward reasoning with the conditional *if P then Q* derives the positive conclusion Q. This is a classically correct application of *modus ponens* (together with any instantiations of the variables in the conditional needed to match the observation with the condition P).

If the conclusion Q is observable, and there is a reason to check Q, because there is some doubt whether the conditional is actually *true*, then the agent can actively observe whether Q is *true*. If Q fails to be *true*, then the conditional is *false*. If Q is *true*, then the instance of the conditional matching the observation P is *true* (although other instances may be *false*).

Affirmation of the consequent

In Computational Logic, conditionals are also used to explain observations. Given an observation of Q, backward reasoning derives P as a candidate explanation of Q. This derivation can be viewed both as abduction with the conditional *if P then Q* and as deduction with the biconditional Q *if and only if P*. In classical logic, this form of reasoning is called the fallacy of *affirmation of the consequent*.

As in the case of *modus ponens*, if P is observable, then the agent can actively observe whether P is *true*. If P fails to be *true*, then the belief in its conditional form fails to explain the observation, even though the belief itself may be *true*; but the belief in its biconditional form is definitely *false*.

Modus tollens

The main problem with *modus tollens* is that real observations are positive and not negative. Negative conclusions have to be derived from positive observations.[2] The longer the derivation and the larger the number of distracting, irrelevant derivations, the more difficult it is for the agent to make the necessary, relevant derivation.

The positive observation in the card version of the selection task is the fact:

the fourth card has number 7 on the number side.

To perform *modus tollens* with the belief:

if a card X has letter d on the letter side
then the card X has number 3 on the number side.

it is necessary first to derive the negative conclusion:

it is not the case that the fourth card has number 3 on the number side.

But this derivation is hard to motivate. Why not also derive the irrelevant conclusions:

it is not the case that the fourth card has number 1 on the number side.
it is not the case that the fourth card has number 2 on the number side.
it is not the case that the fourth card has number 4 on the number side.
etc.

However, the effect of *modus tollens* can be obtained more directly, without the distraction of these additional conclusions, by using the integrity constraint:

---

[2] A negative observation can also be obtained from the failure to make a positive observation. However, the standard selection task examples involve only positive observations from which "negative observations" need to be derived before *modus tollens* can be applied.

if a card X has number N on the number side
and the card X has number M on the number side
then N is identical to M.

Forward reasoning with the observation:

the fourth card has number 7 on the number side.

using the constraint derives:

if the fourth card has number M on the number side
then 7 is identical to M.

Backward reasoning using the conditional derives:

if the fourth card has letter d on the letter side
then 7 is identical to 3.

At this point, the standard pattern of forward and backward reasoning suggests that the condition *the fourth card has letter d on the letter side* should be checked before deriving the conclusion *7 is identical to 3*. However, this condition can be checked only by performing an active observation. But the active observation is unnecessary if the conclusion is *true*, because a conditional with a *true* conclusion is always *true*, no matter whether its conditions are *true* or *false*.

In fact, if the constraint had been in the form:

if a card X has number N on the number side
and the card X has number M on the number side
*and N is **not** identical to M then false.*

then we could check instead, the condition *7 is **not** identical to 3*, using negation as failure and the definition *X is identical to X*. We would then obtain the desired result:

if the fourth card has letter d on the letter side then false.
i.e. *it is not the case that the fourth card has letter d on the letter side.*

The single condition can then be checked by performing an active observation.
This reasoning is a minor variation of the standard pattern:

- Reason forwards to match an observation with a condition of a goal.
- Reason backwards to verify the other conditions.
- Reason forwards to derive the conclusion.
- Reason backwards to solve the conclusion.

The derivation can also be viewed as activating links in a connection graph of constraint and beliefs:

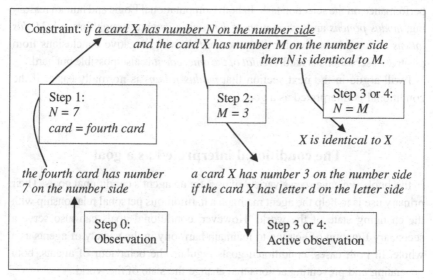

Arguably, viewed in these terms, the derivation is hard because the connection between the positive observation and the conditional belief needs to be made through a constraint/goal that is only loosely related with the problem statement. I will argue in the next section that when the conditional is interpreted as a goal, the connection is typically stronger and the derivation is easier.

We considered the problem of *modus tollens* in the concrete case of the original card version of the task. However, similar considerations apply in other cases in which the conditional is interpreted as a belief. In general, the harder an agent needs to work to derive a conclusion, the less likely it is that the agent will be able to do so.

It is a lot easier to recognise a solution than it is to generate it, because generating a solution requires search, but recognising the solution does not. This would explain why many people fail to apply *modus tollens* in the selection task, but still recognise its correct application when they see it.

Denial of the antecedent

A less common mistake in the selection task is to conclude *not Q* from an observation of *not P*. On the one hand, the inference can be justified for the same reasons that affirmation of the consequent can be justified. On the other hand, the inference is hard for the same reasons that *modus tollens* is hard. However, since it is not a major issue in the selection task, we ignore it here.

Conclusions

Thus if the conditional is interpreted as a belief, then reasoning with Computational Logic in the agent cycle is compatible with psychological studies of human performance on the selection task. In both Computational Logic and human reasoning, *modus ponens* and *affirmation of the consequent* are straightforward. *Modus tollens* is possible but hard, mostly because deriving negative conclusions from positive observations is hard. *Denial of the antecedent* is also possible but hard.

I will argue in the next section that *modus tollens* is normally easier if the conditional is interpreted as a goal.

The conditional interpreted as a goal

In this book, we have seen a variety of uses for an agent's conditional goals. Their primary use is to help the agent maintain a harmonious personal relationship with the changing state of the world. However, conditional goals can also serve a secondary function of helping to maintain harmony in the society of agents as a whole. In both cases, conditional goals regulate the behaviour of agents, both generating and preventing actions that change the state of the world.

In the examples of both the bar version of the selection task and the security measures on the London Underground:

> *if a person is drinking alcohol in a bar,*
> *then the person is at least eighteen years old.*

> *if a passenger is carrying a rucksack on his or her back,*
> *then the passenger is wearing a label with the letter A on his or her front.*

it is natural to understand the conditional as a social constraint. An agent can use the constraint to monitor states of the world by observing whether instances of the constraint are *true* or *false*. Observations of *false* instances violate the goal/constraint. Observations of *true* instances comply with the goal/constraint.

In well-regulated societies, agents normally conform to the rules, and violations are exceptional. Therefore, in concrete formulations of the selection task, in situations where the context makes it clear that the conditional is to be interpreted as a goal, it is unnecessary to stress that the task is to detect violations, because preventing violations is the normal purpose of such goals. In computing, integrity constraints perform a similar function in monitoring database updates.

I will argue that, when an agent interpets the selection task as one of monitoring compliance with a conditional goal, then the inferences that are easy in Computational Logic are the ones that are also correct according to the standards of classical logic. The two main problems are to explain why affirmation of the consequent does not apply and why *modus tollens* is easy. But first we need to confirm that *modus ponens* is easy.

Modus ponens

The general pattern of reasoning with conditional goals is to reason forwards from a fact or assumption that matches a condition of the goal, backwards to verify the other conditions of the goal, and then forwards one step to derive the conclusion. This pattern of reasoning includes the classically correct application of *modus ponens* as the special case in which the goal has no other conditions to be verified.

If the conditional goal is a personal maintenance goal, then the conclusion is an achievement goal, which the agent can attempt to solve by backward reasoning and eventually by performing actions. If the conditional goal is a social constraint, then the agent can actively attempt to observe whether the conclusion is *true*. If the agent observes that the conclusion is *true*, then the instance of the social constraint triggered by the initial observation or assumption is *satisfied*, but if the agent observes that the conclusion is *false*, then the social constraint is *violated*.

Affirmation of the consequent

If the conditional *if P then Q* is interpreted as a belief, then backward reasoning, either directly with the conditional or with the biconditional can be used to derive *P* as an explanation of an observation of *Q*.

However, if the task is interpreted as monitoring the truth of the conditional understood as a goal, then an observation that *Q* is *true* immediately confirms that the conditional *if P then Q* is *true*. There is no point in actively observing whether or not *P* is *true*, because the truth value of *P* has no influence on the truth value of the conditional. In other words, no observation of the truth value of *P* can uncover a violation of the conditional.

Modus tollens

I argued before that *modus tollens* is hard when the conditional is interpreted as a belief, mostly because it is hard to derive negative conclusions. I will now argue that the derivation of negative conclusions is normally easier when the conditional is interpreted as a goal. The argument is supported by experience with the problem of checking integrity constraints in computing.

In computing, integrity checking is an expensive operation, which needs to be performed whenever the database is updated. Because many different integrity constraints can be affected by a single update, it is common to optimise the constraints by doing as much of the reasoning as possible in advance. For this purpose, a common optimisation is to convert condition–action rules into event–condition–action rules. The optimisation is so common, in fact, that many systems, including active databases (Widom and Ceri, 1996), allow rules only in event–condition–action form.

However, the more general conversion of conditional goals into event–condition–conclusion form can be performed mechanically by reasoning in advance. For example, the maintenance goal:

>   *if there is an emergency then get help.*

can be converted into:

>   *if there are flames then get help.*
>   *if there is smoke then get help.*
>   *if one person attacks another then get help.*
>   *if someone becomes seriously ill then get help.*
>   *if there is an accident then get help.*

The reasoning involved in this example was illustrated in Chapter 9 and is formalised in Chapter A5. But notice that the reduction in Chapter 9 of the conclusion *get help* to atomic actions does not affect efficiency to the same extent as the reduction of the condition *there is an emergency*.

The efficiency advantage of the converted rules is that they can be triggered directly by external observations without the need to reason forwards with intermediate beliefs. The disadvantage is that in some cases the number of converted rules can become prohibitively large.

In the case of the conditional goal in the selection task, if the derivation of negative conclusions from positive observations is by means of a constraint of the form *if Q and Q' then false*, then this optimisation can be performed by activating the link between the conditional and the constraint in advance of any input observations. This compiles the initial conditional goal into a denial:

Conditional goal:	*if P then Q.*
Constraint:	*if Q and Q' then false.*
Compiled goal:	*if P and Q' then false.*
Or equivalently:	*it is not the case that P and Q'.*

In this form, an observation that *Q'* is *true* triggers the compiled goal, which initiates an active observation of the value of *P*. If *P* is *true* then *Q'* violates the conditional goal. If *P* is *false* then *Q'* satisfies the conditional goal. This is not quite simple *modus tollens*, but it is the behaviour associated with *modus tollens*, namely actively observing the truth value of *P*, given an observation of *the contrary of Q*.

For example, in the bar version of the selection task:

Conditional goal: *if a person X is drinking alcohol in a bar*
                                  then the person X has age at least eighteen years old.

Constraint: *if a person X has age at least eighteen years old*
                                  and the person X has age under eighteen years old
                                  then false.

Compiled goal: *if a person X is drinking alcohol in a bar*
                                  and the person X has age under eighteen years old
                                  then false.

Or equivalently: *it is not the case that*
                                  a person X is drinking alcohol in a bar
                                  and the person X has age under eighteen years old.

Denial of the antecedent

Since only beliefs, and not goals, are used to explain observations, it is not possible to conclude *not Q* from an observation of *not P*. In particular, there is no link between:

Conditional goal: *if P then Q.*
Constraint: *if P and P' then false.*

where *P'* is the contrary of *P*.

Conclusions

Thus if the conditional is interpreted as a goal, then neither *affirmation of the consequent* nor *denial of the antecedent* is applicable, and *modus ponens* is straightforward. *Modus tollens* is easy under the assumption that the focus on checking for violations encourages reasoning in advance, compiling the goal into a form that makes violations easier to detect.

This assumption about compiling the goal is similar to the argument of Sperber *et al.* (1995), that subjects are likely to reason in accordance with classical logic and to perform *modus tollens*, if they interpret the conditional *if P then Q* as a denial:

i.e.   *it is not the case that P and not Q.*
or equivalently: *if P and not Q then false.*

This analysis of the selection task is also compatible with the evolutionary psychology view that people have an inbuilt cheater detection algorithm. However, in Computational Logic, cheater detection is just a special case of detecting violations of social integrity constraints.

Applied to the bar version of the selection task compiled into the form:

> *if a person X is drinking alcohol in a bar*
> *and the person X has age under eighteen years old*
> *then false.*

general-purpose integrity checking monitors observations that match one of the conditions of the constraint. Given an observation of a person drinking alcohol, the agent can attempt to actively observe the age of the person, and if the person's age is under eighteen years old, then the agent can infer that there has been violation of the goal. Similarly, given an observation of a person who is under eighteen years old, the agent can actively check whether the person is drinking alcohol, and if he is, then the agent can similarly infer a violation.

Security measures reconsidered

I started Chapter 2 with the imaginary example of improving security on the London Underground:

> *if a passenger is carrying a rucksack on his or her back,*
> *then the passenger is wearing a label with the letter A on his or her front.*

To solve the selection task in this example, the simple analysis of this chapter needs to be refined.

I don't think there is any doubt that the conditional in this example is a social constraint. There are no problems with *modus ponens, affirmation of the consequent* or *denial of the antecedent*. But what about *modus tollens*?

As in all the other examples, the main problem is to derive a negative conclusion from a positive observation. You might notice, for example, that a person on the underground has a rucksack on his back, is accompanied by a dog or smoking a cigarette. But you do not spontaneously observe that the person does not have the letter A pinned on his front, is not accompanied by a Scottish Terrier or is not smoking a Marlboro.

I have argued in this chapter that to obtain the effect of *modus tollens*, it is necessary to connect a passive positive observation Q' with a negative conclusion *not Q*. I suggested that in many cases the necessary connection is through an unstated background constraint *if Q and Q' then false*. But is there such a constraint in this example? For example, the constraint:

> *if a person X has a letter L on the front*
> *and the person X has a letter M on the front*
> *then L is identical to M.*

is obviously not good enough. What if the person is wearing a peace symbol on his front? Or is topless? Or is obscuring his front with a replica Roman shield? There are just too many such possibilities to count as the contrary Q' of the conclusion Q.

To obtain the effect of *modus tollens* we need to compile the conditional into a form that can be triggered by a relevant, passive positive observation. The simplest such representation is probably:

> *if a person is a passenger on the underground*
> *and the person is carrying a rucksack on his or her back,*
> *and the person is **not** wearing a label with the letter A on his or her front*
> *then false.*

This is a minor variation of the form *if P and not Q then false* identified by Sperber *et al.* (1995) as facilitating the application of *modus tollens*.

Given this compiled form of the conditional and a positive observation of a passenger on the underground, you can actively observe either whether the person is carrying a rucksack on his back or whether he is wearing the letter A on his front. If it is easier to check the latter of these two conditions, and you fail to observe the letter A on his front, then you should check the other condition, to see whether he has a rucksack on his back. If not, then the conditional has been violated. This is the behaviour associated with classical *modus tollens*.

The reader who studies Chapter A6 and pays close attention to the analysis of *modus tollens* for the card version of the selection task in this chapter will appreciate that what is involved in both of these examples is an inference rule of the form:

Given an integrity constraint of the form: *if P then Q or R*
derive the integrity constraint: *if P and not Q then R*

for the special case where *R* is just *false*. This inference rule is the converse of the negation rewriting rule of Chapter A6.

What the security measure example shows is that the inference rules of Computational Logic need to be refined for dealing with certain cases of negation, but as they currently stand they are pretty close to what is needed in problems like the selection task.

Conclusions

The selection task is a worthy challenge for any theory of human reasoning. In this chapter, I argued that with certain qualifications, Computational Logic embedded as the thinking component of the agent cycle is capable of meeting that challenge. Computational Logic explains both cases where people reason seemingly incorrectly according to the norms of classical logic and cases where they reason correctly. It also explains why people might be able to recognise a correct solution even when they are unable to produce it themselves.

I have argued that this analysis of the selection task is compatible with other analyses, most notably with that of Sperber *et al.* (1995), but even with that of Cosmides (1985, 1989) if generously understood.

But as the example of the imaginary security measures on the London underground shows, the inference rules of Computational Logic need further elaboration. It is possible that the selection task and other psychological studies of human reasoning may help to suggest some of the ways of filling in the details.

17
Meta-logic

Do you want to get ahead in the world, improve yourself, and be more intelligent than you already are? If so, then meta-logic is what you need.

Meta-logic is a special case of meta-language. A *meta-language* is a language used to represent and reason about another language, called the *object language*. If the object language is a form of logic, then the meta-language is also called *meta-logic*. Therefore, this book is an example of the use of meta-logic to study the object language of Computational Logic.

However, in this book we use *meta-logic*, not only to study Computational Logic, but to do so in Computational Logic itself. In other words, the language of meta-logic, as understood in this book, is also Computational Logic. So, to paraphrase the first paragraph of this chapter, if you want to be more intelligent, you should use Computational Logic as a meta-logic to think about thinking.

In fact, even if you are satisfied with your own level of intelligence, you can use meta-logic to simulate the thinking of other agents, whether you believe they are more or less intelligent than you are. For example, an intelligent fox could use meta-logic to simulate the thinking of a stupid crow.

We have already touched upon some of the applications of meta-logic as early as Chapter 3, where we used it to represent the definition of truth for sentences in the form of conditionals. We also used it in Chapter 6, to represent the purposes of subsection 1.1 and the subgoal of satisfying the Secretary of State, and in Chapter 13, to represent the situation calculus and event calculus. In this chapter, we will focus on its use to represent and reason about reasoning. Here is a simple example, in which the meta-language terms *P*, *(P if Q)*, *Q* and *(P and Q)* name object-language sentences. The parentheses are used to avoid ambiguities:

meta₁: *an agent believes P*
      if the agent believes (P if Q) and the agent believes Q.
meta₂: *an agent believes (P and Q)*
      if the agent believes P and the agent believes Q.

The example may seem fairly pointless, but it is a solid foundation on which other, more significant examples can be built. But even in this simple case, the example illustrates how an agent can be aware of its own thinking, even if that thinking may not be very exciting.

More elaborate variants of this example have widespread, practical use in computing, to implement *meta-interpreters*, which are computer programs written in a meta-language to implement an object-language. Typically, the object-language implemented in this way provides some desirable features missing from the meta-language itself.

In English, it is common to use quotation marks to distinguish sentences and other syntactic entities from their names. So for example, "Mary" is the name of Mary, and "Mary is an intelligent agent" is the name of the sentence inside the quotes. However, in many practical applications in computing, it turns out that quotation marks and other naming devices are unnecessary, because the context makes it clear whether an expression belongs to the object-language or the meta-language.

Here is an example of the use of meta-logic to implement object-level reasoning with disjunction *(P or Q)*, without using disjunction in the meta-language.

meta$_3$:   *an agent believes P*
         if the agent believes (P or Q) and the agent believes (not Q).

The terms *or* and *not* in this meta-sentence are not logical connectives in the meta-language, but are names of logical connectives in the object-language.

We will use meta$_3$ to solve the wise man puzzle later in this chapter. We will also need to reason that if an agent observes whether or not a fact is true, then the agent believes the result of the observation. In the solution of the wise man puzzle, this reasoning is needed only for the case of a negative observation, which is an instance of negation as failure:

meta$_4$:   *an agent believes (not Q)*
         if the agent observes whether Q
         and not (Q holds).

Here the expression *not* occurs at both the object-level and the meta-level. The first occurrence of *not* names the logical connective *not* of the object-language, but the second occurrence of *not* is a logical connective in the meta-language. This use of the same syntax for the object-language and meta-language is called *ambivalent* syntax. It is not ambiguous, provided the different usages can be distinguished by their context.

The semantics of belief

Without the use of quotation marks or some other device for naming sentences, meta-logic looks like a modal logic. In modal logic, *believes* is a logical connective like the connectives *if* and *and*. Even more remarkable, the axioms of belief meta$_1$ and meta$_2$ in meta-logic are virtually indistinguishable from the axioms of belief in modal logic. But meta-logic and modal logic have different semantics.

The modal logic semantics of belief is similar to the possible world semantics of time, which we discussed briefly in Chapter 13. In modal logic, sentences are given a truth value relative to a possible world W embedded in a collection of worlds. In such a collection of possible worlds, an agent *believes* a proposition P in a possible world W, if P is *true* in every possible world accessible to the agent from W.

In meta-logic, an agent believes P if P is a belief in the agent's language of thought. With this meta-logical semantics of belief, the meta-beliefs meta$_1$ and meta$_2$ are literally *false*, because they fail to take into account the limitations of real agents in practice. For this reason, the *believes* meta-predicate might be better called the *can-be-shown-in-theory* predicate. In this respect, it is similar to negation as failure, which might similarly be called *cannot-be-shown-in-theory*.

The relationship between modal logics and meta-logics of belief is a complex issue, about which there is still no general agreement. However in Computing, the combination of ambivalent syntax with meta-logical semantics has proved to be very useful in practice. For this and other reasons, it is this representation of belief that we use in this chapter.

How to make a good impression

Suppose you believe:

> *mary is impressed with a person*
> *if mary believes the person is well-bred.*

> *mary believes everyone who speaks the queen's english*
> *and has a noble character is well-bred.*

Or, to put the second sentence more precisely:

mary believes ((a person is well-bred if the person speaks the queen's english and the person has a noble character) holds for all persons).

Intuitively, it follows that Mary will be impressed with you if she believes you speak the Queen's English and have a noble character. It doesn't matter whether you really do speak the Queen's English or not, or whether you do have a noble character or are a complete scoundrel. What matters is only what Mary thinks

about you. On the other hand, whether or not Mary *believes* she is impressed is
not the issue. It's whether she *actually is* impressed that counts.

Making these intuitions water-tight may not be as simple as you think.
Among other things, you need to reason that, because Mary believes in general
that a property holds for all people, then for every person she believes in
particular that the same property holds for that person. For this, you need an
extra meta-level belief, such as:

meta$_5$:   *an agent believes (S holds for a person)*
            if the agent believes (S holds for all persons).

This belief is similar to the if-half of the definition of truth for universally
quantifed sentences mentioned in passing at the end of Chapter 3 and presented
more formally in Chapter A2. As in Chapters 3 and A2, the meta-belief can be
expressed more generally for arbitrary types, and not only for the type of
persons. However, meta$_5$ is simpler and sufficient for our purposes.

To understand better the consequences of your beliefs, it helps to put all the
relevant beliefs together in the same connection graph. The meta-beliefs meta$_3$ and
meta$_4$ are not relevant in this example, and so their connections are not displayed:

> *mary is impressed with a person*
> *if mary believes the person is well-bred.*

> *agent = mary*
> *P holds for a person = a person is well-bred*

meta$_1$:   *an agent believes P*
            if the agent believes (P if Q) and the agent believes Q.

> *(P if Q) = (S holds for a person)*

> *Q = (P' and Q')*

meta$_2$: *an agent believes (P' and Q')*
        if the agent believes P'
        and the agent believes Q'.

meta$_5$:   *an agent believes (S holds for a person)*
            if the agent believes (S holds for all persons)

> *agent = mary*
> *S = (a person is well-bred if the person speaks the queen's*
> *english and the person has a noble character)*

mary believes ((a person is well-bred if the person speaks the queen's
english and the person has a noble character) holds for all persons).

The connection graph can be simplified by reasoning in advance, selecting any link and deriving the resolvent, as described in detail in Chapter A5. In fact, several links can even be activated in parallel. Suppose, in particular, that we activate the two links among the three meta-beliefs meta$_1$, meta$_2$ and meta$_5$. We can replace the three general meta-beliefs by the resulting more specialised meta-belief:

> *mary is impressed with a person*
> *if mary believes the person is well-bred.*

> *agent = mary*
> *P holds for a person = a person is well-bred*

> *an agent believes P holds for a person*
> *if the agent believes ((P if P' and Q') holds for all persons)*
> *and the agent believes P' holds for the person*
> *and the agent believes Q' holds for the person.*

> *agent = mary*
> *P = a person is well-bred*
> *P' = the person speaks the queen's english*
> *Q' = the person has a noble character*

mary believes ((a person is well-bred if the person speaks the queen's english and the person has a noble character) holds for all persons).

The resulting connection graph can be further simplified, by activating the remaining two links and deriving:

> *mary is impressed with a person*
> *if mary believes the person speaks the queen's english*
> *and mary believes the person has a noble character.*

Now, provided you are indeed a person, then this is the conclusion you were after.

How to satisfy the Secretary of State

Here is another application of the three meta-beliefs meta$_1$, meta$_2$ and meta$_5$, but with a different purpose. Suppose, this time, that you want to think like the Secretary of State, either because you aspire to take his place one day, or because you have applied to naturalise as a British Citizen and you want to anticipate what he will think about your application. Suppose, in particular, that you want to determine whether *the secretary of state is satisfied that you fulfil the requirements of schedule 1 for naturalisation by 6.1,* which is a problem left over from Chapter 6.

To simplify matters, suppose that your application for naturalisation is based on having been resident in the UK and not on any past or future service to the crown. So the two most relevant provisions suitably simplified are:

sec_1:   *the secretary of state may grant a certificate of naturalisation*
           to a person by section 6.1
           if   the person applies for naturalisation
           and   the person is of full age and capacity
           and   the secretary of state is satisfied that
                    the person fulfils the requirements of schedule 1
                    for naturalisation by 6.1
           and   the secretary of state thinks fit
                    to grant the person a certificate of naturalisation.

sec_2:   *a person fulfils the requirements of schedule 1 for naturalisation by 6.1*
           if the person fulfils the residency requirements of subparagraph 1.1.2
           and   the person is of good character
           and   the person has sufficient knowledge of english,
                    welsh, or scottish gaelic
           and   the person has sufficient knowledge about life in the uk
           and   the person intends to make his principal home in the uk
                    in the event of being granted naturalisation.

The problem is how to link the third condition of the first provision sec_1 with the conclusion of the second provision sec_2. The problem is similar to the previous one of trying to determine whether Mary will be impressed.

Obviously, to say that the Secretary of State *is satisfied* that something holds is another way of saying that he *believes* that something holds. Therefore, to simulate what the Secretary of State thinks about your application for naturalisation, you can replace the phrase *is satisfied* that by *believes* and use any relevant meta-beliefs about beliefs.

You also need to reflect one level up, and assume that the Secretary of State believes all the provisions of the British Nationality Act, and the second provision sec_2 in particular. We can put all the relevant provisions and assumptions together with the relevant meta-beliefs in the same connection graph. To avoid unnecessary clutter, the matching instantiations of variables are not displayed.

Perhaps not surprisingly, this connection graph has a similar structure to the connection graph for impressing Mary:

the secretary of state may grant a certificate of naturalisation
to a person by section 6.1
if   the person applies for naturalisation
and   the person is of full age and capacity
and   the secretary of state believes the person fulfils
*   the requirements of schedule 1 for naturalisation by 6.1*
and   the secretary of state thinks fit
*   to grant the person a certificate of naturalisation.*

meta₁: *An agent believes P*
if the agent believes (P if Q) and the agent believes Q.

meta₂: *An agent believes (P' and Q')*
if the agent believes P'
and the agent believes Q'.

meta₅: *An agent believes (S holds for a person)*
if the agent believes (S holds for all persons)

the secretary of state believes
((a person fulfils the requirements of schedule 1 for naturalisation by 6.1
*   if the person fulfils the residency requirements of subparagraph 1.1.2*
*   and   the person is of good character*
*   and   the person has sufficient knowledge of english,*
*   welsh, or scottish gaelic*
*   and   the person has sufficient knowledge about life in the uk*
*   and   the person intends to make his principal home in the uk*
*   in the event of being granted naturalisation)*
holds for all persons).

Here the clauses meta₁ and meta₂ contain additional implicit, internal links between their conditions and conclusions. The internal link in meta₁ is not needed in this example, but the internal link in meta₂ needs to be activated three times, to deal with the four conditions of the requirements of schedule 1. Activating all but the topmost link gives us the simplified connection graph, which now contains the previously missing link between the two original provisions that we started with:

the secretary of state may grant a certificate of naturalisation
to a person by section 6.1
if   the person applies for naturalisation
and   the person is of full age and capacity
and   the secretary of state believes the person fulfils
*   the requirements of schedule 1 for naturalisation by 6.1*
and   the secretary of state thinks fit
*   to grant the person a certificate of naturalisation.*

the secretary of state believes a person fulfils
*   the requirements of schedule 1 for naturalisation by 6.1*
if   the secretary of state believes that
*   the person fulfils the residency requirements of subparagraph 1.1.2*
and the secretary of state believes that the person is of good character
and the secretary of state believes that
*   the person has sufficient knowledge of english, welsh, or scottish gaelic*
and the secretary of state believes that
*   the person has sufficient knowledge about life in the uk*
and the secretary of state believes that
*   the person intends to make his principal home in the uk*
*   in the event of being granted naturalisation.*

To solve the problem left over from Chapter 6, it suffices to replace the term *believes* by the phrase *is satisfied that*.

A more flexible way to satisfy the Secretary of State

I would not blame you if you did not find these arguments entirely convincing. You might think, for example, that the Secretary of State should be more flexible, allowing for example a strong belief that a person has good character to compensate for a weak belief that the person has sufficient knowledge of English, Welsh or Scottish Gaelic. Fortunately, meta-logic makes it possible to represent such more flexible ways of judging whether a conjunction of conditions implies a conclusion. For example, we could replace the two meta-beliefs $meta_1$ and $meta_2$ by:

$meta_1'$:   *an agent believes P*
          if the agent believes (P if Q)
          and the agent believes Q with strength S
          and S > t.
$meta_2'$:   *an agent believes (P and Q) with strength S*
          if the agent believes P with strength S_P

and the agent believes Q with strength S_Q
and $S_P + S_Q = S$.

If you are familiar with neural networks of the brain, you will see a resemblance between such networks and meta$_1'$ and meta$_2'$. The condition $S > t$ is similar to the requirement that, for a neuron to fire, the strength of the inputs to the neuron must exceed a certain threshold t. The sum $S_P + S_Q = S$ corresponds to summing the strengths of all the inputs of a neuron. The neural network analogy could be pursued further, by associating weights with the conditions P and Q. So for example, having good character might have greater weight than the ability to speak one of the native British languages.

At first sight, meta$_1'$ and meta$_2'$ may seem a long way from a represention of Computational Logic as the language of an agent's thoughts. But bear in mind that an implementation of the connection graph proof procedure needs a strategy for activating links. Meta$_1'$ and meta$_2'$ can be thought of as an approximate representation of the best-first strategy sketched in Chapters 4 and A5. But in any case, they show the power of a meta-logic without an explicit notion of strength of belief to represent an object-level logic in which strength of belief is explicit.

The two wise men

In this example, we will investigate a more impressive use of meta-logic to simulate the thinking of another agent, to solve a problem that cannot be solved by object-level thinking alone.

The problem is usually formulated with a king and three wise men. To simplify the problem and to bring it up-to-date, we will consider a queen and two wise men version of the story. To avoid any embarassment to Mary, John and Bob, we will refer to the participants in the story simply as "the Queen", "wise man one" and "wise man two":

> There are two wise men. Both of them have mud on their face. Each can see the mud on the other wise man's face, but not the mud on his own. The Queen tells them both that at least one of them has mud on his face. After a short pause, the first wise man announces that he does not know whether he has mud on his face. The second wise man, who knows how to do meta-level reasoning, then declares that he knows that he has mud on his face.

Wise man two can solve the problem by reasoning in two steps as follows:

Step 1: Wise man one knows that he has mud on his face
        or I have mud on my face.
        So if wise man one can see that I do not have mud on my face,
        then he would know that he has mud on his own face.

Step 2: Since wise man one does not know that he has mud on his face,
he does not see that I do not have mud on my face, and
therefore he must see that I do have mud on my face.

This kind of reasoning is a little more complicated than it may seem, partly because it involves reasoning about knowing and seeing. But "seeing is believing", and "knowing" is a special case of "believing" too. So the solution can be reformulated in terms of belief. Here is a connection graph representation of the reasoning involved in step 1 formulated in terms of belief:

$meta_3$: *an agent believes P*
if the agent believes (P or Q) and the agent believes (not Q).

$wise_1$: *wise man one believes*
(wise man one has mud on his face
or wise man two has mud on his face).

$meta_4$: *an agent believes (not Q)*
if the agent observes whether Q and not(Q holds).

$wise_2$: *wise man one observes whether*
(wise man two has mud on his face).

Step 1 can be broken down into two substeps. The first substep performs forward reasoning with $wise_1$ and $wise_2$, which in effect replaces $meta_3$ by $meta_3{'}$ and $meta_4$ by $meta_4{'}$:

$meta_3{'}$: *wise man one believes wise man one has mud on his face*
if wise man one believes (not wise man two has mud on his face).

$meta_4{'}$: *wise man one believes (not wise man two has mud on his face)*
if not wise man two has mud on his face.

The second substep, which activates the link between $meta_3{'}$ and $meta_4{'}$, is a kind of forward reasoning with an assumption:

---

result of step 1: *wise man one believes wise man one has mud on his face*
if not wise man two has mud on his face.

Step 2 connects the result of reasoning in step 1 with wise man one's assertion that he does not know whether he has mud on his face. Expressed in terms of belief, this assertion has two subparts: He doesn't believe that he has mud on his face, and he doesn't believe that he does not have mud on his face. Only the first subpart is relevant to the solution:

wise$_0$:   *if wise man one believes wise man one has mud on his face*
               then false.

result of step 1: *wise man one believes wise man one has mud on his face*
                       if not wise man two has mud on his face.

result of step 2: *if not wise man two has mud on his face then false.*

The result of step 2 is equivalent to:

conclusion: *wise man two has mud on his face.*

The equivalence can be justified either as reasoning with the totality constraint *not wise man two has mud on his face **or** wise man two has mud on his face* of Chapters A4 and A6 or as using the negation rewriting rule (replace *if not P then false by P*) of Chapter A6.

The connection graph solution above is presented in the style of a typical mathematical proof, rather than in the style of the general pattern of reasoning within the agent cycle.

To present the solution as an instance of the general pattern, we need an observation to trigger the pattern. Actually, in this example, there are two observations, the Queen's assertion that one of the wise men has mud on his face, and wise man one's assertion that he does not know whether he has mud on his face. For simplicity, let's ignore the first observation, since it doesn't really lead anywhere (for the same reason that wise man one says that he doesn't know whether he has mud on his face).

Let's focus instead on wise man two's response to the second observation, expressed as the positive atomic sentence:

wise$_{-1}$: *wise man one asserts I do not know whether*
           (wise man one has mud on his face).

Whereas in the connection graph solution we took the negative conclusion:

$wise_0$: *if wise man one believes wise man one has mud on his face then false.*

as our starting point, now we need to derive the negative conclusion $wise_0$ from the positive observation $wise_{-1}$ using an appropriate constraint (similar to the derivation in the selection task in Chapter 16).

Intuitively, wise man two is justified in deriving the negative conclusion from the positive observation, if wise man two believes that wise man one's asssertion can be trusted. This belief can be represented at different levels of abstraction. Here is a fairly concrete representation of the belief that wise man one is trustworthy:

$wise_{-2}$: *if wise man one asserts I do not know whether P*
   and wise man one believes P then false.

Obviously, this belief could be derived from more general beliefs, for example from a more general belief that all wise men are trustworthy.

We can now present wise man two's solution of the problem as a special case of the general pattern:

Observation, $wise_{-1}$: *wise man one asserts I do not know whether*
    (wise man one has mud on his face).

Forward reasoning with $wise_{-2}$:

$wise_0$: *if wise man one believes wise man one has mud on his face then false.*

Backward reasoning with $meta_3$ to verify the other condition of $wise_{-2}$:

   if ((wise man one believes wise man one has mud on his face) or Q)
   and wise man one believes (not Q) then false.

Backward reasoning with $wise_1$:

   if wise man one believes (not wise man two has mud on his face)
   then false.

Backward reasoning with $meta_4$:

   if wise man one observes whether wise man two has mud on his face)
   and not wise man two has mud on his face then false.

Backward reasoning with $wise_2$:

   if not wise man two has mud on his face then false.

Or equivalently:

   wise man two has mud on his face.

This solution is an instance of the general pattern, used not to derive a plan of actions to solve an achievement goal, generated by the triggering of a main-tenance goal, but to generate an explanation of an observation. In this instance, the general pattern generates *wise man two has mud on his face* as an explanation of the observation *wise man one asserts I do not know whether (wise man one has mud on his face)*.

Combining object-language and meta-language

You may not have noticed that I cheated you. The three examples in this chapter are not represented strictly in meta-logic alone, but rather in a combination of object-language and meta-language. For example, the sentence:

mary is impressed with a person
if mary believes the person is well-bred.

combines an object-level conclusion with a meta-level condition. This combination makes for a much more expressive language than an object or meta-language alone. It is made much simpler by using an ambivalent syntax.

But not all applications of meta-logic can benefit from the simplifications of ambivalent syntax. Some applications of meta-logic only make sense if the distinction between using sentences and mentioning them is made explicit in the syntax. The usual way of doing this in English is to use quotation marks. But it is also possible to name sentences and other syntactic entities by constant symbols and other expressions, like meta$_1$ – meta$_5$, as is common in mathematics.

The use of constants to name sentences makes it possible for sentences to refer to themselves. The most famous self-referential sentence is the *liar paradox*:

This sentence: *This sentence is false.*

The sentence is a paradox, because if it is *true*, then it is *false*, and if it is *false*, then it is *true*.

In formal logic, a common solution to such paradoxes is to ban self-referential sentences completely. But most self-referential sentences are completely innocuous. For example:

This sentence: *This sentence contains 37 characters.*

is *true* if you count spaces, and is *false* if you do not.

In fact, banning self-referential sentences would outlaw one of the most important theorems of mathematics and logic of all time, Gödel's Incompleteness Theorem. The proof of the theorem constructs a true, but unprovable, self-referential sentence of the form:

This sentence cannot be proved.

In Gödel's construction, sentences and other syntactic expressions, including proofs, are named by a numerical code. It is because names are represented by numbers that sentences about numbers can refer to themselves.

A number of commentators, including most notably J.R. Lucas (1959) and Roger Penrose (1989), in his prize-winning book, have argued that the Incompleteness Theorem implies that people are not machines, because they can recognise true sentences that a machine cannot prove. According to Hao Wang (1974), Gödel himself also held similar views.

However, it seems that most logicians and philosophers disagree with this interpretation of the Incompleteness Theorem. Stewart Shapiro (1989), for example, points out that, given any constructible set of axioms of arithmetic to which Gödel's theorem applies, the construction of the true, but unprovable sentence is entirely mechanical. This sentence could be added to the axioms, but then there would be a new, true, but unprovable sentence, which could also be added to the axioms. This process of constructing and adding true, but previously unprovable sentences can be continued *ad infinitum*, and beyond (Feferman, 1962).

Conclusions and further reading

The combination of object-logic and meta-logic is a powerful knowledge representation and problem-solving tool, which can be used by computers and humans alike. In Computing, it is used routinely to implement more powerful object-languages in simpler meta-languages. In human thinking, it allows people to reflect upon their own thoughts and to simulate the thinking of other people.

The combination of object-logic and meta-logic is also the key to the proof of the Incompleteness Theorem. The theorem shows that by looking at an object language, arithmetic in this case, from the perspective of the meta-language, it is possible to solve problems that cannot be solved in the object-language alone.

The formal underpinnings of meta-logic and its combination with object-logic in a logic programming setting are surveyed in Perlis and Subrahmanian (1994), Hill and Gallagher (1998) and Costantini (2002). Gillies (1996) discusses the significance of Gödel's theorem for the question of whether humans can solve problems that are not solvable by machines.

Conclusions of the book

I have made a case for a comprehensive, logic-based theory of human intelligence, drawing upon and reconciling a number of otherwise competing paradigms in Artificial Intelligence and other fields. The most important of these paradigms are production systems, logic programming, classical logic and decision theory.

Unification of competing paradigms

The production system cycle, suitably extended, provides the bare bones of the theory: the observe–think–decide–act agent cycle. It also provides some of the motivation for identifying an agent's maintenance goals as the driving force of the agent's life.

Logic programming opens the door to abductive logic programming, in which beliefs are expressed as conditionals in logic programming form, and goals are expressed in a variant of the clausal form of classical logic. Open predicates represent the interface between thoughts in the agent's mind and things in the external world.

The agent interacts with the external world through its observations, which it assimilates into its web of goals and beliefs, and through the actions it attempts to execute. Decision theory provides the agent with a normative theory for deciding between alternative actions, taking into account the uncertainty and the utility of their expected outcomes. It also provides a bridge to more practical decision-making methods.

In addition to these main paradigms explicitly contributing to the logic-based agent model, other paradigms support the model implicitly.

Relationships with other paradigms

In Computing, the agent model receives support, not only from logic programming, deductive databases and default reasoning, but also from moderate forms of object-orientation. Whereas in extreme object-orientation objects interact only by sending and receiving messages, in moderate forms, objects are like agents that interact with one another through the medium of a shared environment.

However, the agent model receives its greatest support from paradigms outside Computing. Most of these paradigms, like Williams' (1990, 1995) guidelines for good writing style, Checkland's (2000) soft systems methodology, Hammond *et al.*'s (1999) *Smart Choices* and Baron's (2008) characterisation of thinking as search plus inference, are informal theories, which are compatible with the more formal logic-based agent model.

The agent model has also been influenced both by formal and informal theories of legal reasoning. This is most obvious in relation to rule-based theories, which hold that rule-based law promotes consistency, transparency and replicability. Legal rules share with logical conditionals the properties that rules need not be fully specified, may be subject to exceptions, and may hold only by default.

In legal reasoning and many other fields, rule-based reasoning operates in tandem with case-based reasoning. Although the two kinds of reasoning may seem to be conflicting paradigms, it can be argued that they are complementary. For one thing, rules are often generated by induction from cases. For another thing, rules are refined by evaluating their application in particular cases, and modifying them if their consequences are judged to be inappropriate. The conditional form of rules facilitates their modification, because unacceptable conclusions can be withdrawn by adding extra conditions, and missing conclusions can be added by adding extra rules.

This process of using cases to generate and modify rules is the basic technique of inductive logic programming (Muggleton and De Raedt, 1994), which is a branch of machine learning in Artificial Intelligence. Donald Gillies (1996) argues that the achievements of inductive logic programming in such applications as generating expert systems and discovering laws of protein structure have significant implications for the problem of induction in the philosophy of science.

Unfortunately, I have neglected this aspect of Computational Logic, as well as other important areas. In particular, although I have touched upon the need to integrate judgements of uncertainty into the decision-making component of the agent cycle, I have not explored the broader relationships between Computational Logic and Probability Theory. Much of the work in this area combines probabilistic reasoning with inductive logic programming. De Raedt *et al.* (2008) contains a survey of representative work in this active research area.

The other major area that I have neglected is the relationship between Computational Logic, neural networks and other connectionist models of the brain. Although I have suggested a connectionist interpretation of connection graphs, most of the work in this area has concerned the relationship between logic programming and neural networks, starting with Hölldobler and Kalinke (1994) and including d'Avila Garcez *et al.* (2001) and Stenning and van Lambalgen (2008). A good overview of the challenges in this area can be found in Bader *et al.* (2006).

The list of such topics goes on for longer than I can continue, and it has to stop somewhere. But before finishing, I would like to mention briefly one more area, which is too important to leave out, and where Computational Logic may be able to contribute.

Conflict resolution

We have seen that conflicts can arise when a single agent needs to make a choice between two or more actions or goals: The crow wants to eat the cheese and sing at the same time. The louse wants to eat and look for a mate. Bob wants to stay friends with John, but stay out of jail. This kind of conflict within a single agent is the source of conflict resolution in production systems and the bread and butter of decision theory.

Conflict resolution is important enough when there is only one individual involved, but it can be much more important when it involves two or more agents: The man with the rucksack wants to blow up the train, but the passengers want to stay alive. The fox wants to have the crow's cheese, but the crow wants to eat it himself. Bob wants to stay out of jail by turning witness against John, and John wants to stay out of jail by turning witness against Bob.

We have seen in the example of the Prisoner's Dilemma that conflicts among several agents can be treated as a conflict for a single agent who cares as much about other agents as he cares about himself. The application of decision theory to this case is a form of utilitarianism: The greatest good for the greatest number of people.

But unbridled utilitarianism does nothing to protect an individual agent or a minority of agents from having their interests violated by the majority. The protection of individual and minority rights requires constraints, which prevent the maximisation of utility from getting out of hand. We saw how such constraints might operate in the example of the runaway trolley in Chapter 12.

The Computational Logic agent model combines both constraints on individual actions and conflict resolution for deciding between alternative actions. But it also provides opportunities for conflict resolution at the higher levels of an agent's hierarchy of goals. If a conflict cannot be resolved at the action level, it may be possible to resolve the conflict by finding an alternative way of solving goals at a higher level, and of reducing those goals to new alternative actions that no longer create a conflict. The greater the number of levels in the hierarchy and the greater the number of alternative ways of reducing goals to subgoals, the more opportunities there are to avoid and resolve potential conflicts.

This hierarchy of goals and subgoals is determined by the agent's beliefs. Whether or not these beliefs actually help the agent to achieve its goals depends on whether or not they are really true. The greater the number of true beliefs, the greater the number of alternative ways the agent can try to achieve its goals and avoid conflict with other agents.

An agent obtains its beliefs from different sources. Some of these beliefs may be hardwired into the agent from birth; but others, perhaps most, are obtained through personal experience and from communications with other agents. But different agents have different experiences, which lead to different beliefs, which can lead to conflicts between agents even when they have the same top-level goals. Therefore, conflicts can often be reconciled by reconciling different beliefs, acknowledging that they may explain different experiences.

This book has been an attempt to reconcile different paradigms for explaining and guiding human behaviour, most notably to reconcile production systems, logic programming, classical logic and decision theory. To the extent that it has succeeded, it may exemplify the broader potential of Computational Logic to help reconcile conflicts in other areas.

A1
The syntax of logical form

The language of Computational Logic used in this book is an informal and simplified form of Symbolic Logic. Until now, it has also been somewhat vague and imprecise. This additional chapter is intended to specify the language more precisely. It does not affect the mainstream of the book, and the reader can either leave it out altogether, or come back to it later.

Atoms

In all varieties of logic, the basic building block is the *atomic formula* or *atom* for short. In the same way that an atom in physics can be viewed as a collection of electrons held together by a nucleus, atoms in logic are collections of *terms*, like "train", " driver" and "station", held together by *predicate symbols*, like "in" or "stop". Predicate symbols are like verbs in English, and terms are like nouns or noun phrases.

Where we have been writing informally:

the driver stops the train

in Symbolic Logic, this would normally be written in the form:

stop(driver, train)

Here the predicate symbol is written first, followed by the atom's terms, which are called its *arguments*, surrounded by parentheses and separated by commas. Each predicate symbol has a standard number of arguments, written in some fixed but arbitrary order. Here the predicate symbol *stop* has two arguments, with its subject *driver* first and its object *train* second.

The advantage of the symbolic form of logic for writing atoms is that it unambiguously distinguishes between the atom's predicate symbol and its

231

arguments, and moreover it identifies the different roles (such as subject or object) of its arguments by their positions inside the parentheses. It is this precision that makes Symbolic Logic suitable for processing by computer.

However, this advantage is bought at the cost of having to over-specify an atom's components. For example, an equally legitimate representation of the sentence *the driver stops the train* is the atomic formula:

happens(stop, driver, train)

This alternative representation treats *stop* as a term rather than as a predicate symbol. It is also possible, although not very useful, to represent the same sentence with a predicate symbol having zero arguments, say as *happens-stop-driver-train()* written more simply as *happens-stop-driver-train*. In fact, the representation that is closest to the intended, underlying meaning of the English sentence is a collection of atomic sentences:

happens(event-0014)
type(event-0014, stop)
agent(event-0014, 007)
object(event-0014, the-flying-scotsman)
isa(007, train-driver)
isa(the-flying-scotsman, train)

This representation makes explicit that the driver *007* is a unique individual, and that the train is a specific train with its own unique identification *the-flying-scotsman*. Even the event itself is a unique event, with an identifier *event-0014* that distinguishes it from other events in which the same driver stops the same train on other occasions.

Although such representations are rather cumbersome by comparison with English sentences, they are often necessary in computer implementations of logic, where the distinctions they make are unavoidable. Arguably, the same distinctions are unavoidable also in a human agent's language of thought.

The informal representation we use in most of the book has the advantage that it hides the underlying complexity involved in such precise representations. However, the reader should be aware that, to represent the intended meaning of seemingly simple English sentences, they would normally need to be translated into the more precise kind of representation illustrated here.

Predicate symbols

Predicate symbols can have zero, one or more arguments. Atomic formulas whose predicate symbol has zero arguments are sometimes called *propositional formulas*. This includes the two special atoms *true* and *false*. The special case of Symbolic Logic, in which all atoms are propositional formulas, is called *propositional logic*. The more general case, in which predicate symbols can have any number of arguments, is called *predicate logic*.

Propositional formulas are sentences that denote *propositions*. Predicate symbols with one argument denote *properties* of individuals, and predicate symbols with more than one argument denote *relations* between individuals. This distinction between propositions, properties and relations is significant in ordinary natural language, but is an unnecessary and unwelcome complication in Mathematics. It is simpler and more convenient to refer to all three notions as *relations*, which may hold between zero, one or more individuals. Thus, with this terminology, we can say simply that *predicate symbols denote* (or *represent*) *relations*.

However, not all relations need to be represented by predicate symbols. Relations can also be represented by *predicates* that are compound syntactic expressions constructed from simpler expressions by joining them with logical connectives like "and", "or", "not" and "if". For example, the property of being tall and handsome can be denoted by a predicate, say *tall(X) and handsome(X)*, which need not be expressed by a separate predicate symbol. We will often find it convenient to speak of such predicates, without implying that they are expressed by predicate symbols.

Denotation is a semantic relationship between symbols and the objects those symbols represent. It is one of the great achievements of Symbolic Logic, envied even by many of its critics, that it has a proper *semantics*. But before discussing semantics, we need to complete our discussion of *syntax*.

Terms

The simplest kind of term is a *constant*, like *007*, which denotes an *individual*, say the person born on 1 April, 2000 to parents Mary Smith and John Smith in Petworth, England. But terms also include *variables*, which stand for whole classes of individuals. It is common in Symbolic Logic to use letters, like X and Y for variables, as in the algebraic formula:

$$X + Y = Y + X$$

which holds for all numbers X and Y. In this book, we use the convention, borrowed from the logic programming language Prolog, that variables start with an upper-case letter, like X or Y, and constants and predicate symbols start with a lower-case letter.

More complex terms can be constructed from simpler terms, like *mother of X*, written *mother(X)*, or 2 + 3, written +(2, 3), where *mother* and + are *function symbols*. However, functions are a special case of relations, and therefore function symbols are, strictly speaking, unnecessary. Instead of writing, for example:

$$mother(cain) = eve$$
$$+(2,3) = 5$$

we can write :
$$mother(cain, eve)$$
$$+(2,3,5)$$

Representing functions as relations has the advantage that function symbols can be reserved for constructing names of individuals. Function symbols used in this way are sometimes called *Skolem functions*, in honour of the logician Thoralf Skolem.

Used for naming, function symbols make it possible to name an infinite number of individuals with a finite vocabulary. For example, in mathematical logic, it is common to name the *natural numbers* 0, 1, 2, ... by the terms 0, $s(0)$, $s(s(0))$, ... where the function symbol s is called the *successor function*. The term $s(X)$ is equivalent to $X + 1$. Using the successor function and representing the addition function as a relation, we can represent $2 + 3 = 5$ by:

$$+(s(s(0)), \ s(s(s(0))), \ s(s(s(s(s(0))))))$$

Not very pretty, but better suited for theoretical studies than the use of such alternative number systems as decimal, binary or Roman numerals.

Terms that contain no variables are called *ground terms*. They play a special role in the semantics, because they are the pool from which the names of individuals are drawn.

Conditionals

Strictly speaking, a *conditional* is a sentence of the form $A \rightarrow B$, where A and B are sentences. However, we use the term *conditional* more loosely to refer to sentences that may contain variables. Moreover, for the most part, we restrict attention to conditionals that can be written in either one of the two equivalent forms:

$$C_1 \wedge \ldots \wedge C_n \wedge \neg D_1 \wedge \ldots \wedge \neg D_m \rightarrow E$$

i.e. *if C_1 and ... and C_n and not D_1 and ... and not D_m then E*

$$E \leftarrow C_1 \wedge \ldots \wedge C_n \wedge \neg D_1 \wedge \ldots \wedge \neg D_m$$

i.e. *E if C_1 and ... and C_n and not D_1 and ... and not D_m*

where the *conclusion E* is an atomic formula, the *conditions C_i* are atomic formulas, and the *conditions $\neg D_j$* are the negations of atomic formulas. Such conditionals are also sometimes called *clauses*, and sets of such conditionals are also called *logic programs*.

As is common with mathematical definitions, the number of positive conditions *n* and the number of negative conditions *m* can be 0. If *m* is 0, then the conditional is called a *definite clause*.

Definite clauses are important for two reasons. First, they are adequate for representing any computable predicate. Second, as we will see in Chapter A2, they have a very simple semantics in terms of minimal models.

If the number of conditions *n+m* is 0, then the degenerate conditional $E\leftarrow$ (or $\rightarrow E$) is in effect just an atomic sentence, which is normally written without the arrow, simply as *E*.

The backward arrow $\leftarrow$ is read *if*, and the forward arrow $\rightarrow$ is read with the same meaning, but in the opposite direction. The symbol $\wedge$ is used for the logical connective *and*. Expressions connected by $\wedge$ are called *conjunctions*.

Predicate symbols and constant symbols appearing in different clauses are the external glue that links different clauses together. Variables are another kind of glue internal to clauses. For example, the variable *X* in the clause:

$$amazing(X) \leftarrow can\text{-}fly(X)$$

has the effect of expressing that *anything that can fly is amazing*. In contrast, the two variables in the clause:

$$amazing(X) \leftarrow can\text{-}fly(Y)$$

have the effect of expressing that *if something can fly then everything is amazing*!

Variables in clauses are consequently said to be *universally quantified within the scope of the clause in which they appear*. In Symbolic Logic the quantification of variables is normally written explicitly with symbols $\forall$ standing for *for all* and $\exists$ standing for *there exists*, and the scope of the quantifiers is indicated by parentheses. Thus the two conditionals above would be written:

$$\forall X\,(amazing(X) \leftarrow can\text{-}fly(X))$$
$$\forall X\,\forall Y\,(amazing(X) \leftarrow can\text{-}fly(Y))$$

Because all variables appearing in clauses are universally quantified and their scope is the entire clause, there is no ambiguity if the quantifiers are omitted.

Because conditionals can have no conditions, atomic sentences can also contain universally quantified variables. Here is a fanciful example:

$$likes(bob, X)$$

Atomic sentences that do not contain such variables are also called *facts*.

In the simplest versions of Symbolic Logic, variables like X and Y can refer to any kind of individual. So, for example, the clause *amazing(X)* ← *can-fly(X)* implies that if a rock can fly then the rock is amazing. Similarly, the mathematical equation $X + Y = Y + X$, if it were written in logical notation, would imply that you could add two rocks together in either order and the result would be the same.

To overcome the unnatural use of unrestricted variables, *sorted* or *typed logics* have been developed, in which variables are restricted, so that they refer only to individuals in designated classes, which are called *sorts* or *types*. A similar effect can be obtained more tediously in unsorted logic by including for every variable in a clause an extra condition whose predicate expresses the sort of that variable.

For example, to state that any animal that can fly is amazing, we would need to write in unsorted logic, say:

$$amazing(X) \leftarrow can\text{-}fly(X) \wedge animal(X)$$

To conclude that any person who can fly is amazing, we would need a clause expressing that all people are animals:

$$animal(X) \leftarrow person(X)$$

Or as adherents of object-orientation in computing (see Chapter 14) would prefer us to say, the class of all people *inherits* the property of flying from the more abstract class of all animals.

In the informal version of Computational Logic that we use in this book, not only do we omit universal quantifiers, but we also sometimes express unsorted variables by words like *anything* and *everything* and sorted variables by common nouns, like *an animal, a station,* or *a bird*. The virtue of this informal usage is that it is neutral with respect to whether it is formalised in some version of sorted logic or formalised in unsorted logic with explicit predicates for sorts. So, for example, instead of writing:

$$\forall X (amazing(X) \leftarrow can\text{-}fly(X) \wedge animal(X))$$

we simply write:

if an animal can fly then the animal is amazing
or   *any animal that can fly is amazing.*

Moreover, the informal version is compatible with other formal representations, such as:

$$amazing(X) \leftarrow can\text{-}fly(X) \wedge isa(X, animal)$$
$$isa(X, animal) \leftarrow isa(X, person)$$

Recursive definitions

Conditionals are often used to define predicates. For example, here is a definition of the predicate *natural-number*:

$$natural\text{-}number(0)$$
$$natural\text{-}number(s(X)) \leftarrow natural\text{-}number(X)$$

The definition is said to be *recursive*, because the predicate *natural-number* defined in the conclusion of the second sentence recurs in the conditions (and vice versa). The ability to express recursive definitions gives conditionals the full power of a general-purpose programming language.

Here is a recursive definition of addition:

$$+ (0, Y, Y)$$
$$+ (s(X), Y, s(Z)) \leftarrow + (X, Y, Z)$$

For simplicity, I have omitted the qualifying conditions that X, Y and Z are natural numbers. In functional notation, the definition is much simpler and looks like this:

$$0 + Y = Y$$
$$s(X) + Y = s(X + Y)$$

This can also be written in the even simpler form $(X + 1) + Y = (X + Y) + 1$. But this is misleading, because the plus sign $+$ in the expression $+ 1$ is different from the plus sign $+$ for example in $(X + Y)$. I will have more to say about the relationship between functions and relations a little later in this chapter.

Goal clauses

In Computational Logic, we use conditionals (including facts and other atomic sentences) to represent beliefs, all of whose variables are universally quantified. In addition, we use conjunctions to represent goals whose variables are all existentially quantified.

In general, a *goal clause* is an existentially quantified conjunction of atoms and negations of atoms:

$$\exists X_1 \ldots \exists X_m (C_1 \wedge \ldots \wedge C_n \wedge \neg D_1 \wedge \ldots \wedge \neg D_m)$$

i.e.   *there exists X_1 ... and there exists X_m such that*
C_1 and ... and C_n and not D_1 and ... and not D_m

If m is 0, then the *goal clause* is called a *definite goal clause*.

Because all variables in a goal clause are existentially quantified within the scope of the goal clause in which they occur, it is normal to omit the explicit use of existential quantifiers. For example, the goal clause:

$$likes(bob, X)$$

stands for $\exists\, X\, likes(bob, X)$

Such existentially quantified goal clauses are sufficient for representing an agent's achievement goals. However, as we will see in greater detail later, they are not sufficient for representing maintenance goals and constraints.

Both definite clauses (including atomic sentences) and definite goal clauses are also called *Horn clauses* after the logician Alfred Horn, who studied some of their mathematical properties. Horn clauses are equivalent in power to Turing Machines, which are the standard mathematical model of mechanical computation.

In logic programming, *goal clauses* represent the computation to be performed. For example, the goal clause:

$$+(s(s(0)),\ s(s(0)), X) \wedge +(X, Y,\ s(s(s(s(s(0))))))$$

represents the problem of computing the sum X of 2 plus 2 and computing a number Y that added to X gives 5.

Other kinds of sentences

Conditionals, used to represent beliefs, and goal clauses, used to represent achievement goals, have a very simple syntax. However, conditionals are logically equivalent to more complex sentences in the syntax of classical logic. Here are some examples of such equivalences:

$$\forall X\, \forall Y\, (amazing(X) \leftarrow can\text{-}fly(Y))$$

is equivalent to: $\forall X\, (amazing(X) \leftarrow \exists\, Y\, can\text{-}fly(Y))$

$$amazing(X) \leftarrow can\text{-}fly(X)$$
$$amazing(X) \leftarrow movie\text{-}star(X)$$

are equivalent to: $amazing(X) \leftarrow (can\text{-}fly(X) \vee movie\text{-}star(X))$

$$generous\text{-}to(X, Z) \leftarrow likes(X, Y) \wedge gives(X, Y, Z)$$

is equivalent to: $(generous\text{-}to(X, Z) \leftarrow likes(X, Y)) \leftarrow gives(X, Y, Z)$

The symbol $\vee$ is used for the logical connective *or*. Expressions connected by $\vee$ are called *disjunctions*. In general, a *disjunction* has the form:

$$C_1 \vee \ldots \vee C_n$$

i.e. $C_1\ or\ \ldots\ or\ C_n$

We will see later that, in addition to allowing the use of existential quantifiers and disjunctions, it is useful to extend the syntax of conditional logic to represent more complex goals and beliefs. In particular, it is useful to include existential quantifiers and disjunctions in the conclusions of maintenance goals. For example:

Maintenance goals: $hungry(me) \rightarrow \exists X \, eat(me, X)$

$attacks(X, me) \rightarrow runaway(me) \lor attacks(me, X)$

Existential quantifiers in the conclusions of conditional goals are so common that it is convenient to omit them, with the convention that variables in the conclusion of a conditional goal that are not in the conditions of the goal are existentially quantified, with scope the conclusion of the goal. For example:

Maintenance goal: $hungry(me) \rightarrow eat(me, X)$

The inclusion of disjunctions in the conclusions of conditionals gives the logic of conditionals the power of *classical logic*. We shall have more to say about the relationship between the logic of conditionals and classical logic in Chapter A2. We focus on the conditional form of logic in this book, because it is easier for both computers and humans to understand.

Arguably, the relationship between classical logic and the logic of conditionals is like the relationship between the language of human communication and the language of human thought. One way to understand this relationship is to view reasoning as involving two kinds of inference rules, applied in two stages. The first kind of rule, applied in the first stage, translates complicated sentences into simpler sentences. The second kind, applied in the second stage, reasons with the resulting simpler sentences.

This two-stage reasoning process is used in many of the proof procedures developed for classical logic in computing. In systems based on the resolution principle (Robinson, 1965a) in particular, the first stage translates sentences of classical logic into *clausal form*. The second stage processes clauses using refinements of the resolution rule of inference. We discuss the resolution principle in the additional Chapter A5.

Understanding human communications in natural language can be viewed as a similar two-stage process. The first stage translates (or compiles) sentences of natural language into simpler sentences in the language of thought. The second stage processes these simpler sentences using rules of inference, like forward and backward reasoning, which are simple cases of resolution. The closer the natural language sentences are to the language of thought, the less effort is needed to translate those sentences into the language of thought, and the easier it is to understand them.

Negation

In classical logic, negative and positive sentences have the same status. *To be or not to be* – there is no reason to prefer one to the other. But in Computational Logic, positive sentences are more basic than negative sentences, and negative sentences typically just fill in the gaps between positive sentences. This more basic status of positive sentences is reflected in the syntax of conditionals, which normally have only positive conclusions, but may have negative conditions ¬ *C* (also written *not C*), for example:

$$liable\text{-}to\text{-}penalty(X) \leftarrow press\text{-}alarm(X) \land not\ emergency$$
$$can\text{-}fly(X) \leftarrow bird(X) \land not\ penguin(X)$$

As we have seen in Chapter 5 and elsewhere, it is natural to conclude that a negative condition *not C* holds if the corresponding positive condition *C* fails to hold. This interpretation of negation is called *negation as failure*. So given a situation in which we are told *bird(john)*, but have no reason to believe *penguin(john)*, it follows by negation as failure that *can-fly(john)*.

Here is a definition of the odd and even numbers, using only positive conclusions and a negative condition:

$$even(0)$$
$$even(s(s(X))) \leftarrow even(X)$$
$$odd(X) \leftarrow not\ even(X)$$

Because it cannot be shown that *even(s(0))*, it follows from these clauses and negation as failure that *odd(s(0))*.

In addition to negative conditions interpreted by negation as failure, negative sentences can have the form of *constraints*, which are conditional goals with conclusion *false*. For example, in the context of an agent monitoring its candidate actions, the constraint:

$$liable\text{-}to\text{-}penalty(X) \rightarrow false$$
i.e.   *Do not be liable to a penalty*

functions as a prohibition, which prevents actions, like your pressing the alarm signal button improperly or your failing to pay your taxes, that are liable to a penalty.

Moreover, as we have seen in Chapter 10, a constraint, such as:

$$even(X) \land odd(X) \rightarrow false$$
i.e.   *Nothing is both odd and even*

which is a property of the definitions of the even and odd numbers, can be used to eliminate candidate explanations of observations.

We will see later that both kinds of negation (negation as failure and constraints) have the same semantics as negation in classical logic. However, they perform different functions in knowledge representation and reasoning.

Functions, relations and equality

In this book, we use function symbols sparingly, only to construct composite names of individuals. Other kinds of functions are treated as relations (or predicates), as in relational databases. Instead of writing $f(X) = Y$, where f is a function symbol, we write $f(X, Y)$, where f is a predicate (or relation) symbol. In this relational representation, the fact that the relation is a function is represented by the constraint:

$$f(X, Y_1) \wedge f(X, Y_2) \rightarrow Y_1 = Y_2$$

We combine this relational representation of functions with a simple notion of equality, understood as identity, and defined by the simple axiom:

$$X = X$$

This representation, of functions as relations and of equality as identity, works well only if individuals have unique names. Thus, for example, it's not good enough to say *bob stops the train* if the same person is also called *robert* and if more than one person is also called *bob*. We have to give *bob* a unique name, *007* for example, and say something like:

> *stops(007, the train)*
> *first-name(007, bob)*
> *first-name(007, robert)*
> *first-name(008, bob)*

Similar considerations apply to the name of the train, of course, and maybe to the name of the event, as we saw earlier in this chapter.

The definition of equality as identity, means that two individuals are identical if and only if they have the same unique name. This contrasts with the more conventional notion of equality, in which the same individual can have several names. For example:

> *the morning star = the evening star*
> *doctor jekyll = mister hyde*

To reason with equalities of this kind, it is normal to use additional axioms, such as the definite clauses:

$$X = X$$
$$f(X_1, \ldots, X_n) = f(Y_1, \ldots, Y_n) \leftarrow X_1 = Y_1 \land \ldots \land X_n = Y_n$$
$$p(X_1, \ldots, X_n) \leftarrow p(Y_1, \ldots, Y_n) \land X_1 = Y_1 \land \ldots \land X_n = Y_n$$

for every function symbol f and every predicate symbol p. However, reasoning with such axioms is computationally expensive. Moreover, their use needs to be exercised with caution, if we want to make such distinctions as:

$$good(doctor\ jekyll) \land bad(mister\ hyde)$$

Classical logic

The syntax of classical logic is an extension of the syntax of the conditional form of logic used in this book. Terms and atomic formulas in classical logic are the same as in the logic of conditionals. However, non-atomic sentences can be constructed using arbitrary combinations of the logical connectives $\rightarrow$, $\land$, $\lor$ and $\neg$, and the quantifiers $\forall$ and $\exists$.

Classical logic is less well-structured than the conditional form of logic. For example, in conditional form, there is only one way to express that *all birds can fly* and *John is a bird*, namely:

$$can\text{-}fly(X) \leftarrow bird(X)$$
$$bird(john)$$

But in classical logic, the same beliefs can be expressed in many logically equivalent ways, including:

$$\neg(\exists X((\neg can\text{-}fly(X) \land bird(X)) \lor \neg bird(john)))$$
$$\neg(\exists X((\neg can\text{-}fly(X) \lor \neg bird(john)) \land (bird(X) \lor \neg bird(john))))$$

To translate classical logic into the conditional form of logic, it is necessary to use such equivalence-preserving rules of inference as:

$$replace\ \neg\exists X \neg A\ by\ \forall X\,A$$
$$replace\ \neg A \lor \neg B\ by\ \neg(A \land B)$$
$$replace\ A \lor \neg B\ by\ A \leftarrow B$$

Classical logic and conditional logic differ also in their use of quantifiers. In conditional logic, all variables in conditionals are universally quantified, and all variables in goal clauses are existentially quantified, and therefore quantifiers can be ommitted. But in classical logic, all variables can be universally or existentially quantified, and therefore quantifiers need to be explicit.

In conditional logic, existential quantifiers are avoided by giving everything that exists a name, which is either a constant or a function symbol applied to other names. Instead of saying, for example, $\exists X \, bird(X)$, we say $bird(john)$ or $bird(007)$. We do so because giving individuals explicit names conveys more information. If you know that *john is a bird*, why conceal John's identity by saying only that *someone is a bird*, especially if you are talking to yourself in your own language of thought.

The relationship among classical logic, clausal logic and Computational Logic

Anything that can be said in classical logic can also be said in the conditional form of logic, but it has to be said using only universally quantified variables, and allowing disjunctions in the conclusions of conditionals. To be more precise, any sentence of classical logic can be translated into a set of *clauses* of the form:

$$C_1 \wedge \ldots \wedge C_n \rightarrow D_1 \vee \ldots \vee D_m$$

where each condition C_i and conclusion D_j is an atomic formula, and all variables in the clause are implicitly universally quantified with scope the entire clause. If n is 0, then $C_1 \wedge \ldots \wedge C_n$ is equivalent to *true*. If m is 0, then $D_1 \vee \ldots \vee D_m$ is equvalent to *false*.

Traditionally, such clauses are written in the logically equivalent form of universally quantified disjunctions (also called *clausal form*):

$$\neg C_1 \vee \ldots \vee \neg C_n \vee D_1 \vee \ldots \vee D_m$$

Although sentences of classical logic can always be translated into clausal form, the original sentence and its translation are not always logically equivalent. For example, the sentence $\forall X \, \exists Y \, (mother(X, Y) \leftarrow person(X))$ can be translated into the clause $mother(X, mom(X)) \leftarrow person(X)$. The clause uses a Skolem function to name names, and is in a sense more informative than the original sentence.

In theory, the use of Skolem functions to replace existential quantifiers entails the need to reason with equality. For example, $mom(cain) = eve$. However, such existential qualifiers typically occur in the conclusions of goals, rather than in beliefs. The proof procedure of Chapter A6 works with explicit existential quantifiers in the conclusions of goals. So the problems of reasoning with equality created by the use of Skolem functions seems not to arise much in practice.

In clausal logic, achievement goals are solved by *reductio ad absurdum*, assuming their negation and deriving *false* from the resulting set of clauses. For example, the negation of the achievement goal:

$$\exists X_1 \ldots \exists X_m (C_1 \wedge \ldots \wedge C_n)$$

is equivalent both to the (universally quantified) denial:

$$C_1 \wedge \ldots \wedge C_n \to false$$

and to the ordinary (universally quantified) clause:

$$\neg C_1 \vee \ldots \vee \neg C_n$$

Maintenance goals in clausal logic are solved in the same way, by converting their negation into clausal form and deriving *false*. However, because maintenance goals are universally quantified, their negations are existentially quantified, and these existential quantifiers need to be replaced by Skolem constants. For example, to solve the maintenance goal:

$$attacks(X, me) \to runaway(me) \vee attacks(me, X)$$

it is necessary to replace the variable X by a Skolem constant, say ☹, and convert the negation of the Skolemised conditional into the clauses:

$$attacks(☹, me)$$
$$\neg\, runaway(me)$$
$$\neg\, attacks(me, ☹)$$

If this way of solving maintenance goals succeeds (by deriving *false*), then it succeeds in solving them once and for all.

However, in this book, we solve maintenance goals differently, by showing that whenever their conditions are *true*, their conclusions are *true*. This alternative treatment of maintenance goals is discussed informally in Chapter 8 and formalised in Chapter A6.

This different treatment of maintenance goals reflects the fact that, neither classical logic nor clausal logic makes a fundamental distinction between goals and beliefs. In contrast, we distinguish between goals and beliefs, by employing a minor variant of clausal form for goals, and the closely related logic programming form:

$$C_1 \wedge \ldots \wedge C_n \wedge \ldots \neg D_1 \wedge \ldots \wedge \neg D_m \to E$$

or $\qquad\qquad E \leftarrow C_1 \wedge \ldots \wedge C_n \wedge \neg D_1 \wedge \ldots \wedge \neg D_m$

for beliefs. As mentioned before, the conclusions of goals (but not of beliefs) may contain both disjunctions and existentially quantified variables.

Somewhat confusingly, as is common in the literature, I use the term *clause* to refer either to clauses written as conditionals, to clauses written as disjunctions or to logic programming clauses. Perhaps even more confusingly, I use the term *conditional* both for clauses written as conditionals with disjunctive conclusions and for logic programming clauses. I also call the resulting combination of the two kinds of conditionals *the conditional form of logic*, as well as *the form of Computational Logic used in this book*. Hopefully, in most cases the context makes the intended meaning obvious.

Conclusions and further references

This whirlwind tour of the syntax of the conditional form of logic and its relationship with both the standard and clausal forms of classical logic has covered a lot of ground, but only touched the surface.

The conditional form of logic is as powerful as, but simpler than, the unstructured form of sentences in classical logic. The inference rules of the conditional form are also correspondingly simpler. The inference rules of classical logic are more complex, because in effect, in addition to the rules needed to reason with conditionals, they also include rules to translate sentences of classical logic into equivalent sentences in conditional form.

This distinction between the two kinds of inference rules in classical logic corresponds to the distinction between two kinds of reasoning in natural language. The inference rules needed to translate classical logic into conditionals corresponds to the reasoning needed to translate natural language into the LOT; and the inference rules needed to reason with conditionals corresponds to the reasoning needed in the LOT.

I have been supported in this view of the relationship between classical logic and conditional logic and between natural language and the LOT by the guidelines for good writing style given in such books as Williams' (1990, 1995). These guidelines, advocating clarity, simplicity and coherence, can be viewed as encouraging a writing style that minimises the difference between the syntax of natural-language communications and the representation of their meanings in the LOT.

The conditional form of logic evolved from the clausal form of logic, and the clausal form of logic evolved from standard classical logic. One of the earliest uses of clausal form was by Martin Davis and Hillary Putnam (1960) in one of the first mechanical proof procedures for classical logic. It was also used for the resolution rule developed by Alan Robinson (1965a).

The application of clausal form to knowledge representation and of resolution to problem solving was pioneered by Cordell Green (1969). However, the resolution theorem provers available at that time did not behave sensibly, and were vulnerable to attacks against the resolution-based approach by advocates of procedural, as opposed to declarative, representations of knowledge (Hewitt, 1971; Winograd, 1971, 1972).

In defence of clausal logic, Kowalski and Kuehner (1971) argued that SL-resolution, essentially a resolution interpretation of Loveland's (1968) model elimination proof procedure, could be understood procedurally in goal-reduction terms. In 1971 and 1972, I collaborated with Alain Colmerauer in Marseille, resulting in Colmerauer's development of Prolog in 1972, and in the procedural interpretation (Kowalski, 1974) of SLD-resolution, a variant of SL-resolution, applied to Horn clauses.

In *Logic for Problem Solving* (Kowalski, 1974, 1979), I argued more generally for the use of clausal form for knowledge representation and reasoning. A detailed analysis of the relationship between clausal logic and classical logic can be found in chapters 2 and 10 of that book. The combination in Computational Logic of clausal logic for goals and logic programming for beliefs comes from abductive logic programming (ALP) (Kakas *et al.*, 1998). The technical underpinnings of ALP are dealt with in Chapter A6.

A2
Truth

This additional chapter explores the semantics of classical logic and conditional logic. In classical logic, the semantics of a set of sentences S is determined by the set of all the interpretations (or semantic structures), called *models*, that make all the sentences in S true. The main concern of classical logic is with the notion of a sentence C being a *logical consequence* of S, which holds when C is true in all models of S.

Semantic structures in classical logic are arbitrary sets of individuals and relationships, which constitute the denotations of the symbols of the language in which sentences are expressed. In this chapter, I argue the case for restricting the specification of semantic structures to sets of atomic sentences, called *Herbrand interpretations*.

The semantics of conditionals, which we use in this book, inherits the semantics of classical logic, but also has a related minimal model semantics. This minimal model semantics associates with every definite clause program a unique minimal model, which has the property that a definite goal clause is true in all models of the program if and only if it is true in the minimal model.

I argue that, for definite clauses, truth in minimal models is more fundamental than truth in all models. I support the argument by observing that the standard model of arithmetic is the minimal model of a simple definite clause program defining addition and multiplication. According to Gödel's Incompleteness Theorem, truth in this minimal model can only be approximated by truth in all models of any computable set of axioms for arithmetic.

Truth and consequences

All variants of Symbolic Logic are formal systems, in which rules of inference are used to manipulate symbolic expressions and derive new symbolic

247

expressions without paying attention to their intended meaning. However, without any meaning, these expressions and their manipulations are not only meaningless, but useless.

In the case of an agent embedded in the real world, symbolic expressions in the agent's language of thought represent actual or potential situations in the world. Beliefs that are *true* in the world help the agent to anticipate the consequences of its actions and to achieve its goals. Goals that the agent can realistically make *true* in the world help the agent to maintain a harmonious relationship with the world and to change the world for its own benefit. Rules of inference, which manipulate thoughts and which derive new thoughts from existing thoughts, help the agent to derive logical consequences of its goals, beliefs and hypotheses, and guide its interactions with the world.

In classical logic, the notion of *logical consequence* provides the criterion for judging whether or not a set of inference rules performs its intended function:

> A sentence *C* is a *logical consequence* of a set of sentences *S*
> (or *S logically implies C*) if (and only if) *C* is *true* whenever *S* is *true*.

> A set of inference rules is *sound* (or *truth-preserving*) if (and only if)
> whenever it derives a sentence *C* from a set of sentences *S*,
> then *C* is a *logical consequence* of *S*.

> A set of inference rules is *complete* if (and only if) whenever a sentence *C* is a
> *logical consequence* of a set of sentences *S*, then there exists a derivation, by
> means of the inference rules, of *C* from *S*.

These concepts of *logical consequence*, *soundness* and *completeness* depend upon the notion of *truth*, which applies only to well-formed formulas that are sentences. A *well-formed formula* is an expression constructed from atomic formulas using the logical connectives →, ∧, ∨ and ¬, and the universal quantifiers ∀ and ∃. A *sentence* is a well-formed formula all of whose variables are explicitly or implicitly quantified using the quantifiers ∀ and ∃.

The notion of truth is *relative* to an interpretation of the symbols of the language in which the sentences are expressed. An *interpretation* is a collection of *individuals* (called the *domain of discourse*), which are the *denotations* (or *meanings*) of the constants and other ground terms of the language, together with a set of *relations*, which are the *denotations* of the predicate symbols. The relations belonging to an interpretation determine the truth of the atomic sentences of the language, and the truth of the atomic sentences, in turn, determines the truth values of all other sentences.

For example, if the conditional

$$amazing(john) \leftarrow can\text{-}fly(john)$$

is interpreted in such a way that the constant *john* denotes my cat, the predicate symbols *amazing* and *can-fly* denote the properties of being lazy and sleeping all day respectively, then the conditional means:

My cat is lazy if my cat sleeps all day.

And because my cat sleeps all day and my cat is lazy, the sentences *can-fly(john)* and *amazing(john)* are both *true*. As a consequence, the conditional *amazing(john)* ← *can-fly(john)* is also *true*.

For convenience, we include the atomic sentences *true* and *false* in the language. We sometimes use the atom *true* to represent an empty conjunction and the atom *false* to represent an empty disjunction. We also use the atom *false* in the conclusions of conditionals, to represent constraints. Unfortunately, these usages are easily confused with the truth values *true* and *false*. When it is necessary to distinguish between these atoms and the truth values, we refer to them as the *atoms true* or *false* and the *truth values true* or *false*, respectively.

The truth values *true* and *false* are asymmetric, because falsity is defined in terms of truth:

A sentence that is not *true* is also said to be *false*.

A negative sentence ¬ *C* is *true* if (and only if) the sentence *C* is *false*.

An *atomic sentence* of the form $p(c_1, \ldots, c_n)$, where $c_1, \ldots, c_n$ are ground terms, is *true* in an interpretation if (and only if) the individuals denoted by the terms $c_1, \ldots, c_n$ are in the relation denoted by the predicate symbol p. If the atomic sentence is a predicate symbol with no arguments (i.e. $n = 0$), then the sentence is *true* if (and only if) the interpretation simply assigns it the truth value *true*. The atomic sentence *true* is always assigned the truth value *true*. The atomic sentence *false* is never assigned the truth value *true* (and therefore has the truth value *false*).

A sentence that is a *conjunction* $C_1 \wedge \ldots \wedge C_n$ is *true* in an interpretation if (and only if) all of C_i are *true*. (Therefore, if $n = 0$, then the conjunction is *true*.)

A sentence that is a *disjunction* $C_1 \vee \ldots \vee C_n$ is *true* in an interpretation if (and only if) at least one of C_i is *true*. (Therefore, if $n = 0$, then the disjunction is not *true*.)

A sentence that is a conditional $C \rightarrow D$ is *true* in an interpretation if (and only if) C has the truth value *false* or D has the truth value *true*. (Therefore a conditional of the form $C \rightarrow false$ is *true* if and only if C has the truth value *false*.)

A universally quantified sentence $\forall X\, C$ is *true* if (and only if) every *ground instance* of C (obtained by replacing every occurrence of the variable X in C by a ground term) is *true*.

An existentially quantified sentence $\exists X\, C$ is *true* if (and only if) some ground instance of C is *true*.

Finally, an interpretation of a set of sentences is said to be a *model* of the set of sentences if (and only if) every sentence in the set is *true* in the interpretation.

It is this sense of the term *model* that explains the use of the term *model-theoretic semantics*. There is another sense of the term *model*, which is more common in English, and which we also use in this book. This is its sense as a synonym for *theory*. It is this more common meaning of the term that we intend when we speak, for example, of an agent *model*, a cognitive *model* or of a *model* of the mind. If necessary, we use the term *semantic model*, to distinguish it from model in the sense of a theory.

The semantics of conditionals

According to the semantics of classical logic, a conditional (also called *material implication*) of the form $C \rightarrow D$ is logically equivalent to a disjunction $\neg\, C \vee D$. This implies that the conditional is *true* whenever the conclusion D is *true*, no matter whether the condition C is *true* or *false*. The conditional is also *true* whenever the condition C is *false*, no matter whether the conclusion D is *true* or *false*. For example, the conditionals:

> *john can fly* $\rightarrow 2 + 2 = 4$
> *the moon is made from green cheese* $\rightarrow$ *john can fly*

are both *true* in any interpretation in which $2 + 2 = 4$ is *true* and *the moon is made from green cheese* is *false*, no matter whether *john can fly* is *true* or *false*.

These properties of the semantics of conditionals are sufficiently unintuitive that they have come to be known as the *paradoxes of material implication*. The desire to avoid such paradoxes has given rise to various non-classical logics, the most influential of which is Relevance Logic (Anderson and Belnap, 1975).

However, there are some cases where these properties seem to make sense. For example:

> *john can fly* $\rightarrow$ *I am a monkey's uncle*

On the obviously intended assumptions that my assertion is *true* and that *I am an monkey's uncle* is *false*, it must be that I mean to imply that *john can fly* is *false*. This implication relies upon the semantics of the material implication as understood in ordinary classical logic.

The semantics of conditionals in this book is the classical semantics. The paradoxes are avoided, partly by invoking pragmatic, rather than semantic, considerations, as argued for example by Grice (1989). The role of pragmatics is most obvious in the case of disjunctions. For example, why assert the *weak disjunction*, even if it is *true*:

> *I am going to the party* ∨ *I will stay at home*

if I have no intention of going to the party, but I am planning to stay at home instead?

In Computational Logic, the paradoxes are avoided for the additional reason that practical proof procedures eliminate weak disjunctions and weak conditionals for the sake of computational efficiency. In the case of propositional logic, they eliminate any disjunction $C \vee D$ that is *subsumed* by a stronger disjunction, say D alone. They also eliminate any weak conditional $B \wedge C \to D$ or $C \to D \vee E$ that is *subsumed* by a stronger conditional $C \to D$.

In the more general case of sentences containing variables, subsumption also eliminates any sentence that is an instance of another sentence. For example, if I believe *likes(bob, X)* and you ask me what Bob likes, I will tell you that Bob likes everything, partly because it is more informative, and partly because if I had a more specific belief, say that *likes(bob, mary)*, I would have eliminated it to avoid cluttering my mind with unnecessary details. We will discuss subsumption and related matters in greater detail in Chapter A5.

Universal quantifiers and Herbrand interpretations

According to the semantics of universal quantifiers, a sentence of the form ∀*X C* is *true* if and only if every *ground instance* of *C* is *true*. This simple definition (called the *substitution interpretation of quantifiers*) works correctly only if there are enough ground terms in the language to name all the individuals in the interpretation. The set of ground terms needs to include not only the names of all the individuals in the set of sentences under consideration, but also a pool of names for talking about any individuals that might need talking about in the future.

Assuming that there are enough names to talk about all the individuals that might need talking about makes it possible to do away with the mystery of what counts as an individual and what counts as a relation. It allows us simply to identify an interpretation with the set of all the atomic sentences that are assigned the truth value *true* in the interpretation.

The fact that an interpretation directly identifies only those atomic sentences that are *true*, and that the definition of truth for a negative sentence ¬ *C* reduces to the failure of *C* to be *true*, reflects the asymmetry between truth and falsity. In the conditional form of logic, this asymmetry is further reflected in the fact that sentences with positive conclusions are more basic than sentences with negative conclusions. In the agent model, it is reflected in the fact that an agent's basic observations are represented by positive atomic sentences.

Sets of atomic sentences regarded as interpretations or as semantic models are called *Herbrand interpretations* or *Herbrand models*, in honour of the logician

Jacques Herbrand. The mathematical attraction of Herbrand interpretations is the property that if there exists any other kind of model then there exists a Herbrand model as well. Arguably, for our purpose, such Herbrand interpretations are more useful than arbitrary interpretations.

Indeed, for our purpose, the only interpretation that really matters is the real world, and the only semantic relationship that really matters is the relationship between an agent's thoughts and the succession of states of the world.

The interface between the real world and the agent's goals and beliefs is the set of observations that the agent encounters and the set of actions that the agent performs. This interface is as close as the agent needs to get to the real world, to determine whether its beliefs are *true* and whether its goals can be made *true*. The use of Herbrand interpretations restricts the agent's knowledge of the world to this interface, and avoids trying to identify the true nature of the world without describing it in some other language.

Minimal models of definite clause programs

In classical logic, a sentence *C* is a *logical consequence* of a set of sentences *S* if (and only if) *C* is *true* in every model of *S*. Typically, the set of sentences *S* has many, often infinitely many, models. However, in the case of definite clauses, there is a single model that stands out from all the others. It is the Herbrand model *M* that is generated by instantiating universally quantified variables with ground terms and by reasoning forwards.

Consider, for example, the recursive definite clauses *E*:

$$even(0)$$
$$even(s(s(X))) \leftarrow even(X)$$

Forward reasoning generates the infinite sequence of atomic sentences:

$$even(0), \; even(s(s(0))), \; even(s(s(s(s(0))))), \; \dots \; ad \; infinitum.$$

This set is a Herbrand model of *E*. In fact, it is the smallest Herbrand model that makes the two sentences in *E* both *true*.

The smallest Herbrand model of a definite clause program *H* always exists, and it is called the *minimal model* of *H*. This model is *minimal* in the sense that it is contained in every other Herbrand model of *H*.[1] In fact, every larger set of

---

[1] However, the minimal model depends upon the vocabulary of the underlying language of *H*. This vocabulary includes all the ground terms that can be constructed from the terms occurring in *H*, but it could also include other constants or function symbols. These other, unused symbols might be held in reserve to be used in future extensions of *H*. But in any case, these ground terms need to be *sorted* (or *well-typed*), to exclude such terms as *s(bob)*.

atomic sentences is also a model. This includes the *maximal model* in which all the ground atoms are *true*.

The maximal model is one of those models that give the semantics of classical logic a bad name. The minimal model, on the other hand, has all the good properties that the critics desire. In particular, it has the remarkable property that, as far as goal clauses (or achievement goals) are concerned, truth in the minimal model is equivalent to truth in all models:

For every definite clause program H, there exists a unique minimal model M such that for all definite goal clauses G:

G is a logical consequence of H (i.e. G is *true* in all models of H) if and only if G is *true* in M.

This property is a direct consequence of a theorem proved in van Emden and Kowalski (1976) for the case where G is an atomic fact. It also holds for disjunctions of definite goal clauses, i.e. sentences of the form $G_1 \lor \ldots \lor G_n$ where each G_i is an (existentially quantified) definite goal clause. However, it does not hold for sentences containing negation or universal quantification.

For example, the sentences:

$$not \; even(s(s(s(0))))$$
$$\forall X \, (even(s(s(X))) \rightarrow even(X))$$

are both *true* in the minimal model M of E, but they are not logical consequences of E. The first sentence is *true* in M, because the atomic sentence $even(s(s(s(0))))$ is not *true* in M. However, it is not a logical consequence of E, because it is not *true*, for example, in the maximal model of E.

The second sentence $\forall X \, (even(s(s(X))) \rightarrow even(X))$ is *true* in M, because for all ground terms t that can be constructed from the constant 0 and the function symbol s:

if $even(s(s(t)))$ is *true* in M, then it must have been derived by forward reasoning using the ground instance $even(s(s(t))) \leftarrow even(t)$ of the conditional in E. But then the condition $even(t)$ of this ground instance must also be *true* in M.

Notice that this second sentence is the converse of the second conditional in E. It is not *true* in all models of E, because there exist non-Herbrand models containing weird individuals, for example the individual named WEIRD, such that $even(s(s(\text{WEIRD})))$ is *true*, but $even(\text{WEIRD})$ is not *true*. The simplest and smallest such model is just the minimal model augmented with the one additional atomic sentence $even(s(s(\text{WEIRD})))$.

Arguably, it is the minimal model of a definite clause program H that is the *intended model* of H, and it is relative to this model that the truth or falsity of arbitrary sentences in the syntax of classical logic should be judged.

This way of looking at models separates sentences into two kinds: sentences like definite clauses that determine minimal models, and arbitrary sentences of classical logic that are *true* in such minimal models.

The difference between these two kinds of sentences is analogous to the difference between an agent's beliefs and its goals. Beliefs have the form of logic programs, and represent a minimal model of the agent's world. Goals have the form of arbitrary sentences of classical logic, and represent properties of the world that the agent would like to hold.

This difference between beliefs and goals is most striking in the case of maintenance goals, which are universally quantified conditionals. We will see in Chapter A6 that the semantics of a maintenance goal G can be naturally understood as generating a set of atomic sentences Δ describing atomic actions, such that G is *true* in the minimal model of $B \cup \Delta$, where B is the set of the agent's beliefs. With this semantics, forward reasoning can be viewed as trying to make G *true* by making its conclusion *true* whenever its conditions are made *true*. This process of forward reasoning goes on forever, unless no new atomic sentences can be observed or derived.

Any model generated by forward reasoning in this way is minimal, not only in the sense that $B \cup \Delta$ has a minimal model, but also in the sense that atomic sentences are made *true* by adding them to Δ only when necessary. In particular, there is no need to make conditions of maintenance goals *true* for no reason.

Truth in arithmetic

The case for viewing minimal models as intended models is supported by the fact that the standard model of arithmetic is the minimal model of a definite clause program. Here is a definite clause representation of addition and multiplication in terms of relations, along with a more conventional representation in terms of functions on the right:

$+(0, Y, Y)$ i.e. $0 + Y = Y$

$+(s(X), Y, s(Z)) \leftarrow +(X, Y, Z)$ i.e. $s(X) + Y = s(X + Y)$

$\times(0, Y, 0)$ i.e. $0 \times Y = 0$

$\times(s(X), Y, V) \leftarrow \times(X, Y, U) \wedge +(U, Y, V)$ i.e. $s(X) \times Y = (X \times Y) + Y$

The functional representation is undoubtedly easier to understand, but the relational representation more clearly distinguishes between the undefined function symbol s, used to construct the natural numbers, and addition and multiplication, which are defined by the conditionals. Moreover, the relational representation avoids the need for a separate equality predicate.

Arguably, the relational representation also has a more obvious semantics in terms of the minimal model A defined by the four definite clauses. It is this model that we mean when we speak of the *intended model of arithmetic* and of *truth* in arithmetic (as remarked in effect by Martin Davis (1980)).

Consider, for example, the sentence:

$$\forall X(+(X, 0, X))$$

where X is a natural number. This sentence is not a goal clause, because X is universally quantified. However, it is easy to show that the sentence is *true* in the minimal model A. Here is a proof by mathematical induction:

Base case: $X = 0$. Then $+(X, 0, X)$ is just $+(0, 0, 0)$,
which is true in A
because it is an instance of the clause $+(0, Y, Y)$.

Inductive case: $X = s(n)$. By induction hypothesis, $+(n, 0, n)$ is true in A.
We need to show $+(s(n), 0, s(n))$ is true in A.
But this follows by one step of forward reasoning,
using the clause $(s(X), Y, s(Z)) \leftarrow +(X, Y, Z)$.

This semantic argument can be expressed purely syntactically, by augmenting the definite clauses with additional axioms, including axioms for induction. The induction axiom needed for this example is an instance of the axiom schema:[2]

$$P(0) \wedge \forall N(P(N) \rightarrow P(s(N))) \rightarrow \forall X P(X).$$

where $P(X)$ is any predicate in which X is the only unquantified variable. The instance of $P(X)$ needed in the example is $+(X, 0, X)$.

In the example, the universally quantified sentence $\forall X (+(X, 0, X))$ is both *true* and provable using induction. However, Gödel's Incompleteness Theorem shows that there are universally quantified sentences of arithmetic that are *true* but unprovable using any constructible set of axioms for arithmetic. Intuitively, this is because to show that a universally quantified sentence is *true*, it is necessary to show that every ground instance of the sentence is *true*, and there are infinitely many such ground instances, one for every natural number.

---

[2] An *axiom scheme* is a collection of axioms, one for each predicate $P(X)$ (not restricted to predicate symbols). However, induction can also be represented as a single sentence in either meta-logic or so-called second-order logic. In meta-logic, P ranges over names of formulas. In second-order logic, P ranges over subsets of the natural numbers. From a mathematical point of view, the big difference between the meta-logical and second-order representations is that the set of formulas is infinite but countable, whereas the set of all subsets of the natural numbers is infinite but uncountable.

In many cases, the infinitely many instances display a recurrent pattern that can be captured finitely with proof by induction. But in the case of the sentence constructed in the proof of the Incompleteness Theorem, it cannot. The sentence is constructed by coding sentences of arithmetic by natural numbers, and by representing the provability predicate of arithmetic as an arithmetical predicate. In this way, arithmetic becomes its own meta-language, and sentences about arithmetic become sentences of arithmetic.

The *true*, but unprovable sentence, is a sentence that says of itself that it is unprovable. If the sentence is *false*, then it is not *true* that the sentence is unprovable, and the sentence can actually be proved, in which case the axioms of arithmetic are inconsistent. If the sentence is *true*, then it cannot be proved, in which case the axioms of arithmetic are incomplete. Therefore any constructive axiomatisation of arithmetic that is consistent is incomplete. Moreover, any such axiomatisation is certain to have non-minimal, unintended models, in which sentences that are *true* in the intended model of arithmetic are *false*.

Conclusions

In this chapter, we investigated the notions of truth, logical consequence and minimal models. I sketched an argument for restricting attention to Herbrand interpretations, which are sets of atomic sentences. In the case of an agent embedded in the real world, the advantage of Herbrand interpretations is that they avoid the philosophical problems of trying to identify the true nature of the world, and they focus instead on just specifying the interface between the agent's thoughts and the world.

I also sketched a further argument for regarding minimal models as intended models, and pointed out that, in the case of definite clauses, a definite goal clause is true in all models if and only if it is true in the minimal model.

I argued that in the case of arithmetic, the truth or falsity of arbitrary sentences is best understood as truth or falsity in the minimal model of the definite clause program defining addition and multiplication. I also sketched an argument that the semantics of an agent's maintenance goals can similarly be understood as generating a minimal model in which the maintenance goals are all *true*.

The fact that forward reasoning can be understood as generating minimal models also draws support from mental model theory, which argues that people reason by constructing model-like structures in the mind. In Chapters A3 and A6, we will see how the inference rules of forward reasoning, backward reasoning and negation as failure can be understood in semantic terms, as determining the truth of sentences in minimal models.

A3

Forward and backward reasoning

We have already looked informally at forward and backward reasoning with conditionals without negation (definite clauses). This additional chapter defines the two inference rules more precisely and examines their semantics.

Arguably, forward reasoning is more fundamental than backward reasoning, because, as shown in Chapter A2, it is the way that minimal models are generated. However, the two inference rules can both be understood as determining whether definite goal clauses are true in all models of a definite clause program, or equivalently whether the definite goal clauses are true in the minimal model.

Forward reasoning

Of the two rules of inference, only forward reasoning is *truth-preserving*, in the sense that, if the sentences it starts with are *true* in an interpretation, then the derived sentence is also *true* in the same interpretation. It follows that any sentence obtained by repeatedly applying forward reasoning, starting from an initial set of *premises*, is a logical consequence of the premises. Therefore, forward reasoning is a sound rule of inference. We will see later that forward reasoning with definite clauses is also complete.

To see how forward reasoning preserves truth, consider the case of John who buys a lottery ticket in the hope of becoming rich:

$$buys\text{-}ticket(john, 150541)$$
$$buys\text{-}ticket(X, Y) \wedge chosen(Y) \rightarrow rich(X)$$

Forward reasoning can be applied if the variables can be instantiated in such a way that the fact and one of the conditions of the conditional become identical. If such an instantiation is possible, then forward reasoning instantiates the conditional:

Step 1:   *buys-ticket(john, 150541)* ∧ *chosen(150541)* → *rich(john)*

This is *logically equivalent* to the non-standard conditional:

$$buys\text{-}ticket(john, 150541) \rightarrow (chosen(150541) \rightarrow rich(john))$$

Forward reasoning with this equivalent conditional then derives the conclusion. This is just classical *modus ponens*:

Step 2:   *chosen(150541)* → *rich(john)*

Both steps are truth-preserving. Step 1 is truth-preserving, because a conditional is *true* if and only if every instance is *true*. Step 2 is truth-preserving, because if a conditional is *true* and its conditions are *true* then its conclusion must also be *true*.

In the more general case, *forward reasoning* involves an atomic sentence and a conditional, both of which may contain universally quantified variables. For example:

$$likes(bob, X)$$
$$likes(X, Y) \wedge gives(X, Y, Z) \rightarrow generous\text{-}to(X, Z)$$

If the atomic sentence and the conditional can be instantiated, so that the resulting atomic sentence and one of the conditions of the conditional are identical, then instantiation is performed:

Step 1:   *likes(bob, X)*
                 likes(bob, X) ∧ *gives(bob, X, Z)* → *generous-to(bob, Z)*
Equivalently: *likes(bob, X)* → (*gives(bob, X, Z)* → *generous-to(bob, Z)*)

Notice that the variable X in the original sentences is actually two different variables, because the "scope" of a variable is limited to the sentence in which it occurs. Outside of that scope, the name of the variable loses its significance, and inside that scope, all occurrences of the variable can be *renamed*, without affecting the semantics of the sentence. Notice also that the instantiation of the two sentences is the most general instantiation that does the job of making the two atoms identical.

In the next step, forward reasoning deletes from the instantiated conditional the condition that is identical to the instantiated atom:

Step 2:   *gives(bob, X, Z)* → *generous-to(bob, Z)*

In general, starting from an atomic sentence and a conditional:

atomic sentence
conditions → *conclusion*

forward reasoning first instantiates both sentences, so that the instantiated atomic sentence is identical to one of the conditions of the instantiated conditional:

Step 1:   *atomic sentence'*
              atomic sentence' ∧ *other-conditions'* → *conclusion'*.

This instantiation of terms for variables is the most general instantiation that makes the two atoms identical, and is called the (*most general*) *unifier* of the two atoms. All other common instances of the two atoms are instances of this most general unifier. The operation of most general instantiation is called *unification*; and the resulting atoms are said to be *unified*. The unifier of two atoms, if there is one, is *unique* up to the renaming of variables.

Having performed unification, forward reasoning deletes from the instantiated conditional the condition that is now identical to the instantiated atomic sentence:

Step 2:   *other-conditions'* → *conclusion'*.

Note that *atomic sentence'* can occur anywhere in the conditions of the conditional. However, for simplicity, both here and elsewhere, it is written first, because the order in which formulas appear in a conjunction doesn't matter, and because it makes the description of the inference rule simpler.

Backward reasoning

With backward reasoning, truth is preserved in the opposite direction: If the subgoals that are derived are *true*, and the conditional used to derive the subgoals is *true*, then the initial goal from which the subgoals are derived is *true*. To see this, consider first the simple case of a single atomic goal clause:

Initial goal clause: *generous-to*(X, *mary*)
Conditional: *likes*(X, Y) ∧ *gives*(X, Y, Z) → *generous-to*(X, Z)

Here the variable X in the goal clause is existentially quantified and different from the universally quantified variable X in the conditional, despite having the same (local) name.

Backward reasoning attempts to unify the atomic goal and the conclusion of the conditional. If the attempt succeeds, then both sentences are instantiated by applying the unifier:

Step 1:   *generous-to*(X, *mary*)
              likes(X, Y) ∧ *gives*(X, Y, *mary*) → *generous-to*(X, *mary*)

Instantiation of the conditional is truth-preserving, because all of its variables are universally quantified, and if the conditional is *true* then all of its instances are *true*. In this example, the instantiation of the goal clause is unnecessary.

However, in the general case, when the goal clause needs to be instantiated, this instantiation is not truth-preserving, because all of the variables in the goal clause are existentially quantified. But if an instance of a goal clause is *true*, then the goal clause itself is *true*, because an existentially quantified sentence is *true* if an instance is *true*.

Having instantiated the goal clause and the conditional, backward reasoning continues by replacing the goal atom by the conditions of the conditional, as subgoals:

Step 2, subgoals: $likes(X, Y) \land gives(X, Y, mary)$

Here the variables X and Y are existentially quantified. (To find someone who is generous to Mary, it suffices to find someone who gives *something* he/she likes to Mary. He/she does not need to give *everything* he/she likes to Mary.) If the subgoals and the conditional are *true*, then the initial goal clause is also *true* in the same interpretation.

In general, starting from a selected atomic goal in an initial goal clause and a conditional:

$$selected\text{-}goal \land other\text{-}goals$$
$$conditions \rightarrow conclusion$$

backward reasoning attempts to unify the *selected-goal* with the *conclusion* of the conditional. If the unification is possible, then the unifier is applied to both sentences:

Step 1, instantiation: $selected\text{-}goal' \land other\text{-}goals'$
$$conditions' \rightarrow selected\text{-}goal'.$$

Backward reasoning then replaces the instantiated selected goal by the conditions of the instantiated conditional:

Step 2: $conditions' \land other\text{-}goals'.$

In the special case where there are no *other-goals*, the second step is simply *modus ponens* in reverse. In the special case where there are no *conditions*, the *conditions* are equivalent to *true*, and the *conditional* is in effect a *fact*.

Below is an example of the way in which backward reasoning is used for computation in logic programming. The example uses the theoretically elegant, though hopelessly inefficient representation of the natural numbers using only 0 and the successor function *s*. The inefficiency of the computation is not an inherent property of logic programming, but rather a property of this specific representation.

Consider the goal of adding 2 plus 2, using the definition of addition given in Chapter A1. Here the names of variables are chosen to make the matching instantiations more obvious:

Initial goal clause: $+(s(s(0)), s(s(0)), X)$
New goal clause: $+(s(0), s(s(0)), X')$ where $X = s(X')$
New goal clause: $+(0, s(s(0)), X'')$ where $X' = s(X'')$
New goal clause: *true* where $X'' = s(s(0))$

The cumulative instantiations of the existentially quantified variables compute the sum $X = s(s(s(s(0))))$.

Soundness and completeness

As we have seen, forward reasoning is sound. Backward reasoning, on the other hand, is *backwards sound*: Given an *initial goal clause* and a *derived goal clause* obtained by reasoning backwards with a *conditional*, the *initial goal clause* is *true* in any interpretation in which the *derived goal clause* and the *conditional* are *true*. Moreover, if the *derived goal clause* is the atom *true* (an empty conjunction of subgoals), then the *initial goal clause* is *true*, simply if the *conditional* is *true*.

Thus forward and backward reasoning are two different, but sound ways to solve a goal clause $C_1 \wedge \ldots \wedge C_n$. *Forward reasoning* can be understood as solving the goal clause by deriving atomic sentences $C_1' \ldots C_n'$ such that the conjunction $C_1' \wedge \ldots \wedge C_n'$ is an instance of the goal clause $C_1 \wedge \ldots \wedge C_n$. *Backward reasoning* can be understood as solving the goal clause by deriving the goal atom *true* from the initial goal clause.

The soundness of forward reasoning and the backward soundness of backward reasoning ensure that if a goal clause is solved using either forward or backward reasoning, then the goal clause is *true* in every interpretation in which the conditionals used in the derivation are *true*.

The backward soundness of backward reasoning can be turned into ordinary soundness if goal clauses G are turned into denials $G \rightarrow false$, and if solving a goal clause is understood as deriving *true* → *false*, which is equivalent to *false*.[1] This way of looking at backward reasoning makes it easier to see that both

---

[1] Note that the denial of a goal clause $\neg (\exists X_1 \ldots \exists X_m (C_1 \wedge \ldots \wedge C_n))$ is equivalent to a conditional constraint $\forall X_1 \ldots \forall X_m (C_1 \wedge \ldots \wedge C_n \rightarrow false)$.

backward and forward reasoning are special cases of the resolution rule, presented in Chapter A5. It also makes it easier to obtain completeness by means of refutation completeness:

> Let C be any sentence of classical logic,
> and S any set of sentences of classical logic.
> Then C is a *logical consequence* of S
> if (and only if) the sentences S and $C \rightarrow false$ have no model;
> if (and only if) S and $C \rightarrow false$ logically imply *false*.

> Therefore, a set of inference rules is *refutation complete*
> if (and only if) whenever C is a *logical consequence* of S,
> then there exists a derivation (called a *refutation*)
> by means of the inference rules, of *false* from S and $C \rightarrow false$.

Both forward and backward reasoning are *refutation complete* for Horn clauses. If G is a definite goal clause and S is a definite clause program, then the following are equivalent:

- G is a logical consequence of S.
- G is *true* in the minimal model of S.
- There exists a derivation of *false* from the clauses S and $G \rightarrow false$ both by forward reasoning and by backward reasoning.

Conclusions

In this chapter, we saw that forward and backward reasoning are both sound and refutation complete for Horn clauses. In Chapter A4, we will see how to extend reasoning with Horn clauses by means of negation as failure. In Chapter A5, we will see how to extend forward and backward reasoning to the resolution rule, which is sound and refutation complete for the clausal form of full classical logic.

A4
Minimal models and negation

To a first approximation, the *negation as failure* rule of inference is straight-forward. Its name says it all:

>*to show that the negation of a sentence holds*
>*try to show the sentence holds, and*
>*if the attempt fails, then the negation holds.*

But what does it mean to *fail*? Does it include infinite or only finite failure? To answer these questions, we need a better understanding of the semantics.

Consider, for example, the English sentence:

>*bob will go if no one goes*

Ignore the fact that, if Bob were more normal, it would be more likely that *bob will go if no one else goes*. Focus instead on the problem of representing the sentence more formally as a logical conditional.

The variable X in the obvious representation:

>*bob will go* ← *not(X will go)*

is universally quantified with scope the entire conditional:

>$\forall X$ (*bob will go* ← *not(X will go)*)

i.e.   *bob will go* ← $\exists X$ *not(X will go)*

i.e.   *bob will go* ← *not* $\forall X$ (*X will go*)

i.e.   *bob will go if not everyone will go*

What we really want is:

>*bob will go* ← *not* $\exists X$ (*X will go*)

In fact, that is what we actually get if we apply the negation as failure inference rule in the obvious way, ignoring quantification:

Initial goal: *bob will go*
Subgoal: *not X will go*

Naf: *X will go*
Subgoal: *not X' will go (where X = bob)*
           Naf: *X' will go*
                      Subgoal: *not X" will go (where X' = bob)*

ad infinitum   ...

But then we have two problems: The problem we started with, that all variables in conditionals are implicitly universally quantified, when what we need is an existentially quantified variable inside negation; and the problem of the infinite loop.

But as we have just seen, the first problem is not a problem, but a solution to a problem that we may not have realised we had. In general, negation as failure interprets variables in negative conditions that do not occur elsewhere as existentially quantified inside the negation; and for most applications this is exactly what we want! We will see later that this is also what we want and what we get with variables in the conclusions of maintenance goals that do not occur in the conditions.

It is the infinite loop that is the real problem. But before we try to tackle the problem in this particular example, let's sharpen our intuitions by considering some simpler cases first. The simplest case is the one without any negation at all.

Negation in minimal models

We have seen in Chapter A2 that every set H of conditionals without negation (i.e. Horn clause program) has a unique minimal model M, which is generated by instantiating universally quantified variables with ground terms and by forward reasoning. I have argued that it is this minimal model that is the *intended model* of H. Viewed this way, the semantics of negation as failure is simply the normal semantics of negation in classical logic:

> a sentence *not p* holds by *negation as (potentially infinite) failure*
> if and only if *not p* is *true* in M
> if and only if *p* is not *true* in M.

In fact, the negation as failure inference rule can be understood simply as reasoning backwards with the definition of truth, to show that *not p* is *true* in M, by showing that *p* is not *true* in M.

Remember the simple definite clause program E:

$$even(0)$$
$$even(s(s(X))) \leftarrow even(X)$$

with its infinite Herbrand model M consisting of the atomic sentences:

even(0), *even*(*s*(*s*(0))), *even*(*s*(*s*(*s*(*s*(0))))), . . . *ad infinitum*.

Consider the problem of determining if *not even*(*s*(*s*(*s*(0)))) is *true* in *M*:

if and only if	*even*(*s*(*s*(*s*(0))))	is not *true* in *M*
if and only if	*even*(*s*(*s*(*s*(0))))	does not belong to *M*,
which is the case.		

The negation as failure inference rule gives the same result without the need to generate the model *M* explicitly:

	even(*s*(*s*(*s*(0)))) can be shown	
if and only if	*even*(*s*(0)) can be shown	
but only if	*s*(0) can be unified either with 0 or with *s*(*s*(0)).	
But it cannot. So	*even*(*s*(*s*(*s*(0)))) cannot be shown.	
So	*not even*(*s*(*s*(*s*(0)))) can be shown.	

Intended models of general logic programs

The minimal model semantics of definite clauses can be extended to conditionals with negative conditions, which are also called *general logic programs*. The first step, given such a general logic program *P*, is literally to extend *P* with a set Δ of negations *not a* of atom sentences *a*, treating these negations as though they were positive atoms (as in strong negation).

The second step is then to treat the extended set *P* ∪ Δ as though it were a definite clause program, with its own unique minimal model M_Δ. If the set Δ is appropriately restricted, so that, among other things, M_Δ does not include both an atom *a* and its negation *not a*, then M_Δ is an *intended model* of *P*. We will see later that a program *P* can have several such extensions Δ.

Before discussing in greater detail the conditions necessary to ensure that Δ is appropriately restricted, consider the *even/odd* program:

$$even(0)$$
$$even(s(s(X))) \leftarrow even(X)$$
$$odd(X) \leftarrow not\ even(X)$$

Ignoring, to begin with, the definition of *odd*, let Δ be the set of all ground negations that are *true* in the minimal model of the Horn clause program *E*, i.e. let Δ be the set:

$$not\ even(s(0)),\ not\ even(s(s(s(0)))),$$
$$not\ even(s(s(s(s(s(0)))))),\ \ldots\ ad\ infinitum.$$

Let *M* be the minimal model of *even/odd* ∪ Δ, treating Δ as a set of positive atoms. This adds to the minimal model of *E* the additional positive atoms:

$$odd(s(0)),\ odd(s(s(s(0)))),$$
$$odd(s(s(s(s(s(0)))))),\ \ldots\ ad\ infinitum.$$

Arguably, M is the unique intended model of the program *even/odd*. Notice that the constraint $even(X) \wedge odd(X) \rightarrow false$ is *true* in M.

There exists a large class of general logic programs having a unique minimal model that can be generated in this way. This is the class of so-called *locally stratified programs* (Przymusinski, 1988). Intuitively, locally stratified programs can be layered into strata in such a way that negative conditions in higher strata are defined in lower strata, in the way that *odd* is defined in terms of *even*.

In the next section, we will investigate the unstratified program:

$$bob\ will\ go \leftarrow not\ john\ will\ go$$
$$john\ will\ go \leftarrow not\ bob\ will\ go$$

But first, we need to identify the restrictions necessary to ensure that Δ is appropriate, in both the stratified and unstratified cases. The most important restriction is obviously that:

Δ is *consistent* with P.

i.e.   If *not a* is in Δ then a is not *true* in the minimal model M of $P \cup \Delta$.

i.e.   for all atoms a, the constraint $a \wedge not\ a \rightarrow false$ is *true* in M.

The only other restriction that Δ needs to satisfy is that Δ should be sufficiently large. This condition can be understood in different ways, the simplest of which is that:

Δ is *total*.

i.e.   if a is not *true* in M, then *not a* is *true* in M,
       and therefore *not a* is in Δ.

i.e.   For all atoms a, the "constraint" $a \vee not\ a$ is *true* in M.

These two restrictions, *consistency* and *totality*, define the *stable model semantics* of general logic programs (Gelfond and Lifschitz, 1988):

The minimal Herbrand model M obtained by treating $P \cup \Delta$
as a definite clause program is a *stable model* of P if and only if
not a is in M if and only if a is not in M.

In the stable model semantics, *not a* can be understood both as *not a* is *true* and as *a cannot be shown*.

Examples of stable models

Let us return now to the example we started with. Call it the program B:

$$bob\ will\ go \leftarrow not\ \exists X\,(X\ will\ go)$$

The only ground atom that can be constructed from the vocabulary of B is the atom *bob will go*. However, the language in which the sentence is expressed might contain other constants for other individuals and objects not mentioned in the sentence. We can ignore this slight complication, because it has no impact on the following argument.

The problem is to determine whether there is a stable model and whether *bob will go* is *true* or *false* in this model. Suppose there is such a stable model M_Δ, which is the minimal model of some extension $B \cup \Delta$ of B. Now consider whether the negative sentence *not bob will go* is in Δ:

> If *not bob will go* is in Δ, then *bob will go* is in M_Δ,
> and then Δ is not consistent with the program B.
> If *not bob will go* is not in Δ, then neither *bob will go*
> nor *not bob will go* is in M_Δ, and then Δ is not total.

Therefore the program B has no such stable extension Δ and therefore no stable model. It is simply inconsistent.

In the stable model semantics, a logic program can have more than one stable model, as in the case of the program BJ:

> bob will go $\leftarrow$ not john will go
> john will go $\leftarrow$ not bob will go

The program has one stable model in which *not john will go* and *bob will go*, and another stable model in which *not bob will go* and *john will go*.

In cases where a program has more than one minimal model, an agent can be either *credulous* or *sceptical*. In the stable semantics, a *credulous* agent may choose to believe a sentence if and only if it is *true* in **some** minimal model. But a *sceptical* agent believes a sentence if and only if it is *true* in **all** minimal models. Of course, an agent may be credulous in some situations, but sceptical in others.

In the last example, according to a sceptical semantics, it is impossible to say whether or not *bob will go* or *john will go*. This is like the situation in classical logic, where the two conditionals above would be written as a disjunction:

> bob will go $\lor$ john will go.

Conclusions

In classical logic, a sentence C is a *logical consequence* of a set of sentences S if and only if C is *true* in every interpretation in which S is *true*. However, for the applications in this book, it is intended interpretations, rather than arbitrary interpretations, that matter.

For beliefs in the form of definite clauses, these intended interpretations are minimal models, which can be generated by instantiation and forward reasoning. For more general beliefs that are general logic programs, the intended interpretations are minimal models obtained by extending the beliefs with the negations of atomic sentences. Viewing semantics in terms of such minimal models is in the spirit of virtually all of the logics that have been developed for default reasoning in Artificial Intelligence. These logics include circumscription (McCarthy, 1980), default logic (Reiter, 1980), modal non-monotonic logic (McDermott and Doyle, 1980) and autoepistemic logic (Moore, 1985).

Thus, the argument for viewing thinking in terms of determining truth in minimal models, rather than in terms of logical consequence, is supported by the examples of default reasoning, arithmetic and the real world. Johan van Benthem discusses some of these and many other examples (van Benthem, 1989).

A5
The resolution rule

This additional chapter shows that both forward and backward reasoning are special cases of the resolution rule of inference. Resolution also includes compiling two clauses, like:

you deal with the emergency appropriately ← you get help.

you get help ← you alert the driver.

into one: *you deal with the emergency appropriately ← you alert the driver.*

In the propositional case, given two clauses of the form:

$$D \rightarrow E \vee A$$

$$A \wedge B \rightarrow C$$

where B and D are conjunctions of atoms including the atom *true*, and C and E are disjunctions of atoms including the atom *false*, *resolution* derives the *resolvent*:

$$D \wedge B \rightarrow E \vee C.$$

The two clauses from which the resolvent is derived are called the *parents* of the resolvent, and the atom A is called the atom *resolved upon*.

Resolution was originally defined by Robinson (1965a) for clauses that are disjunctions represented as sets of *literals*, where a literal is an atom or the negation of an atom. For example, the conditional $D \wedge B \rightarrow E \vee C$, where B, C, D and E are single atoms, is interpreted as the disjunction $\neg D \vee \neg B \vee E \vee C$ and is represented by the set of literals $\{\neg D, \neg B, E, C\}$.

The representation of clauses as sets of literals, interpreted as disjunctions, builds into the resolution rule several inference rules of classical logic, which

269

would otherwise have to be stated separately and explicitly. For example, the following logical equivalences are implicit in the set representation of clauses:

$A \vee A$ is equivalent to A

$A \vee B$ is equivalent to $B \vee A$

$A \vee (B \vee C)$ is equivalent to $(A \vee B) \vee C$.

In the propositional case, the *resolvent* of two clauses represented as sets:

$$\{A\} \cup F \text{ and } \{\neg A\} \cup G$$

is the clause $F \cup G$.

In this book, we represent clauses as conditionals, but we treat the conditions and conclusions of clauses as sets of atoms. This simplifies the statement of the resolution rule, because it means that the atom A that is resolved upon can occur anywhere in the conclusion of one parent and anywhere in the conditions of the other parent. It also means that if an atom occurs in the conditions of both parents or in the conclusions of both parents, then the duplicate occurrences of the atom are automatically merged into one occurrence in the resolvent. Merging duplicate atoms is also called *factoring*.

Resolution is sound and *refutation complete*. If a set of clauses has no model, then there exists a derivation of *false* using only the resolution rule of inference (including factoring).

The refutation completeness of resolution suffices for showing *logical consequence* in classical first-order logic: To show that a set of sentences S logically implies a sentence C in classical logic, translate S and the negation of C into clausal form and use resolution to derive *false*.

The unrestricted resolution rule is very elegant, but also very inefficient. To improve efficiency, numerous refinements have been developed. Most of these refinements are generalisations of forward and backward reasoning. For example, hyper-resolution (Robinson, 1965b) is a generalisation of forward reasoning and SL-resolution (Kowalski and Kuehner, 1971) is a generalisation of backward reasoning. The connection graph proof procedure (Kowalski, 1975 and chapter 8, 1979), on the other hand, performs unrestricted resolution, but deletes links when resolutions are performed to avoid redundancies.

In the case of propositional definite clauses, forward reasoning is the special case of resolution in which $B \rightarrow C$ is derived from A and $A \wedge B \rightarrow C$. Backward reasoning is, in effect, the special case in which $D \wedge B \rightarrow false$ is derived from $D \rightarrow A$ and $A \wedge B \rightarrow false$.

Unification and factoring

In the non-propositional case, in which clauses can contain (universally quantified) variables, the resolution rule needs to be extended with unification, to make the two atoms resolved upon identical. Given two clauses:

$$D \rightarrow E \vee A_1$$

$$A_2 \wedge B \rightarrow C$$

such that A_1 and A_2 are unifiable, the resolvent is:

$$D' \wedge B' \rightarrow E' \vee C'$$

where B', C', D' and E' are obtained by applying the most general unifier of A_1 and A_2 to B, C, D and E respectively.

The original resolution rule is a little more complicated than this, because it includes additional unifications, to make two literals in the same clause identical, to factor them into one literal. Factoring is unnecessary in the case of Horn clauses, but is necessary in some other cases.

Consider the example of the barber paradox, in which a barber, John, shaves everyone who does not shave himself, but shaves no one who does shave himself. Ignoring the complication that the variable standing for the shaved person ought to be restricted to some appropriate sort (as mentioned in Chapters A1 and 6), the example can be represented in the clausal form:

$$shaves(john, X) \vee shaves(X, X)$$
$$shaves(john, X) \wedge shaves(X, X) \rightarrow false$$

These two clauses have four resolvents (two of which are duplicates):

$$shaves(X, X) \rightarrow shaves(X, X)$$
$$shaves(john, john) \rightarrow shaves(john, john)$$
$$shaves(john, john) \rightarrow shaves(john, john)$$
$$shaves(john, X) \rightarrow shaves(john, X)$$

No matter how many further resolutions are performed, it is impossible to derive *false*, because every resolution step deletes two atoms, leaving two atoms behind in the resolvent.

In cases such as these, the simple resolution rule needs to be augmented with factoring: Given a clause of one of the two forms

$$D \rightarrow E \vee A_1 \vee A_2$$
or $$A_1 \wedge A_2 \wedge B \rightarrow C$$

such that A_1 and A_2 have a most general instance A, *factoring* derives the clause

$$D' \to E' \vee A$$

or $$A \wedge B' \to C'$$

where B', C', D' and E' are obtained by applying the most general unifier of A_1 and A_2 to B, C, D and E respectively.

Applied to the barber paradox, factoring generates two additional clauses from the two original clauses:

$$shaves(john, john) \to false$$
$$shaves(john, john)$$

Resolution derives *false* in one step, proving that no such barber exists.

Connection graphs

The efficiency of resolution can be greatly enhanced by storing clauses, their unifying links and their unifiers in connection graphs. These links can then be activated later when needed, without having to search for the connections.

Reasoning is performed by activating a link – any link at all – adding the resolvent to the graph, deleting the activated link, and adding new links between the newly added resolvent and other clauses in the graph.

The deletion of a link may cause a parent clause to contain an unlinked atom. When this happens, the parent clause can be deleted along with all its other links. This deletion can sometimes have a rippling effect, leading to the deletion of other clauses and their links. Here is an example from Kowalski (1979):

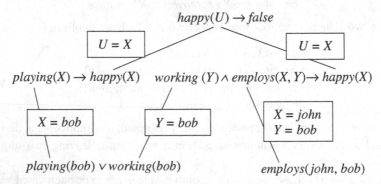

The connection graph proof procedure, like resolution, is a refutation procedure. So it succeeds, if the clause *false* is derived. Notice that the clause *playing(bob)* ∨ *working(bob)* is a non-Horn clause. So strict forward or backward reasoning is not possible.

Any link in the graph can be activated. Let's see how close we can come to reasoning forward with breadth-first search. The obvious place to start is with the link connected to the "fact" *employs(john, bob)*. When the associated resolvent is generated and the link is deleted, both parent clauses have unlinked atoms, and therefore both parents can be deleted, along with all their other links. Doing so, in effect, replaces the two parents by the resolvent, because the resolvent inherits its parents' links. However, the unifiers associated with these inherited links are now the result of combining the unifier of the activated link with the unifiers of the inherited links:

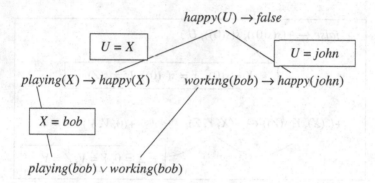

Again we can activate any link. Reasoning forward with the disjunction this time, choosing the link with the unifier $X = bob$, the resolvent clause replaces both its parents again:

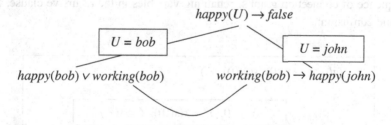

Activating the link between the two occurrences of the atom *working(bob)*, we obtain:

$$happy(U) \rightarrow false$$

$$\boxed{U = bob} \qquad \boxed{U = john}$$

$$happy(bob) \lor happy(john)$$

The two remaining links can be activated in any order, and even in parallel. Either way, the clause *false* is derived in two steps, and the rest of the connection graph is empty. The happy person we are looking for is $U = bob$ or $U = john$.

A recursive clause, like $+(s(X), Y, s(Z)) \leftarrow +(X, Y, Z)$, can resolve with a copy of itself, giving in this case the resolvent $+(s(s(X)), Y, s(s(Z))) \leftarrow +(X, Y, Z)$. Self-resolving clauses give rise to internal links within the same clause, standing for links between two different copies of the clause. In such cases, similar rules about deletion and inheritance of links apply. Here is a connection graph for computing the sum of $2 + 2$:

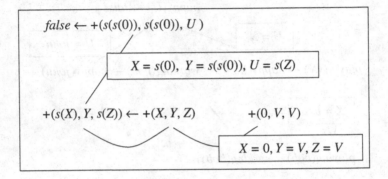

In theory, any link, including the internal link, could be selected for activation. However, the standard program execution strategy activates links backwards from the goal. Applying this strategy systematically gives rise to the following sequence of connection graphs, renaming variables in the recursive clause, to avoid confusion:

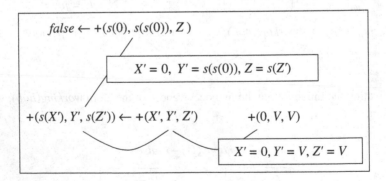

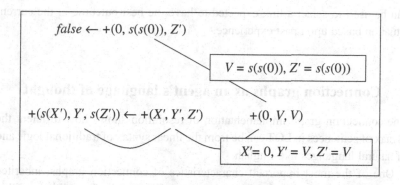

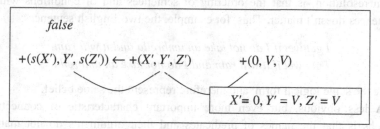

The cumulative instantiations $U = s(Z)$, $Z = s(Z')$, $Z' = s(s(0))$ compute the sum $U = s(s(s(s(0))))$.

In examples like this, if you ignore the fact that the connection graph is just facilitating resolution, it looks like the goal clause is being repeatedly over-written, in the way that computers execute conventional computer programs. If you can stretch your imagination a little further, then you might even imagine that the unifying substitutions are like signals that are transmitted along a network of neural connections in a brain.

This imaginative view of connection graphs, as a kind of connectionist model of the mind, is supported by their similarity with Maes' (1990) spreading activation networks. As in activation networks, different levels of strength can be associated with different initial goals, reflecting their relative importance. Different levels of strength can also be associated with different observations, reflecting perhaps some instinctive judgement of their significance. As in activation networks, these activation levels can be transmitted from clause to clause along links in the connection graph.

Such activation levels are similar to utility measures in decision theory; and, like utility measures, they can be weighted by measures of uncertainty. In the case of connection graphs, these weights might reflect the frequency with which the activation of a link has contributed to successful outcomes in the past. The resulting level of activation weighted by likelihood of leading to a useful result can be used to select a link expected to have the best outcome in the current situation based upon past experience.

Connection graphs as an agent's language of thought

The connection graph implementation of resolution shows how different the syntax of sentences in LOT can be from the linear syntax of traditional logic and of natural languages like English.

One of the most important characteristics of connection graphs, inherited from resolution, is that the ordering of sentences and of conditions within sentences doesn't matter. Thus, for example, the two English sentences:

> *I get wet if I do not take an umbrella and it will rain.*
> *I get wet if it will rain and I do not take an umbrella.*

have the same logical form, and therefore represent the same belief.

A less obvious, but even more important characteristic of connection graphs is that the names of predicates and their arguments do not matter. The only thing that, matters is the connections, both the connections within the graph and the connections to the real world outside the agent's mind. For example:

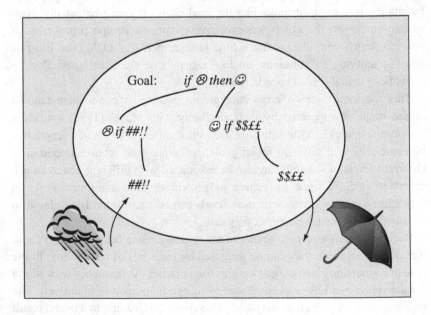

Subsumption

The connection graph proof procedure is only one among a great number of refinements of resolution that have been developed to improve the efficiency of automated reasoning. Another such enhancement, which is compatible with connection graphs, is the deletion of subsumed clauses. This improves efficiency, because if there exists a refutation using a subsumed clause, then there exists an even shorter refutation using the subsuming clause. There is no need to keep both clauses, because the subsuming clause is both more informative and more efficient than the subsumed clause. Provided it is done carefully, deletion of subsumed clauses does not affect soundness or completeness.

Suppose, for example, that I believe:

> *mary is going to the party.*
> *mary is going to the party* → *X is going to the party.*
> *I am going to the party* ∨ *I will stay at home.*

From the first two clauses, I can derive that everyone (or everything) is going to the party:

> *X is going to the party.*

This subsumes the disjunction *I am going to the party* ∨ *I will stay at home*, which therefore can be deleted.

As noted in Chapter A2, deletion of subsumed clauses is a pragmatic way of dealing with the paradoxes of material implication without abandoning classical logic.

Paraconsistency

The paradoxes of material implication are closely related to the property of classical logic that an inconsistent set of sentences logically implies every sentence. This unintuitive property of classical logic comes from interpreting *whenever* in the definition of logical consequence:

> A sentence *C* is a *logical consequence* of a set of sentences *S*
> (or *S logically implies C*) if (and only if) *C* is *true* whenever *S* is *true*.

as material implication in the meta-language. Interpreting *whenever* in this way, if *S* is inconsistent, then it is *false* that *S* is *true* in any interpretation. Therefore *C* is a logical consequence of *S*, and it doesn't matter whether or not *C* is *true* in any interpretation. However, it would be more informative to say:

Given that C is a *logical consequence* of S and that S is inconsistent,
it is impossible to say whether or not C is *true* in any interpretation.

Looked at like this, there is nothing wrong with interpreting *whenever* as
material implication. What's wrong is thinking that it is informative to tell
someone that a sentence is a logical consequence of an inconsistent set of
sentences.

In fact, resolution, whether or not it is augmented with subsumption, derives
only informative consequences of a set of clauses. Consider the simplest
possible case of two clauses, p and *not p*. Only one application of resolution
is possible, and it derives *false* in one step. It doesn't derive that *the moon is
made of green cheese*, or that *the world is coming to an end*.

However, there is a perverse sense in which resolution can be used to show
that any sentence q is a logical consequence of p and *not p*:

To show q is a logical consequence of p and *not p*,
represent *not q* as a set of clauses *not-Q*,
use resolution to refute the set of clauses $\{p, not\, p\} \cup not\text{-}Q$, and
ignore the fact that none of the clauses in *not-Q*
participate in the refutation.

But with backward reasoning (generalised to arbitrary clauses as in SL-
resolution), even this perverse approach will not work. Backwards reasoning
from the conclusion reduces goals to subgoals using only relevant clauses. If the
inconsistent clauses are not relevant to the solution, then they will not contribute
to a proof. For example, if q is an atomic sentence, then q cannot be shown at
all by backward reasoning using the inconsistent and irrelevant clauses p and
not p.

In the same way that the paradoxes of material implication have led to
relevance logic and other non-classical logics, the fact that inconsistent sets of
sentences logically imply any sentence has led to the development of non-
classical, paraconsistent logics (Priest, 2002). As the discussion in this section
shows, these problems can be solved in classical logic, by treating them as
pragmatic problems in the spirit of Grice (1989).

Conclusions

The resolution rule is an elegant and powerful rule of inference, which includes
forward and backward reasoning as special cases. When it was first invented (or
discovered?) by its author, John Alan Robinson (1965a), it was presented as a
machine-oriented inference principle, suitable for computer implementation,

but not for human use. In my 1979 book, I argued, on the contrary, that special cases of resolution have a natural interpretation in human-oriented terms.

These two contrary views of resolution are in fact complementary, and are supported by dual process theories of human reasoning. Moreover, the connection graph implementation of resolution is compatible with the view that the human mind is like a machine. Its software is the clausal form of logic, and its hardware is the resolution principle. Reasoning in connection graphs is sound, because resolution is sound. However, despite many attempts to prove completeness (Siekmann and Wrightson, 2002), it is not known whether or not it is complete.

Although completeness is an important theoretical property, the difficulty of demonstrating its completeness is somewhat paradoxically an argument in its favour. Completeness is easy to show when a proof procedure allows many different, but essentially equivalent ways of generating the same proof. It is more difficult to show counter-examples of when there are fewer ways of generating a proof. As long as there are no proofs that cannot be generated, the difficulty of demonstrating completeness suggests that the connection graph proof procedure is efficient because it contains few redundancies.

In Chapter A2, I argued that subsumption solves the paradoxes of material implication, and in this chapter I argued that resolution solves the problem that an inconsistent set of sentences logically implies every sentence. In both cases, the solution treats these as pragmatic problems, which do not affect the semantics and proof procedures of classical logic.

Resolution and the connection graph proof procedure were developed as refutation procedures for showing *logical consequence* in classical first-order logic. However, I have argued in other chapters that it is truth in minimal models rather than logical consequence that we should be aiming for.

In fact, without acknowledging it, many of the connection graphs presented in other chapters do not conform to the official resolution rule, because they contain links between atoms in the conclusions of conditional goals and atoms in the conclusions of conditional beliefs. These non-conformist connection graphs are needed for showing that conditional goals are true in minimal models, as shown implicitly in Chapter A6.

A6
The logic of abductive logic programming

This additional chapter provides the technical support for abductive logic programming (ALP), which is the basis of the Computational Logic used in this book. ALP uses abduction, not only to explain observations, but to generate plans of action.

ALP extends ordinary logic programming by combining the closed predicates of logic programming, which are defined by clauses, with open predicates, which are constrained directly or indirectly by integrity constraints represented in a variant of classical logic. Integrity constraints in ALP include as special cases the functionalities of condition–action rules, maintenance goals and constraints.

More formally, an *abductive logic program* $<P, O, IC>$ consists of a logic program P, a set of open predicates O and a set of integrity constraints IC. The open predicates are restricted so they do not occur in the conclusions of clauses in P. This restriction is not essential, but it simplifies the technicalities.

There are many variants of ALP, with different syntax, semantics and proof procedures. In this book, we express integrity constraints in the form of generalised conditionals, which are like ordinary conditionals, but which may have existential quantifiers and disjunctions in their conclusions. The inclusion of disjunctions in the conclusions of integrity constraints means that, in the propositional case, they have the full power of classical logic.[1] The inclusion of existential quantifiers in conclusions means that, in the non-propositional case, the use of Skolem functions to eliminate existential quantifiers, as discussed in Chapter A1, is reduced in comparison with ordinary causal form.

In ALP, we are concerned with the problem of solving a goal clause G, which may simply be an atomic sentence in the case of explaining an observation, or

---

[1] In the propositional case, they have the expressive power of *range-restricted* clauses, in which every universally quantified variable occurring in the conclusion of an integrity constraint also occurs in the conditions of the constraint.

may be a conjunction of conditions in the case of planning. In both cases, a *solution* of G is a set Δ of ground instances of the open predicates O such that:

G holds with respect to the program $P \cup \Delta$ and

$P \cup \Delta$ satisfies *IC*.

The notions of *holding* and *satisfying* are deliberately vague (or abstract). This is because many different notions of *holding* and *satisfying* have been explored, and there is still no general agreement about which notions are most appropriate.

Several competing views of the semantics of integrity constraints, associated with different proof procedures for checking database integrity, were investigated intensively in the field of deductive databases in the 1980s. To begin with, the two main views were the consistency view and the theoremhood view. In the *consistency view*, an integrity constraint is satisfied if it is consistent with the database. In the *theoremhood view*, it is satisfied if it is a theorem, true in all models of the database. Reiter (1988) also proposed an *epistemic view*, according to which integrity constraints are *true* statements about what the database knows.

Reiter (1988) also showed that in many cases these three views are equivalent for databases with the closed-world assumption. For relational databases, the three views are also equivalent to the standard view that a database satisfies an integrity constraint if the integrity constraint is *true* in the database regarded as a Herbrand interpretation.

However, there are also many cases in which these different views result in different judgements of integrity satisfaction. The simplest example is the program consisting of the single Horn clause $C \leftarrow C$ and the integrity constraint $C \rightarrow false$. According to the consistency and epistemic views, the integrity constraint is satisfied; but according to the standard theoremhood view, it is not.

The different views can be understood as different ways of interpreting negation as failure. The consistency and epistemic views understand it as infinite failure, and the theoremhood view interprets it as finite failure. For Horn clause programs, the consistency and epistemic views are equivalent to the view that an integrity constraint is satisfied if and only if it is *true* in the unique minimal model.

Having been involved in the debates about the semantics of integrity constraints, developed proof procedures for both integrity checking (Sadri and Kowalski, 1988) and ALP (Fung and Kowalski, 1997; Kowalski *et al.*, 1998) and argued against conventional model-theoretic semantics (Kowalski, 1995), I am now convinced that semantics in general, and the semantics of ALP in particular, is best understood in terms of truth in minimal models:

A set Δ of ground instances of the open predicates O is a *solution* of G if and only if $\{G\} \cup IC$ is *true* in some minimal model of $P \cup \Delta$.

The notion of *minimal model* is clear-cut in the case in which $P \cup \Delta$ is a Horn clause program. Although this case may seem very restricted, it is the basis for all other cases and extensions. The extension to the case where P and IC are not ground is quite straightforward, involving mainly just performing instantiation or unification. The extension to the case with negation is similar to the extension from minimal models of Horn clause programs to stable models of logic programs with negation. We will discuss the treatment of negation and other extensions later in the chapter.

A system of inference rules for ground Horn ALP

A *ground Horn* abductive logic program $<P, O, IC>$ consists of a program P, which is a ground (variable-free) Horn clause program, a set of open predicates O and integrity constraints IC, which are ground conditionals of the form:

$$A \wedge B \rightarrow C$$

where A is an *open atom* (i.e. an atom with an open predicate in O), and B and C are conjunctions of atoms.[2] Integrity constraints of this form are like the event–condition–action rules of active databases (Widom and Ceri, 1996). The atom A is like an event that is not defined by the database.

The problem is to solve a ground Horn goal clause G_0, which is a conjunction of variable-free atoms.

The following definition of *abductive derivation* is adapted from the IFF proof procedure for ALP (Fung and Kowalski, 1997). Whereas the IFF proof procedure uses logic programs expressed in the biconditional, *if and only if* form, the abductive proof procedure of this chapter employs similar inference rules for logic programs in conditional form. The two proof procedures differ mainly in their semantics. The IFF proof procedure employs the theoremhood view of integrity satisfaction, whereas the abductive proof procedure of this chapter employs the minimal model view.

The proof procedure uses forward and backward reasoning in an attempt to generate a solution Δ of G_0 by generating an abductive derivation G_0, G_1, ..., G_N such that G_N contains the set Δ but no other goals that need to be solved. Each G_{i+1} is obtained from the previous G_i by one of the following inference rules:

---

[2] Note that the atom A can occur anywhere in the conditions of the constraint. Note also that if there is no B, then this is equivalent to B being *true*. If there is no C, then this is equivalent to C being *false*. We will discuss the case where C is a disjunction of conjunctions later.

F_1: *Forward reasoning* with a selected open atom A in G_i and an integrity constraint in IC. Suppose the integrity constraint has the form $A \wedge B \rightarrow C$ and G_i has the form $A \wedge G$. Then G_{i+1} is $(B \rightarrow C) \wedge A \wedge G$.

(Notice that this introduces a conditional into the goal clause. For this reason, we call the resulting goal clauses *generalised goal clauses*.)

F_2: *Forward reasoning* can also be used with a selected open atom A and a conditional in G_i. Suppose G_i has the form $(A \wedge B \rightarrow C) \wedge A \wedge G$.

Then G_{i+1} is $(B \rightarrow C) \wedge A \wedge G$.

B_1: *Backward reasoning* with a selected atom C in G_i and a clause in P. Suppose the clause has the form $C \leftarrow D$ and G_i has the form $C \wedge G$.

Then G_{i+1} is $D \wedge G$.

B_2: *Backward reasoning* with a selected atom C in a *conditional* in G_i having the form $(C \wedge B \rightarrow H) \wedge G$. Suppose $C \leftarrow D_1 \cdots C \leftarrow D_m$ are all the clauses in P having conclusion C.

Then G_{i+1} is $(D_1 \wedge B \rightarrow H) \wedge \ldots \wedge (D_m \wedge B \rightarrow H) \wedge G$.

Fact: *Factoring* between two copies of an open atom A in G_i. If G_i has the form $A \wedge A \wedge G$, then G_{i+1} is $A \wedge G$.

(Any previous applications of F_1 and F_2 to any occurrence of A are deemed to have been done to the resulting single copy of A.)

S: *Logical simplification*: Replace *true* $\rightarrow C$ by C.
   Replace *true* $\wedge C$ by C.
   Replace *false* $\wedge C$ by *false*.

An abductive derivation $G_0, G_1, \ldots, G_N$ using these inference rules is a *successfully terminating derivation* of a set of open atoms Δ if and only if:

G_N is not *false*,
G_N has the form $(B_1 \rightarrow C_1) \wedge \ldots \wedge (B_m \rightarrow C_m) \wedge A_1 \wedge \ldots \wedge A_n$, $m \geq 0, n \geq 0$, where each A_i is an open atom,
no further applications of the inference rules can be performed on G_N
no matter which atom is selected, and $\Delta = \{A_1, \ldots, A_n\}$.

The residual conditionals $B_i \rightarrow C_i$ in a successfully terminating derivation are conditionals introduced by F_1 but whose remaining conditions B_i are not *true* in the minimal model of $P \cup \Delta$. The conditions B_i of these residuals may consist solely of open atoms not in Δ; or they may contain closed atoms C that are not the conclusions of any clauses in P. In the latter case, it is as though there were a clause of the form $C \leftarrow false$ in P (as a result of which B_i is *false*, and the residual can be simplified to *true* and be ignored).

Note that if G_i has the form $C \wedge G$, where C is a closed atom that is the conclusion of no clause in P, then G_i cannot be part of a successfully terminating derivation. It is as though there were a clause of the form $C \leftarrow false$ in P (as a result of which C is *false*, and G_i can be simplified to *false*).

Together the inference rules F_1, F_2, and B_2 check whether the conditions of an integrity constraint hold *true* in the minimal model of $P \cup \Delta$; and if they do, logical simplification adds the conclusion of the integrity constraint to the goals. The inference rule B_1 uses ordinary backward reasoning to solve both the initial goal and any new goals introduced from the conclusions of integrity constraints. In effect, the factoring rule *Fact* treats the open predicates added to Δ as though they were facts added to P. The inference rules F_1, F_2, B_1, B_2, *Fact* and S are *sound*.

Theorem: Given a ground Horn abductive logic program $<P, O, IC>$ and ground Horn goal clause G_0:

> If there exists a successfully terminating derivation of Δ,
> then $\{G_0\} \cup IC$ is *true* in the minimal model of $P \cup \Delta$.

The inference rules are not complete, because they do not recognise infinite failure.

Infinite success and incompleteness

Consider the abductive logic program $< \{C \leftarrow C\}, \{A\}, \{A \wedge C \to false\}>$ and the goal A. The inference rules generate the non-terminating derivation:

G_0	A	given
G_1	$(C \to false) \wedge A$	by F_1
G_2	$(C \to false) \wedge A$	by B_2
	ad infinitum $\quad \cdots$	by B_2

This infinite derivation is the only derivation possible. However, $\Delta = \{A\}$ is a solution of G_0 because both the integrity constraint and the initial goal are true in the minimal model of $P \cup \{A\}$. The integrity constraint $A \wedge C \to false$ is *true*, because C is *false*.

It is possible to capture this kind of non-terminating "successful" derivation by broadening the notion of successful derivation:

An abductive derivation $G_0, G_1, \ldots, G_N$ is a *successful derivation* of a set of open atoms Δ if and only if:

> G_N is not *false*,
> G_N has the form $(B_1 \to C_1) \wedge \cdots \wedge (B_m \to C_m) \wedge A_1 \wedge \cdots \wedge A_n, m \geq 0, n \geq 0$,
> where each A_i is an open atom,
> no further applications of the inference rules can be performed on the A_i,
> $\Delta = \{A_1, \ldots, A_n\}$ and
> the conditions B_i of the residues are not *true*
> in the minimal model of $P \cup \Delta$.

Implementing the requirement that the conditions of the residues are not *true* in $P \cup \Delta$ can be done by trying to show that the conditions are *true* and failing. However, as the example above shows, this necessitates recognising infinite failure. This is impossible in general, but can be solved effectively in many cases (including the ground case) by the use of *tabling* (Sagonas *et al.*, 1994).

With the new definition, the inference rules are complete in the following sense.

Theorem: Given a ground Horn abductive logic program $<P, O, IC>$, a ground Horn goal clause G_0 and a set of ground open atoms Δ:

> If $\{G_0\} \cup IC$ is *true* in the minimal model of $P \cup \Delta$,
> then there exists a successful derivation of Δ', such that $\Delta' \subseteq \Delta$.

Proof procedures for ground Horn ALP

The inference rules F_1, F_2, B_1, B_2, *Fact* and S determine the form of abductive derivations. To obtain a proof procedure, it is necessary to specify how the search space of derivations is generated and explored. It is important to note that only B_1 generates alternative derivations, corresponding to alternative ways of reasoning backwards from a selected atomic goal C in G_i using alternative clauses $C \leftarrow D$ in P. All the other inference rules simply transform one (generalised) goal clause G_i into another. Moreover, the order in which the inference rules are applied doesn't matter, because they all have to be applied (except for the alternative ways of applying B_1) in order to generate a successful derivation. However, for efficiency, the simplification rules S and *Fact* should be applied as soon as they are applicable.

The search space of all possible derivations has the form of an *or-tree* (or *search tree*):

R The initial goal G_0 is the *root* of the tree.

S/Fact Given any node G_i in the search tree,
   if a rule in S or *Fact* can be applied,
   then the node has a single successor G_{i+1}
   obtained by applying one such rule.

Select Otherwise, some atom C either in the position $C \wedge G$
   or in the position $(C \wedge B \rightarrow H) \wedge G$ in G_i
   is selected for application of the inference rules.

F If the selected atom C is an open atom in the position $C \wedge G$, and F_1 can be applied with an integrity constraint in IC or F_2 can be applied with some conditional in G_i, then one such application is performed to generate G_{i+1}. In both cases, this application of F_1 or F_2 should not have been performed before.

B_1 If the selected atom C is a closed atom in the position $C \wedge G$, then there are as many successor nodes G_{i+1} as there are ways of applying B_1 with some clause in P with conclusion C.

B_2 If the selected atom C is in the position $(C \wedge B \to H) \wedge G$, then B_2 is used to generate G_{i+1}.

It is important to note that there are as many such search trees as there are ways of applying a simplification or factoring rule in step *S/Fact*, of applying forward reasoning in step *F*, and of selecting an atom in step *Select*. It is necessary to explore only one such search tree in an attempt to generate a successful derivation. This makes it worthwhile to put some effort into deciding which search space to generate, to make the resulting search as efficient as possible. Any search strategy, including depth-first, breadth-first, best-first, serial or parallel, can be used to explore the selected search space. In particular, the search tree could be embedded in a connection graph, and the best-first search strategy sketched in Chapter 4 could be used to guide the search.

Integrity constraints with disjunctive conclusions

Several of the examples in the book involve integrity constraints with disjunctive conclusions:

$$C \to D_1 \vee \ldots \vee D_m$$

To deal with such integrity constraints, it suffices to add the additional inference rule:

Splitting: If G_i has the form $(D_1 \vee \ldots \vee D_m) \wedge G$, then there are as many successor nodes G_{i+1} of the form $D_i \wedge G$ as there are disjuncts D_i.

Splitting needs to be performed when the conditions of an integrity constraint have been reduced to *true*, and the disjunctive conclusion has been conjoined to the subgoals in G_i.

In the propositional case, integrity constraints with disjunctive conclusions have the expressive power of the clausal form of classical logic. The splitting rule, together with the forward reasoning rules F_1 and F_2, turns the proof procedure into a model generator for clausal logic. In fact, the proof procedure for the case $<P, O, IC>$, where P is empty and O is the set of all predicates in the language, is equivalent to the SATCHMO (Manthey and Bry, 1988) model generator (and proof procedure) for the clausal form of classical logic.

We will see how splitting can be used to implement the totality restriction of the stable model semantics of negation as failure, in the next section.

Negation through abduction with contraries and constraints

The minimal model semantics of ALP blends smoothly with the stable model semantics of logic programs with negation. In both cases, the semantics is defined in terms of the minimal model of a Horn clause program P extended with a set Δ. In the case of abduction, Δ consists of open ground atoms; and in the case of logic programs with negation, Δ consists of negations of ground atoms treated as though they were positive atoms.

The stable model semantics can be interpreted as a special case of ALP, by treating all negations of atoms *not a* as positive, open atoms, say *non-a*, and by using integrity constraints to express that *a* and *non-a* are contraries.[3] The most important integrity constraint needed for this is the *consistency constraint*:

$$non\text{-}a \land a \rightarrow false$$

We also need to ensure that Δ is sufficiently large. To capture the stable model semantics, we need the *totality constraint*:

$$true \rightarrow non\text{-}a \lor a$$

With this representation, for every logic program with negation P, there is a *corresponding* abductive logic program $<P', O, IC>$, where O is the set of positive contraries of the negations of atoms in P, P' is the Horn clause program obtained from P by replacing negations of atoms with their positive contraries in O, and IC is the set of consistency and totality constraints.

With this correspondence the stable models of P coincide with the minimal models of $P' \cup \Delta$, where Δ is a solution of the initial goal *true* (Eshghi and Kowalski, 1989). In fact, the very definition of stable model coincides with the definition of abductive solution in this special case.

However, there is a problem with the correspondence: It requires the satisfaction of all the totality constraints whether they are relevant to the initial goal G_0 or not. We will investigate this problem and discuss its solution in the following sections.

The case for ignoring the totality constraints

Consider the program from Chapter A4:

P: *bob will go $\leftarrow$ not john will go.*
        john will go $\leftarrow$ not bob will go.

---

[3] Treating negations as positive contraries makes it easier to compare the treatment of negation in ALP with the treatment of negation in the stable model semantics. However, it is also possible to treat negations directly as open formulas, as in the IFF proof procedure.

To reformulate the program in ALP terms, re-express the negative conditions as positive open predicates, say in the form:

P':   *bob will go* ← *john stays away.*
         john will go ← *bob stays away.*
O: {*john stays away, bob stays away*}
IC: *bob will go* ∧ *bob stays away* → *false.*
         john will go ∧ *john stays away* → *false.*

Ignore the totality constraints for now, and consider the initial goal G_0 = *bob will go*. The proof procedure generates only one successfully terminating derivation with solution Δ = {*john stays away*} as follows:

G_0 *bob will go*
G_1 *john stays away*
G_2 (*john will go* → *false*) ∧ *john stays away*
G_3 (*bob stays away* → *false*) ∧ *john stays away*

Similarly, the proof procedure generates the solution Δ = {*bob stays away*} for the initial goal G_0 = *john will go*. The results are the same as those obtained with the stable model semantics, but without the totality constraints.

The case for the totality constraints

The following example shows that we need the totality constraints, or something like them. Consider the program consisting of the clauses:

P: *john can fly* ← *john is a bird* ∧ *not(john is abnormal)*
       john is a bird

Under the closed-world assumption and the stable model semantics, since it cannot be shown that *john is abnormal*, it follows that *not(john is abnormal)* and therefore that *john can fly*. But it cannot be shown that *not(john can fly)*.

But without the totality constraints it is possible to show *not(john can fly)* re-expressed as a positive predicate *john is flightless*, using the corresponding abductive logic program <P', O, IC>, where:

P' *john can fly* ← *john is a bird* ∧ *john is normal*
        john is a bird
O {*john is flightless, john is normal*}
IC: *john is flightless* ∧ *john can fly* → *false.*
        john is normal ∧ *john is abnormal* → *false.*

According to the semantics of ALP without totality constraints, *john is flightless* has the undesirable solution Δ = {*john is flightless*}. This same solution is also generated by the abductive proof procedure:

G_0 *john is flightless*
G_1 *(john can fly → false) ∧ john is flightless*
G_2 *(john is a bird ∧ john is normal → false) ∧ john is flightless*
G_3 *(john is normal → false) ∧ john is flightless*

It seems that we need the totality constraint (or something like it), after all.[4]
With the totality constraint:

true → john is normal ∨ john is abnormal

the undesired solution disappears, because neither *john is normal* nor *john is abnormal* is *true* in the minimal model of $P' \cup \Delta$, where $\Delta = \{john\ is\ flightless\}$.

Here is what the proof procedure (with one particular selection strategy) does with the same problem augmented with the totality constraint above (ignoring the other totality constraint, to avoid clutter). The first three steps of the derivation are the same. However, the initial goal can be regarded as containing the disjunctive conclusion of the totality constraint, because the condition of the constraint is *true*:

G_0 *(john is normal ∨ john is abnormal) ∧ john is flightless*
G_1 *(john is normal ∨ john is abnormal) ∧*
       (john can fly → false) ∧ john is flightless
G_2 *(john is normal ∨ john is abnormal) ∧*
       (john is a bird ∧ john is normal → false) ∧ john is flightless
G_3 *(john is normal ∨ john is abnormal) ∧*
       (john is normal → false) ∧ john is flightless
G_4 *john is normal ∧ (john is normal → false) ∧ john is flightless*
G_5 *john is normal ∧ john is flightless ∧ false*
G_6 *false*
G_4' *john is abnormal ∧ (john is normal → false) ∧ john is flightless*

The generalised goal clause G_3 has two successor nodes G_4 and G_4'. The successor node G_4 leads to a failing derivation of *false*. The successor node G_4' terminates unsuccessfully, because *john is abnormal* is not an open atom and no inference rules can be applied to G_4'. So with the totality constraint, the undesired solution disappears, both in the semantics and in the proof procedure.

An alternative to the totality constraints

Unfortunately, the totality constraints are computationally very expensive. They require the global consideration of a totality constraint for every ground atom in the

---

[4] This is also a counter-example to replacing the totality requirement of the stable model semantics by the requirement that $P \cup \Delta$ or $P' \cup \Delta$ be maximally consistent.

language, whether the ground atom is relevant to the goal or not. This is bad enough in the ground case; but in the case with variables, it is prohibitively expensive.

An alternative to checking all the totality constraints is to check only those totality constraints that are locally relevant to the problem at hand. In addition to avoiding the computational problems of the global constraints, the local alternative has other merits. Among its other properties, the alternative is inconsistency tolerant, deals with the problem of preventative maintenance, and has a nice interpretation in terms of arguments for and against the initial goal. The effect of restricting the totality constraints to those that are locally relevant can be obtained by adding a minor variant of the negation rewriting rule of the IFF proof procedure, together with an additional simplification rule:

Neg: If G_i has the form $(non\text{-}C \wedge B \rightarrow H) \wedge G,$
      then G_{i+1} is $(B \rightarrow H \vee C) \wedge G.$
      Replace *non-C* $\wedge$ *C* by *false*
      Replace *false* $\vee$ *C* by *C*.

We assume that the set of integrity constraints *IC* is a set of clauses possibly with disjunctive conclusions, but without negation. Therefore, negation rewriting deals only with negation introduced from the conditions of logic programs by backward reasoning using B_2. But if a negation *non-C* is introduced by B_2 into the conditions of an integrity constraint representing a maintenance goal, then *Neg* makes it possible to satisfy the maintenance goal by making *C true*, thereby preventing the need to achieve the conclusion of the maintenance goal.

To see how negation rewriting compares with the totality constraints, reconsider the example of the last section $G_0 = john \ is \ flightless$ using the same abductive logic program:

P'   *john can fly* $\leftarrow$ *john is a bird* $\wedge$ *john is normal*
     john is a bird
O   {*john is flightless, john is normal*}
IC: *john is flightless* $\wedge$ *john can fly* $\rightarrow$ *false*.
     john is normal $\wedge$ *john is abnormal* $\rightarrow$ *false*.

The first three steps are the same as they were before without the totality constraint:

G_0 *john is flightless*
G_1 $(john \ can \ fly \rightarrow false) \wedge john \ is \ flightless$
G_2 $(john \ is \ a \ bird \wedge john \ is \ normal \rightarrow false) \wedge john \ is \ flightless$
G_3 $(john \ is \ normal \rightarrow false) \wedge john \ is \ flightless$

Whereas before, without totality, the derivation terminated successfully with G_3, now negation rewriting applies, and the derivation terminates unsuccessfully with G_4:

G_4 *john is abnormal* ∧ *john is flightless*

The derivation terminates unsuccessfully, for the same reason that G_4' failed when we used the totality constraint before, because the subgoal *john is abnormal* is not an open atom, and no further inference rules can be applied.

Thus negation rewriting eliminates the same undesired solution eliminated by the totality constraint before, but now by means of a local inference rule, which applies only when it is relevant.

Before we discuss the semantics of the proof procedure with negation rewriting, reconsider the goal G_0 = *bob will go* using the abductive logic program:

P':   *bob will go* ← *john stays away.*
        john will go ← *bob stays away.*
O: {*john stays away, bob stays away*}
IC: *bob will go* ∧ *bob stays away* → *false.*
        john will go ∧ *john stays away* → *false.*

The example is significant both because the proof procedure obtains the same results as the stable model semantics, and because these results are different from those of the IFF proof procedure, on which the abductive proof procedure is based.

The first three steps are the same as they were without the totality constraint:

G_0 *bob will go*
G_1 *john stays away*
G_2 (*john will go* → *false*) ∧ *john stays away*
G_3 (*bob stays away* → *false*) ∧ *john stays away*

Before the derivation terminated successfully with G_3. Now negation rewriting applies, and the derivation terminates successfully with G_6:

G_4 *bob will go* ∧ *john stays away*
G_5 *john stays away* ∧ *john stays away*
G_6 *john stays away*

The derivation terminates, because the only inference rule, namely F_1, that can be applied to *john stays away* has already been applied to the earlier copy of *john stays away* and is treated as having been applied to the new single copy in accordance with the definition of *Fact*.

Preventative maintenance

The combination of *Neg* and *Splitting* makes it possible to satisfy maintenance goals by preventing the need to achieve their conclusions. For example, if you have an exam coming up and you fail the exam then you need to retake the exam later. If you don't like the idea of retaking the exam, you can reason as follows:

P: *you fail the exam ← you do not study.*

O: {*you have an exam, you study, you do not study, you retake the exam*}

IC: *you have an exam ∧ you fail the exam → you retake the exam.*

      you study ∧ you do not study → false.

G_0 *you have an exam*

G_2 *you have an exam ∧ (you do not study → you retake the exam)*

G_3 *you have an exam ∧ (you study ∨ you retake the exam)*

G_4 *you have an exam ∧ you study*

G_4' *you have an exam ∧ you retake the exam*

So the choice is up to you. Either you study or you retake the exam.

An argumentation-theoretic interpretation

An abductive derivation $G_0, G_1, \ldots, G_N$ using *Neg* for logic programs P with negation, but without other open predicates and other integrity constraints, can be viewed as constructing an argument to support and defend the claim G_0:

> The inference rule B_1 reduces the initial goal, and all other goals needed to support it, to subgoals, and ultimately to open subgoals of the form *non-a*. If the derivation is successful then the set of all these open subgoals is the set Δ.
>
> When an open atom *non-a* is generated by B_1, to be added to Δ, the inference rule F_1 is used with the consistency constraint to derive $a \rightarrow false$, in an attempt to attack the argument being constructed by B_1 by undermining *non-a*. However, no attempt is made to undermine *non-a* if *non-a* already belongs to Δ. Instead, *Fact* is used to merge the two copies of *non-a* into a single copy, and to avoid attacking and defending *non-a* redundantly.
>
> The inference rule B_2 reduces a in $a \rightarrow false$ to alternative arguments attacking *non-a*. Each such attacking argument is ultimately reduced to a conjunction of open subgoals of the form *non-b*.

For each such attacking argument, reduced to open atoms, the proof procedure attempts to undermine one such open atom *non-b* and defeat the attack. This is done by using the inference rules *Neg* and *Splitting*, to generate a counter-attack, by showing *b*. However, no attempt is made to counter-attack *non-b* if *non-b* belongs to Δ. Instead, F_2 is used to eliminate *non-b* from the attack. This also ensures that Δ does not attack itself.

In a successful derivation, this dialectic process of support, attack and counter-attack continues until every attack against the open atoms in Δ has been considered and counter-attacked, and all the goals and subgoals needed for this purpose have been reduced to open atoms in Δ.

An argumentation-theoretic semantics

This view of abductive derivations in terms of arguments and counter-arguments can be given an argumentation-theoretic semantics. Moreover, it suggests that the stable model semantics itself can also be understood in argumentation terms: given an abductive logic program $<P', O, IC>$ corresponding to a normal logic program P, the stable model semantics can be understood as sanctioning a set Δ of open atoms as a solution of a goal G_0 if and only if:

$P' \cup \Delta$ supports an argument for G_0.
No argument supported by $P' \cup \Delta$ attacks Δ.
For every *non-b* not in Δ,
$P' \cup \Delta$ supports an argument that attacks *non-b*.

In the stable model semantics, argumentation is all-out warfare: for Δ to be stable, every *non-b* has to take a side, either with or against Δ. If *non-b* is not with Δ, then Δ attacks *non-b*.

With abductive derivations, Δ is an *admissible* solution of G_0, if and only if:

$P' \cup \Delta$ supports an argument for G_0.
No argument supported by $P' \cup \Delta$ attacks Δ.
For every argument supported by $P' \cup \Delta'$ that attacks Δ,
$P' \cup \Delta$ supports an argument that attacks Δ'.

In the admissibility semantics, argumentation is merely self-defence.

The inference rules F_1, F_2, B_1, B_2, *Fact*, *S* and *Neg* are *sound*:

Theorem: Given an abductive logic program $<P', O, IC>$ corresponding to a ground logic program P with negation, but without other open predicates and other integrity constraints, and given a goal clause G_0:

> If there is a successfully terminating derivation of Δ,
> then Δ is an *admissible* solution of G_0.

As in the case of ground Horn ALP, to obtain completeness, the definition of successful derivation needs to be extended to the possibly non-terminating case. A discussion of these and related issues can be found in Dung *et al.* (2006) in the context of proof procedures for abstract argumentation.

Extensions of the abductive proof procedure

The most important extension is, of course, to the case of non-ground abductive logic programs. In the case of the IFF proof procedure, on which the abductive proof procedure is based, this extension involves a number of additional inference rules, for dealing with substitutions represented by means of equations. However, in the case of the abductive derivations of this chapter, the extension to the non-ground case requires mainly just adding unification for forward reasoning, backward reasoning and factoring. It also requires the range-restriction on variables, which is not too difficult to live with in practice.[5] Unfortunately, there is not sufficient space to deal with this extension and the issues it raises in this book.

Four other extensions are needed to deal with the topics in this book:

We need to generalise forward reasoning, so that the atom A in G_i used for forward reasoning can be a closed atom. This allows the consequences of hypothetical actions and explanations to be considered without the need to reduce them to open atoms.

We need to extend clauses/beliefs to include conditionals in the conditions of conditionals; for example, to represent the wood louse designer's beliefs in Chapter 9.

We need to extend forward reasoning, to reason forwards using beliefs, and not only using integrity constraints. This involves relaxing the restriction that every integrity constraint contains an atom with an open predicate.

We need to integrate the abductive and the connection graph proof procedures.

The first extension is trivial. The restriction that A be an open atom was imposed for simplicity. The restriction can be removed without further ado.

---

[5] With a minor modification of this restriction, integrity constraints can contain existentially quantified variables in their conclusions, and these existential quantifiers may be left implicit.

The second extension is also very easy. We already have conditionals in generalised goal clauses introduced by forward reasoning with integrity constraints. They could just as easily have been introduced by backward reasoning with clauses.

The third extension requires a little more work. Integrity checking methods that reason forwards with clauses were developed for deductive databases in the 1980s (Sadri and Kowalski, 1988). These could be integrated with the abductive proof procedure presented in this chapter. However, it is interesting to note that many practical systems in computing restrict rules to the form of event–condition–action rules, which are obtained in effect by reasoning in advance.

The fourth extension is not very difficult in theory, because forward and backward reasoning are special cases of resolution, and the connection graph proof procedure is just a vehicle for implementing resolution more efficiently. However, as remarked at the end of Chapter A5, the connection graph proof procedure was developed as a refutation procedure to show logical consequence. To adapt it to the generation of minimal models in ALP, conclusions of conditional goals need to be linked to the conclusions of conditional beliefs.

Note that the combination of abduction with open predicates and default reasoning with negative predicates requires no extension at all, but simply the inclusion of both kinds of predicates, their associated integrity constraints, and negation rewriting in the same abductive logic program.

Conclusions

This chapter has presented the technical support for the main reasoning techniques studied in this book. However, there remain a number of extensions needed for a comprehensive framework. Many of these extensions are straightforward, because all of them have been developed as individual components or in combination with other components in other frameworks. Their harmonious integration into a single encompassing framework is a topic for further research.

This chapter also introduced an argumentation semantics and proof procedure for abductive logic programming. The semantics and proof procedure build upon recent advances in logic-based argumentation in AI. One of the most important achievements of this argumentation-based approach is the demonstration that almost all of the original logic-based formalisms developed for default reasoning in AI can be understood uniformly in argumentation terms (Bondarenko *et al.*, 1997). This approach has been especially influential in the field of AI and law (Prakken and Sartor, 1996). A recent survey can be found in Rahwan and Simari (2009).

References

Allen, L. E. and Saxon, C. S. 1984. Computer aided normalizing and unpacking: some interesting machine-processable transformation of legal rules. In *Computing Power and Legal Reasoning*, C. Walter (ed.). St. Paul, MN: West Publishing Company; 495–572.

Almor, A. and Sloman, S. 2000. Reasoning versus text processing in the Wason selection task: a non-deontic perspective on perspective effects. *Memory & Cognition* **28**(6): 1060–70.

Anderson, A. R. and Belnap, N. 1975. *Entailment: The logic of relevance and necessity, Vol. I*. Princeton, NJ: Princeton University Press.

Anderson, J. R. and Lebiere, C. 1998. *The Atomic Components of Thought*. Mahwah, NJ: Erlbaum.

d'Avila Garcez, A. S., Broda, K. and Gabbay, D. M. 2001. Symbolic knowledge extraction from trained neural networks: a sound approach. *Artificial Intelligence* **125**(1–2): 155–20.

Bader, S., Hitzler, P. and Hölldobler, S. 2006. The integration of connectionism and first-order knowledge representation and reasoning as a challenge for artificial intelligence. *Information* **9**(1).

Baron, J. 2008. *Thinking and Deciding*, 4th edn. Cambridge: Cambridge University Press.

van Benthem, J. 1989. Semantic parallels in natural language and computation. In *Logic Colloquium 1981*, H.-D. Ebbinghaus (ed.). Amsterdam: Elsevier Science Publishers; 331–75.

Bertossi, L. and Chomicki, J. 2003. Query answering in inconsistent databases. In *Logics for Emerging Applications of Databases*, J. Chomicki, G. Saake and R. van der Meyden (eds). New York: Springer; 43–83.

Bondarenko, A., Dung, P. M., Kowalski, R. and Toni, F. 1997. An abstract argumentation-theoretic approach to default reasoning. *Journal of Artificial Intelligence* **93**(1–2): 63–101.

Brooks, R. A. 1991. Intelligence without reason. MIT AI Lab Memo 1293, April 1991. Reprinted in *Proceedings of the 12th International Joint Conference on Artificial Intelligence*, Sydney, Australia, 1–21.

Brown, G. and Yule, G. 1983. *Discourse Analysis*. Cambridge: Cambridge University Press.

Bundy, A., Byrd, L., Luger, G., Mellish, C. and Palmer, M. 1979. Solving mechanics problems using meta-level inference. *Proceedings of the 6th International Joint Conference on Artificial Intelligence.*

Byrne, R. M. J. 1989. Suppressing valid inferences with conditionals. *Cognition* **31**: 61–83.

Carruthers, P. 2004. Practical reasoning in a modular mind. *Mind & Language* **19**(3): 259–78.

Checkland, P. 2000. Soft systems methodology: a thirty year retrospective. *Systems Research and Behavioral Science Systems Research* **17**: S11–58.

Cheng, P. W. and Holyoak, K. J. 1985. Pragmatic reasoning schemas. *Cognitive Psychology* **17**: 391–416.

Cheng, P. D. and Juang J. Y. 1987. A parallel resolution procedure based on connection graph. *Sixth National Conference on Artificial Intelligence.*

Chisholm, R. 1963. Contrary-to-duty imperatives and deontic logic. *Analysis* **24**: 33–6.

Clark, K. L. 1978. Negation by failure. In *Logic and Databases*, H. Gallaire and J. Minker (eds). New York: Plenum Press; 293–322.

Clark, K. L. and Tärnlund, S.-A. 1978. A first-order theory of data and programs. In *Proceedings of the IFIP Congress* **77**: 939–44.

Colmerauer, A. and Roussel, P. 1992. The birth of Prolog. *The Second ACM SIGPLAN Conference on History of Programming Languages*, 37–52.

Costantini, S. 2002. Meta-reasoning: a survey. In *Computational Logic: Logic Programming and Beyond*, Vol. 2, A. C. Kakas and F. Sadri (eds). New York: Springer; 253–88.

Cosmides, L. 1985. Deduction or Darwinian algorithms: an explanation of the "elusive" content effect on the Wason selection task. PhD thesis, Harvard University.

Cosmides, L. 1989. The logic of social exchange: has natural selection shaped how humans reason? Studies with the Wason selection task. *Cognition* **31**: 187–276.

Dávila, J. and Uzcátegui, M. 2005. Agents that learn to behave in multi-agent simulations. *Proceedings of Fifth IASTED International Conference on Modelling, Simulation and Optimization (MSO'2005)*; 51–5. See also http://galatea.sourceforge.net.

Davis, M. 1980. The mathematics of non-monotonic reasoning. *Journal of Artificial Intelligence* **13**: 73–80.

Davis, M. and Putnam, H. 1960. A computing procedure for quantification theory. *Journal of the ACM* **7**(3): 201–15.

Dennis, L. A., Farwer, B., Bordini, R. H., Fisher, M. and Wooldridge, M. A. 2008. *Common Semantic Basis for BDI Languages, LICS 4908*. New York: Springer; 124–39.

De Raedt, L., Frasconi, P., Kersting, K. and Muggleton, S. (eds) 2008. *Probabilistic Inductive Logic Programming*. New York: Springer.

Dung, P. M. 1991. Negation as hypothesis: an abductive foundation for logic programming. *Proceedings of the 8th International Conference on Logic Programming.* Cambridge, MA: MIT Press.

Dung, P. M., Kowalski, R. and Toni, F. 2006. Dialectic proof procedures for assumption-based, admissible argumentation. *Journal of Artificial Intelligence* **170**(2): 114–59.

van Emden, M. and Kowalski, R. 1976. The semantics of predicate logic as a programming language. *JACM* **23**(4): 733–42.

Eshghi, K. and Kowalski, R. 1989. Abduction compared with negation by failure. In *Sixth International Conference on Logic Programming*, G. Levi and M. Martelli (eds). Cambridge, MA: MIT Press; 234–54.

Feferman, S. 1962. Transfinite recursive progressions of axiomatic theories. *Journal of Symbolic Logic* **27**: 259–316.

Fodor, J. 1975. *The Language of Thought*. Cambridge, MA: Harvard University Press.

Fung, T. H. and Kowalski, R. 1997. The IFF proof procedure for abductive logic programming. *Journal of Logic Programming*.

Gardner, H. 1983. *Frames of Mind: The Theory of Multiple Intelligences*. New York: Basic Books.

Gelfond, M. and Lifschitz, V. 1988. The stable model semantics for logic programming. *Proceedings of the Fifth International Conference on Logic Programming (ICLP)*; 1070–80.

Gillies, D. 1996. *Artificial Intelligence and Scientific Method*. Oxford: Oxford University Press.

Gödel, K. 1931. Über formal unentscheidbare Sätze der Principia Mathematica und verwandter Systeme, I. *Monatshefte für Mathematik und Physik* **38**: 173–98.

Gödel, K. 1951. Some basic theorems on the foundations of mathematics and their implications. In *Collected works / Kurt Gödel*, Vol. III, S. Feferman (ed.) (1995). Oxford: Oxford University Press; 304–23.

Green, C. 1969. Application of theorem proving to problem solving. *Proceedings of the 1st International Joint Conference on Artificial Intelligence*. San Francisco: Morgan Kaufmann; 219–39.

Grice, H. P. 1989. *Studies in the Way of Words*. Cambridge, MA: Harvard University Press.

Hammond, J., Keeney, R. and Raiffa, H. 1999. *Smart Choices – A practical guide to making better decisions*. Cambridge, MA: Harvard Business School Press.

Hauser, M., Cushman, F., Young, L. and Mikhail, J. 2007. A dissociation between moral judgments and justifications. *Mind and Language* **22**(1): 1–21.

Hewitt, C. 1971. Procedural embedding of knowledge in planner. *Proceedings of the 2nd International Joint Conference on Artificial Intelligence*. San Francisco: Morgan Kaufmann.

Hill, P. M. and Gallagher, J. 1998. Meta-programming in logic programming. In *Handbook of Logic in Artificial Intelligence and Logic Programming*, Vol. 5 D. Gabbay, C. J. Hogger and J. A. Robinson (eds). Oxford: Oxford University Press; 421–97.

Hodges, W. 1993. The logical content of theories of deduction. *Behavioral and Brain Sciences* **16**(2): 353–4.

Hodges, W. 2006. Two doors to open. In *Mathematical Problems from Applied Logic I: Logics for the XXIst Century*, Vol. 4, D. Gabbay, S. Goncharov and M. Zakharyaschev (eds). New York: Springer; 277–316.

Hölldobler, S. and Kalinke, Y. 1994. Toward a new massively parallel computational model for logic programming, *Proceedings of Workshop on Combining Symbolic and Connectionist Processing, ECAI-94*, Amsterdam; 68–77.

IPCC. 2007. Fourth Assessment Report: Climate Change.

Johnson-Laird, P. 1983. *Mental Models*. Cambridge: Cambridge University Press.

Johnson-Laird, P. N. and Byrne, R. M. J. 1991. *Deduction*. London: Psychology Press.

Kahneman, D. and Frederick, S. 2002. Representativeness revisited: attribute substitution in intuitive judgment. In *Heuristics of Intuitive Judgment: Extensions and Application*, T. Gilovich, D. Griffin and D. Kahneman (eds). New York: Cambridge University Press.

Kakas, A., Kowalski, R. and Toni, F. 1998. The role of logic programming in abduction. *Handbook of Logic in Artificial Intelligence and Programming*, Vol. 5. Oxford: Oxford University Press; 235–324.

Kowalski, R. 1975. A proof procedure using connection graphs. *JACM* **22**(4): 572–95.

Kowalski, R. 1974, 1979. *Logic for Problem Solving*. DCL Memo 75, Department of Artificial Intelligence, University of Edinburgh (1974). Expanded edition published by North Holland Elsevier (1979). Also at http://www.doc.ic.ac.uk/~rak/.

Kowalski, R. 1992. Database updates in the event calculus. *Journal of Logic Programming* **12**(162): 121–46.

Kowalski, R. 1995. Logic without model theory. In *What is a Logical System?*, D. Gabbay (ed.). Oxford: Oxford University Press.

Kowalski, R. and Kuehner, D. 1971. Linear resolution with selection function. *Artificial Intelligence* **2**: 227–60.

Kowalski, R. A. and Sadri, F. 1990. Logic programs with exceptions. *Proceedings of the Seventh International Conference on Logic Programming*. Cambridge, MA: MIT Press; 598–613.

Kowalski, R. A. and Sadri, F. 2010. An agent language with destructive assignment and model-theoretic semantics. In *CLIMA XI – Computational Logic in Multi-Agent Systems*, J. Dix, G. Governatori, W. Jamroga and J. Leite (eds). New York: Springer.

Kowalski, R. and Sergot, M. 1986. A logic-based calculus of events. *New Generation Computing* **4**(1): 67–95. Also in *The Language of Time: A Reader*, I. Mani, J. Pustejovsky and R. Gaizauskas (eds). Oxford: Oxford University Press (2005).

Kowalski, R. and Toni, F. 1996. Abstract argumentation. *Journal of Artificial Intelligence and Law* **4**(3–4): 275–96.

Kowalski, R., Toni, F. and Wetzel, G. 1998. Executing suspended logic programs. *Fundamenta Informatica* **34**(3): 1–22.

Laird, R., Newell, J. and Paul, A. 1987. Soar: an architecture for general intelligence. *Artificial Intelligence* **33**: 1–64.

Lenat, D. and Guha, R. V. 1989. *Building Large Knowledge-Based Systems; Representation and Inference in the Cyc Project*. Boston: Addison-Wesley Longman Publishing. (An up-to-date overview can be found at http://www.cyc.com/.)

Loveland, D. W. 1968. Mechanical theorem-proving by model elimination. *Journal of the ACM* **15**: 236–51.

Lucas, J. R. 1959. Minds, machines and Gödel. *Philosophy*, **XXXVI**, 1961. Reprinted in *The Modeling of Mind*, K. M. Sayre and F. J. Crosson (eds). Paris: Notre Dame Press (1963) and in *Minds and Machines*, A. R. Anderson (ed.). New York: Prentice-Hall (1964).

Luger, G. 2009. *Artificial Intelligence, Structures and Strategies for Complex Problem Solving*. London: Pearson Education Limited.

Manthey, R. and Bry, F. 1988. SATCHMO: A theorem prover implemented in Prolog. *Proceedings CADE 1988*. Lecture Notes in Computer Science 310. New York: Springer; 415–34.

Maes, P. 1990. Situated agents can have goals. *Robotic and Autonomous Systems* **6**(1–2): 49–70.

McCarthy, J. 1980. Circumscription – a form of non-monotonic reasoning. *Artificial Intelligence* **13**: 27–39.

McCarthy, J. and Hayes, P. J. 1969. Some philosophical problems from the standpoint of artificial intelligence. In *Machine Intelligence 4*, D. Michie (ed.). New York: Elsevier.

McDermott, D. and Doyle, 1980. Nonmonotonic logic I. *Artificial Intelligence* **13**: 41–72.

Mikhail, J. 2007. Universal moral grammar: theory, evidence, and the future. *Trends in Cognitive Sciences* **11**(4): 143–52.

Moore, R. C. 1985. Semantical considerations on nonmonotonic logic. *Artificial Intelligence* **25**: 75–94.

Mueller, E. 2006. *Commonsense Reasoning*. Amsterdam: Elsevier.

Muggleton, S. H. and De Raedt, L. 1994. Inductive logic programming: theory and methods. *Journal of Logic Programming* **19**(20): 629–79.

Newell, A. 1973. Production systems: models of control structure. In *Visual Information Processing*, W. Chase (ed.). New York: Academic Press; 463–526.

Nilsson, N. 1998. *Artificial Intelligence: A New Synthesis*. San Francisco: Morgan Kaufmann.

Nute, D. 1997. *Defeasible Deontic Logic*. Dordrecht: Kluwer Academic.

Panton, C., Matuszek, D., Lenat, D., Schneider, M., Witbrock, N. *et al.* 2006. Common sense reasoning – from Cyc to Intelligent Assistant. In *Ambient Intelligence in Everyday Life*, LNAI 3864, Y. Cai and J. Abascal (eds). Berlin: Springer; 1–31.

Peirce, C. S. 1931. *Collected Papers*, C. Hartshorn and P. Weiss (eds). Cambridge, MA: Harvard University Press.

Penrose, R. 1989. *The Emperor's New Mind: Concerning Computers, Minds, and The Laws of Physics*. Oxford: Oxford University Press.

Pereira, L. M. and Saptawijaya, A. 2007. Moral decision making with ACORDA. In: *14th International Conference on Logic for Programming Artificial Intelligence and Reasoning* (LPAR'07), N. Dershowitz and A. Voronkov (eds).

Pereira, L. M. and Saptawijaya, A. 2009. Modelling morality with prospective logic. In: *International Journal of Reasoning-based Intelligent Systems (IJRIS)* **1**(3/4): 209–21. [Also to appear in M. Anderson and S. Anderson (eds), *Machine Ethics*, Cambridge University Press, Cambridge.]

Perlis, D. and Subrahmanian, V. S. 1994. Metalanguages, reflection principles and self-reference. In *Handbook of Logic in Artificial Intelligence and Logic Programming*, Vol. **2**, D. M. Gabbay, C. J. Hogger and J. A. Robinson (eds). 328–58.

Pollock, J. 1995. *Cognitive Carpentry*. Cambridge, MA: MIT Press.

Poole, D. 1997. The independent choice logic for modeling multiple agents under uncertainty. *Artificial Intelligence* **94**: 7–56.

Poole, D., Goebel, R. and Aleliunas R. 1987. Theorist: a logical reasoning system for defaults and diagnosis. In *The Knowledge Frontier: Essays in the Representation of Knowledge*, N. Cercone and G. McCalla (eds). New York: Springer; 331–52.

Poole, D. and Mackworth, A. 2010. *Artificial Intelligence: Foundations of Computational Agents*. Cambridge: Cambridge University Press.

Post, E. 1943. Formal reductions of the general combinatorial decision problem. *American Journal of Mathematics* **65**(2): 197–215.

Prakken, H. and Sartor, G. 1996. A dialectical model of assessing conflicting arguments in legal reasoning. *Journal of Artificial Intelligence and Law* **4**(3–4).

Priest, G. 2002. Paraconsistent logic. *Handbook of Philosophical Logic*, 2nd edn, Vol. 6, D. Gabbay and F. Guenthner (eds). Dordrecht: Kluwer Academic; 287–393.

Przymusinski, T. 1988. On the declarative semantics of deductive databases and logic programs. In *Foundations of Deductive Databases and Logic Programming*. New York: Morgan Kaufmann; 193–216.

Quine, W. V. O. 1963. Two dogmas of empiricism. *From a Logical Point of View*. New York: Harper & Row; 20–46.

Rahwan, I. and Simari, G. (eds). 2009. *Argumentation in Artificial Intelligence*. New York: Springer.

Reiter, R. 1980. A logic for default reasoning. *Artificial Intelligence* **13**: 81–132.

Reiter, R. 1988. On integrity constraints. *2nd Conference on Theoretical Aspects of Reasoning about Knowledge*, 97–111.

Robinson, J. A. 1965a. A machine-oriented logic based on the resolution principle. *Journal of the ACM* **12**(1): 23–41.

Robinson, J. 1965b. Automatic deduction with hyper-resolution. *International Journal of Computer Mathematics* **1**(3): 227–34.

Russell, S. J. and Norvig, P. 2010. *Artificial Intelligence: A Modern Approach*, 3rd edn. Upper Saddle River, NJ: Prentice Hall.

Sadri F. and Kowalski R. 1988. A theorem-proving approach to database integrity. In *Foundations of Deductive Databases and Logic Programming*, J. Minker (ed.). New York: Morgan Kaufmann; 313–62.

Sagonas, K., Swift, T. and Warren, D. S. 1994. XSB as an efficient deductive database engine. *SIGMOD Record* **23**(2): 442–53.

Sergot, M. J., Sadri, F., Kowalski, R. A., Kriwaczek, F., Hammond, P. and Cory, H. T. 1986. The British Nationality Act as a logic program. *CACM* **29**(5): 370–86.

Shanahan, M. P. 1997. *Solving the Frame Problem: A Mathematical Investigation of the Common Sense Law of Inertia*. Cambridge, MA: MIT Press.

Shapiro, S. 1989. Incompleteness, mechanism, and optimism. *The Bulletin of Symbolic Logic* **4**(3): 273–302.

Siekmann, J. and Wrightson, G. 2002. Strong completeness of R. Kowalski's connection graph proof procedure. In *Computational Logic: Logic Programming and Beyond*, A. Kakas and F. Sadri (eds). New York: Springer Lecture Notes on AI, Vol. 2408; 231–52.

Simon, H. A. 1957. *Administrative Behaviour*, 2nd edn. New York: Macmillan.

Simon, H. A. 1960. *The New Science of Management Decision*. New York: Harper & Row. (1977 Revised edition, Prentice-Hall, Englewood Cliffs, NJ.)

Simon, H. A. 1999. Production systems. In *The MIT Encyclopedia of the Cognitive Sciences*, R. Wilson and F. Keil (eds). Cambridge, MA: MIT Press; 676–7.

Sperber, D. and Wilson, D. 1986. *Relevance*. Oxford: Blackwell.

Sperber, D., Cara, F. and Girotto, V. 1995. Relevance theory explains the selection task. *Cognition* **52**: 3–39.

Stenning, K. and van Lambalgen M. 2008. *Human Reasoning and Cognitive Science*. Cambridge, MA: MIT Press.

Thagard, P. 2005. *Mind: Introduction to Cognitive Science*, 2nd edn. Cambridge, MA: M.I.T. Press.

van Lambalgen, M. and Hamm, F. 2005. *The Proper Treatment of Events*. Oxford: Blackwell.

Vickers, G. 1965. *The Art of Judgment*. London: Chapman & Hall.

Wang, H. 1974. *From Mathematics to Philosophy*. London: Routledge & Kegan Paul.

Wason, P. 1968. Reasoning about a rule. *The Quarterly Journal of Experimental Psychology*. **20**(3): 273–81.

Widom, J. and Ceri, S. 1996. *Active Database Systems: Triggers and Rules for Advanced Database Processing*. San Francisco: Morgan Kaufmann.

Williams, J. 1990, 1995. *Style: Toward Clarity and Grace*. Chicago: University of Chicago Press.

Winograd, T. 1971. Procedures as a representation for data in a computer program for understanding natural language, MIT AI TR-235.

Winograd, T. 1972. *Understanding Natural Language*. New York: Academic Press.

Index

Printed in the United States
by Baker & Taylor Publisher Services